STUDY BOOK

Certificate in Corporate Finance

Syllabus version 3

In this November 2007 edition

- A **user-friendly format** for easy navigation
- **Exam tips** to put you on the right track
- A **Test your Knowledge** quiz at the end of each chapter
- A **full index**

APPROVED WORKBOOK

BPP
LEARNING MEDIA

Published November 2007

ISBN 9780 7517 4587 0

British Library Cataloguing-in-Publication Data
A catalogue record for this book
is available from the British Library

Published by

BPP Learning Media Ltd
BPP House, Aldine Place
London W12 8AA

www.bpp.com/learningmedia

Printed and bound in Great Britain by
William Clowes Ltd, Beccles, Suffolk

Your learning materials, published by BPP Learning Media Ltd, are
printed on paper sourced from sustainable, managed forests.

£80.00

Contents

0207 786 5908

1

The Regulatory Environment

INTRODUCTION

The current system of regulation for the UK financial services industry was set up with the establishment of the Financial Services Authority (FSA) as the overall regulator in 2001.

The FSMA 2000 establishes the statutory role of the Financial Services Authority. In this chapter, we look at the range of investments which are covered by the Act, and at the range of activities which are regulated by the FSA under the legislation.

The FSA Handbook is the main source for the rules that must be followed. The rule book is continuing to evolve and recent moves from 'rules-based' regulation to 'principles-based' regulation are intended to lead to a reduction in the volume of detailed rules.

Individuals carrying out 'controlled functions' are subject to the 'approved persons' regime, which is a distinct from the process of authorisation of the firms in which such individuals work.

We explain the FSA's enforcement powers and their wide powers to require information from firms.

CHAPTER CONTENTS

BPP
LEARNING MEDIA

CHAPTER LEARNING OBJECTIVES

The Regulatory Infrastructure

- **Know** the regulatory infrastructure generated by the Financial Services and Markets Act 2000 (FSMA 2000) and the status and relationship between FSMA 2000, the Treasury and the Financial Services Authority (FSA), and between the FSA and the RIEs, ROIEs, DIEs, RCHs, DPBs and MTFs.

- **Understand** the implications of S19 FSMA 2000 – the General Prohibition.
  - Offences under the Act.
  - Enforceability of agreements entered into with an unauthorised business.

- **Know** what regulated activities constitute designated investment business in the UK.

- **Know** which designated investments are covered by the Regulated Activities Order 2001.

- **Know** what are excluded activities in relation to designated investment business in the UK.

- **Know** what constitutes exempt persons in relation to designated investment business in the UK.

The Role of the FSA

- **Know** the FSA's statutory objectives.

- **Know** the FSA's rule making powers in relation to authorisation (threshold conditions), supervision, enforcement, sanctions and disciplinary action.

- **Understand** the Principles for Businesses.

- **Understand** the risk-based supervision of firms by the FSA.

- **Understand** the importance of principles based regulations.

- **Know** the Statements of Principle and Code of Practice for approved persons.

- **Know** the senior management responsibilities: purpose; apportionment of responsibilities; recording the apportionment; systems and controls, compliance, internal audit and risk functions.

- **Understand** the FSA's controlled functions: the five functional areas; the main roles within each; the four areas of significant influence functions, the requirement for the FSA approval prior to appointment, the ongoing requirement to be fit and proper, the consequences of qualified versus 'clean' withdrawal on termination of employment.

- **Understand** the criteria applied to ensure approved persons are fit and proper to conduct investment business.

- **Know** the FSA's power to require information (S165 of FSMA) and its investigatory powers.

- **Know** the role, scope and consequences of the Regulatory Decisions Committee's responsibility for decision-making.

- **Know** the FSA's disciplinary powers with respect to authorised firms, approved persons and other persons.

- **Know** the role of the Financial Services and Markets Tribunal.

European Union Legislation

■ **Know** the purpose and scope of the Markets in Financial Instruments Directive (MiFID) including

- The concept of passporting within the EEA.
- The definition of MiFID and non-MiFID firms.
- The categories of MiFID financial instruments.
- What constitutes core and ancillary investment services or activities.

■ **Know** the responsibilities of the home and host state regulators.

1 BACKGROUND TO THE UK REGULATORY SYSTEM

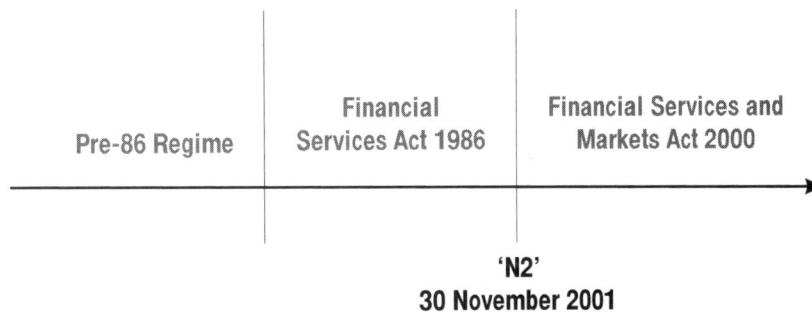

Pre-86 Regime	Financial Services Act 1986	Financial Services and Markets Act 2000

'N2'
30 November 2001

Prior to the advent of the 1986 Financial Services Act, the industry was completely self-regulating. Standards were maintained by an assurance that those in the financial services industry had a common set of values and were able, and willing, to ostracise those who violated them.

The 1986 Act moved the UK to a system that became known as self-regulation within a statutory framework. A key element of the system was that those conducting investment business in the UK must obtain authorisation. Once authorised, firms and individuals would be regulated by self-regulating organisations (SROs), such as IMRO, SFA or PIA. It should be noted that the Financial Services Act 1986 only covered investment activities. Retail banking, general insurance, Lloyd's of London and mortgages were all covered by separate Acts and Codes.

The system was created in the belief that it could combine both the flexibility and understanding of practitioner self-regulation, with the enforceability of statute and, consequently, deliver the appropriate level of protection.

The late 1990s saw a more radical reform of the financial services system by unifying most aspects of financial services regulation within a **single statutory regulator – the Financial Services Authority (FSA)**. The 'patchwork quilt' of regulation would be swept away and the FSA would regulate investment business, insurance business, banking, building societies, Friendly Societies, Mortgages and Lloyd's.

On 30 November 2001, the **Financial Services and Markets Act 2000 (FSMA)** came into force to create a system of **statutory regulation**. Whilst practitioners and consumers are actively consulted, it is the FSA that co-ordinates the regulation of the industry.

The new regime seeks to learn from many of the regulatory failures that occurred during the 1980s and 1990s. Undoubtedly, the most important has been that of pensions misselling, where salesmen encouraged some 2.2 million people to move out of their employers' schemes into personal pension plans. These transfers were often unsuitable and have given rise to some major compensation claims. This has led to an increased importance in the new regime on educating investors to ensure that they understand the risks of transactions they undertake.

BCCI, an important international bank with many UK offices and customers, was the subject of an £8bn fraud. The subsequent insolvency of the bank caused great harm to many creditors. This has led to the FSA taking on regulatory responsibility for banks and increased regulation in the field of money laundering.

The Barings crisis was caused by the actions of a single rogue trader, Nick Leeson, whose unauthorised trading, coupled with the inadequacy of controls, led to the collapse of the bank. This has led to a big drive towards ensuring that senior management take their responsibilities seriously and ensure that systems and controls are adequate.

Finally, world copper prices were manipulated by the unauthorised trading of Mr Hamanaka of Sumitomo. As much of his trading took place on the London Metal Exchange, there was cause for UK regulatory concern. Ultimately, the unauthorised trading cost Sumitomo $2.7bn. As a result, the new regime introduces more stringent rules to deal with market abuse.

The regulation of the UK financial services industry continues to evolve.

2 THE FINANCIAL SERVICES AND MARKETS ACT 2000

2.1 Primary and secondary legislation

Before looking further at the detail of FSMA, it is important to understand the legislative structure that exists. FSMA itself only provides the skeleton of the regulatory system, much of the detail being provided by secondary legislation. The secondary legislation links into various sections of FSMA, fleshing out the requirements and, thus, requiring the two to be read in conjunction. An example of this concerns the authorisation requirement. FSMA requires that any firm undertaking a **regulated activity** must be authorised or exempt from authorisation. Whilst the routes that a firm may follow to obtain authorisation are contained in FSMA, the meaning of the term 'regulated activity' and the exemptions are found in secondary legislation – namely the Regulated Activities Order. Both FSMA and the secondary legislation are drafted by **HM Treasury**.

Arguably, the FSA's role as **legislator** has been diminished by the requirements of EU Single Market Directives – in particular, the far-reaching Markets in Financial Instruments Directive (MiFID), implemented on 1 November 2007 – as the FSA has increasingly needed to apply rules which have been formulated at the **European level**.

The FSA derives its power to make rules in the FSA Handbook from **S138 FSMA**. The Handbook starts with the **Principles for Businesses** and includes the rules contained in the *Conduct of Business Sourcebook*. It is hardly surprising, then, that the FSA Handbook is a lengthy document.

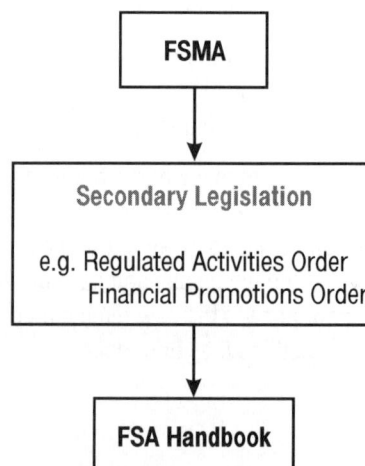

```
          ┌─────────────┐
          │    FSMA     │
          └─────────────┘
                 │
                 ▼
    ┌──────────────────────────────┐
    │     Secondary Legislation     │
    │                               │
    │   e.g. Regulated Activities Order │
    │        Financial Promotions Order │
    └──────────────────────────────┘
                 │
                 ▼
          ┌─────────────┐
          │ FSA Handbook │
          └─────────────┘
```

2.2 The four regulatory objectives

Section 2 of FSMA spells out the purpose of regulation by specifying four **regulatory objectives** (these are sometimes called statutory objectives). These objectives are summarised below.

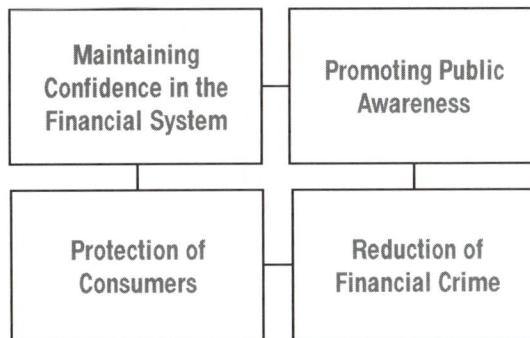

```
┌─────────────────────┐   ┌─────────────────────┐
│   Maintaining       │   │  Promoting Public   │
│ Confidence in the   │   │     Awareness       │
│ Financial System    │   │                     │
└─────────────────────┘   └─────────────────────┘

┌─────────────────────┐   ┌─────────────────────┐
│  Protection of      │   │   Reduction of      │
│   Consumers         │   │  Financial Crime    │
└─────────────────────┘   └─────────────────────┘
```

The emphasis placed on these objectives makes FSMA unusual compared to the Acts that it supersedes – none of which clearly articulated their objectives. The FSMA is seeking to inject much needed clarity into what the regulatory regime is trying to achieve and, perhaps more importantly, seeking to manage expectations regarding what it cannot achieve.

2.3 The general prohibition

Section 19 contains what is known as the **general prohibition**. This states that no person can carry on a regulated activity in the UK, or purport to do so, unless they are authorised or exempt. The definition of 'person' here includes both companies and individuals. The lists of exemptions and exclusions are set out in the Regulated Activities Order.

The sanctions for breaching S19 are fairly severe, namely criminal sanctions and unenforceability of agreements, compensation and actions by the FSA to restrain such activity.

- **Criminal Sanctions**

  Breach of the general prohibition is an offence punishable in a court of law. UK courts have both a lower level, known as a Magistrates' Court, where summary offences are heard and a higher level with a judge and jury, known as the Crown Court, where indictable offences are heard. The maximum penalties for conducting unauthorised regulated activities are set out in S23 of FSMA as follows.

  - **Magistrates' Court**: six months' imprisonment and/or a £5,000 fine.

  - **Crown Court**: two years' imprisonment and/or an unlimited fine.

  It is a defence to show that all reasonable precautions were taken, and all due diligence exercised, to avoid committing the offence.

- **Unenforceable Agreements**

  Any agreement made by an unauthorised firm will be unenforceable against the other party. FSMA makes it clear that agreements are not illegal or invalid as a result of a contravention of the general prohibition, merely 'voidable'. This ensures that the innocent party to the agreement may still be able to enforce the agreement against the other party, even though the performance may be a criminal offence.

- **Compensation**

  The innocent party will be entitled to recover compensation for any loss sustained if the agreement is made unenforceable.

- **Injunctions and Restitution Orders**

  The FSA may seek injunctions and restitution orders to restrain the contravention of the general prohibition and seek to remove the profits from offenders.

2.4 Authorisation

We shall now look at the circumstances when a firm must seek authorisation. The following decision chart indicates the questions to be asked in establishing whether a firm needs to be authorised.

Does My Firm Need Authorisation

We noted earlier that the FSA regulates all areas of financial services in the UK. For this exam you are only required to know the activities that relate to investment banking that are known as **designated investment business**.

2.4.1 Regulated activities of designated investment business

- **Dealing as principal or agent in investments.** This covers buying, selling, subscribing or underwriting investments.

- **Arranging deals in investments.** This covers making, offering or agreeing to make any arrangements with a view to another person buying, selling, subscribing or underwriting investments.

- **Managing investments.**

- **Safeguarding and administering investments or arranging such activities.**

- **Sending dematerialised instructions**. This relates to the use of computer-based systems for giving instructions for investments to be transferred.

- **Establishing, operating or winding up a collective investment scheme or stakeholder pension.** This would include the roles of the trustee and the depository of these schemes.

- **Advising on investments**.

- **Operating a multilateral trading facility**. This covers the operation of electronic order matching systems away from recognised exchanges.

The activities that are to be regulated by FSMA are set out in the Regulated Activities Order. As well as the activities covering the investment industry, it also covers banking, insurance, mortgage lending industries, funeral plans and Lloyd's insurance.

Note that the regulated activity must be carried on **'by way of business'**. Whether something is carried on by way of business is, ultimately, a question of judgement. However, in general terms it will take into account the degree of continuity and profit. HM Treasury has also (via secondary legislation) made explicit provisions for certain activities, such as the activity of accepting deposits. This will not be regarded as carried on by way of business if a person does not hold himself out as doing so on a day-to-day basis, i.e. he only accepts deposits on particular occasions. An example of this would be a car salesman accepting a down payment on the purchase of a car.

2.4.2 Specified investments

Only activities with regard to specified investments are covered by FSMA. Specified investments are defined in the Regulated Activities Order.

We are required to know the following investments that are relevant to designated investment business.

- **Rights under contracts of insurance** with an investment element.

- **Shares** or stock in the capital of a company **wherever the company is based** other than an open ended investment company.

- **Debentures, loan stock and similar instruments, e.g. certificate of deposit, Treasury bills of exchange, floating rate notes, bulldog bonds and unsecured loan stock** (but **not** cheques or other bills of exchange, banker's drafts, letters of credit, trade bills or premium bonds).

- **Government and public securities**, e.g. gilts, US Treasury bonds (not National Savings products, e.g. premium bonds and National Savings certificates).

- **Warrants**.

- **Certificates representing certain securities**, e.g. American Depository Receipts.

- **Units in collective investment schemes** including shares in, or securities of, an open-ended investment company. Note that a collective investment scheme will be a specified investment regardless of the underlying property the scheme invests in.

- **Rights over a stakeholder pension**.

- **Personal pensions**.

- **Options** to acquire or dispose of any specified investment or currencies, gold, silver, platinum or palladium.

- **Futures** on anything for investment purposes. This differs from the treatment of options as it will cover all futures regardless of the underlying investment, provided it is for investment purposes.

    The definition of 'investment purposes' is complex. However, in general terms, any futures contract traded either on an exchange, or in an over-the-counter (OTC) market or form similar to that traded on an exchange, will constitute an investment. The type of future, in effect, excluded by this definition would be a short-term contract between a producer and a consumer of a good to purchase that good in the future, e.g. a wheat buyer buying from a farmer. This can sometimes be referred to as a commercial purpose future. As a rule of thumb, unless the examiner indicates otherwise, candidates should assume a future is for investment purposes.

- **Contracts for differences**. A contract for a difference is a contract in a product which itself has no physical basis. This essentially means cash-settled derivatives such as interest rate swaps and stock index futures, as well as spread betting and speculative forward rate agreements, e.g. a rolling spot Forex contract.

- **Rights to or interests in specified investments**. Repos (sale and repurchase agreements) in relation to specified investments (e.g. a government bond) are specified investments.

Note that spot Forex trades, general loans (e.g. car loan), property deals and National Savings and Investments products are not specified investments.

2.5 Excluded activities

- **Dealing as principal where the person is not holding themselves out to the market as willing to deal**. The requirement to seek authorisation does not apply to the personal dealings of unauthorised individuals for their own account, i.e. as **customers** of an authorised firm. It would also exclude companies issuing their own shares.

- **Media, e.g. TV, radio and newspapers**. Most newspapers and other media give investment advice. However, provided this is not the primary purpose of the newspaper, then under the exceptions granted within FSMA, it need not seek formal authorisation. On the other hand, the publication of **'tip sheets'** (written recommendations of investments) will require authorisation.

- **Trustees, nominees and personal representatives**. These persons, so long as they do not hold themselves out to the general public as providing the service and are not separately remunerated for the regulated activity, are excluded from the requirement to seek authorisation.

- **Employee share schemes**. This exclusion applies to activities which further an employee share scheme.

- **Overseas persons**. Overseas persons are firms which do not carry on regulated activity from a permanent place within the UK. This exception covers two broad categories. Firstly, where the activity requires the direct involvement of an authorised or exempt firm or, secondly, where the activity is carried on as a result of an unsolicited approach by a UK individual. Thus, if a UK individual asks a fund manager in Tokyo to buy a portfolio of Asian equities for them, the Japanese firm does not need to be authorised under FSMA.

Exam tip

> Use the word **DEMOTE** to help you to learn the five excluded activities.
>
> **D**ealing as principal, where the person is not holding themselves out to the market as willing to deal
> **E**mployee share schemes
> **M**edia
> **O**verseas persons
> **T**rustees
> Nomin**E**es and personal representatives

2.6 Exempt persons

There are a number of persons who are exempt from the requirement to seek authorisation under FSMA.

- **Appointed representative**. In markets such as life assurance, the bulk of sales takes place through self-employed individuals who act on behalf of the companies. As the companies do not employ them, if this exemption were not in place, such persons would need separate authorisation. The exemption removes them from the scope of authorisation so long as they act solely on behalf of one firm and that firm takes complete responsibility for their actions.

- **Certain persons listed in the Financial Services and Markets Act (Exemption) Order**, e.g. supranational bodies, municipal banks, local authorities, housing associations, the National Grid, trade unions, the Treasury Taskforce, the English Tourist Board, government organisations (such as the Bank of England, other central banks, an enterprise scheme, the International

Monetary Fund and the UK's National Savings Bank). In addition, charities and the Student Loans Company are exempt in respect of deposit taking activities. The Financial Services and Markets Act (Exemption) Order 2001 is written by HM Treasury under powers set out in S38 of FSMA.

- **Members of professions**. Solicitors, accountants and actuaries have been giving investment advice for many years. As long as giving such advice does not constitute a major proportion of their business (i.e. is incidental) and they are not separately paid for those activities, they are exempt from the requirement to seek authorisation. However, they will still be governed by their professional bodies (e.g. the Law Society for solicitors). These professional bodies are known as **Designated Professional Bodies (DPBs)** and are subject to scrutiny by the FSA.

- **Members of Lloyd's**. The requirement to seek authorisation is disapplied for members of Lloyd's writing insurance contracts. The Society of Lloyd's, however, must be authorised. This exemption covers **being** a Lloyd's member but does not cover the activities of **advising** on Lloyd's syndicate participation or **managing** underwriting activities.

- **Recognised Investment Exchanges (RIEs), Recognised Overseas Investment Exchanges (ROIEs) and Recognised Clearing Houses (RCHs)**. These are considered in more detail below.

Exam tip

Use the word APRIL to help you remember the five exempt persons.

Appointed representatives
Professional people, e.g. solicitors, accountants and actuaries
RIE, ROIEs and RCHs
Institutions who are exempt, e.g. the Bank of England
Lloyd's members

2.6.1 Recognised Investment Exchanges (RIEs)

The act of running an investment exchange is, in itself, a regulated activity (arranging deals in investments) and therefore requires regulatory approval. It is, however, exempt from the requirement if it has been given **Recognised Investment Exchange** status. This status assures any parties using the exchange that there are reasonable rules protecting them.

Many firms are members of an RIE and are also regulated by the FSA. It is important to note that firms are obliged to seek authorisation from the FSA. Membership of an RIE merely gives the member privileges of membership associated with the exchange, such as the ability to use the exchange's systems. **Membership of an RIE does not confer authorisation to conduct regulated activities**.

The following are UK exchanges which have been given RIE status.

- London Stock Exchange (LSE).
- Euronext.liffe.
- London Metal Exchange (LME).
- ICE Futures.
- virt-x. → SWX (EUROPE). LTD.
- EDX London.
- PLUS Markets

In addition to the UK exchanges which are permitted to operate under the RIE status above, certain overseas exchanges are also permitted to operate in the UK. These are often known as **Recognised Overseas Investment Exchanges (ROIEs)**. Examples of these include

- NASDAQ.
- Chicago Mercantile Exchange (CME).
- EUREX.

A ROIE is also granted recognition by the FSA.

2.6.2 Recognised Clearing Houses (RCHs)

This recognition permits the organisation to carry out the clearing and settlement functions for an exchange. At present there are two RCHs.

- Euroclear UK and Ireland.
- LCH.Clearnet.

2.6.3 Designated Investment Exchanges (DIEs)

In addition to those RIEs in the UK and overseas which the FSA recognises as being effectively run, there are also overseas exchanges which have been given a form of approval yet are unable to conduct regulated activities in the UK. Designated Investment Exchange (DIE) status assures any UK user of that overseas market that the FSA believes there are appropriate forms of local regulation that guarantee the investor's rights. Note that the term 'designated' does not mean exempt from the requirement to seek authorisation.

Examples of DIEs include

- The Tokyo Stock Exchange.
- The New York Stock Exchange.

2.6.4 Multilateral Trading Facilities (MTFs)

A **Multilateral Trading Facility (MTF)** is a system that brings together multiple parties (e.g. retail investors, or other investment firms) who want to buy and sell financial instruments, and enables them to do so. Anyone operating a MTF **does require authorisation.**

MTFs may be crossing networks or matching engines that are operated by an investment firm or a market operator. Instruments traded on a MTF may include shares, bonds and derivatives.

Changes to FSA rules bring the rules into line with MiFID requirements from 1 November 2007. MiFID requires operators of MTFs to ensure their markets operate on a fair and orderly basis. It aims to ensure this by placing requirements on MTF operators regarding how they organise their markets and the information they give to users.

Additionally, MiFID provides for the operators of MTFs to **passport their services** across borders.

2.7 Obtaining authorisation

FSMA creates a single authorisation regime for the regulated activities within its scope. If a firm requires authorisation, it may obtain it by one of two main routes.

- Authorisation by the FSA.
- Passporting.

2.8 Authorisation by the FSA

By far the most common way to obtain authorisation is obtaining permission from the FSA to carry out one or more regulated activities. The 'permission' that a firm receives will play a crucial role in defining the firm's business scope. This permission is sometimes referred to as **'Part IV permission'** as it is set out in Part IV of FSMA. Where a firm obtains permission to do one or more regulated activities, it is then authorised to do those activities. In their application the applicant must set out which regulated activities and specified investments it wishes permission for. The permission will set out what activities and investments are covered and any limitations and requirements that the FSA wishes to impose.

2.9 Passporting under MiFID

The UK's regulatory structure is determined by both UK and European law. Much European law seeks to support the creation of a single, competitive and efficient European market.

To this end, a large number of directives have been agreed amongst the member states and have subsequently entered domestic legislation. These directives seek to 'harmonise' regulations in order to create a fair market place. Differences in regulation between states need to be justified so that their impact is not unduly anti-competitive.

The key financial services directive we need to be aware of is the **Market in Financial Instruments Directive (MiFID)**. It is envisaged that MiFID will come into force on 1 November 2007. The aim of MiFID is to promote fair, efficient and integrated financial markets while facilitating competition between different trade execution venues.

The central feature of MiFID is that it facilitates European cross-border business and the opening of branch offices. This is done through the idea of a 'passport' which enables firms to use their domestic authorisation to operate not only in their home state, but also in other host states within the **European Economic Area**. Most credit institutions, financial institutions, insurance undertakings or investment firms may apply for a passport. In order to apply for a passport into the UK, a firm would contact its home state regulator.

The following table outlines the basic split of responsibilities between the home state regulator and the host state regulator.

Home	Host
Authorisation Fitness and Propriety Capital Adequacy Client Assets All **cross border** services Conduct of Business rules Most Conduct of Business throughout EEA branches for MiFID business Conduct of Business rules within home state only for non-MiFID business	Very limited Conduct of Business **via a branch** in host state in relation to MiFID business All Conduct of Business in host state in relation to **non-MiFID** business

The scope of FSMA and MiFID differ in certain respects. The most important are outlined below.

2.9.1 MiFID financial instruments

Only those investments which are specified in MiFID constitute MiFID investments. Consequently, the passport may only be used for such investments.

MiFID investments include

- Transferable securities, e.g. shares and bonds.
- Units in collective investment undertakings.
- Money market instruments (including repos).
- Financial and commodity derivative contracts (including futures, options, contracts for differences and credit derivatives)
- Forward rate agreements (FRAs).

- Interest rate, currency and equity swaps.
- Options over any of the above investments, e.g. interest rate or currency options.
- All other products are outside the scope of the directive.

2.9.2 MiFID firms and non-MiFID firms

The MiFID definition of investment services is narrower than that of FSMA. In particular, financial analysis and research is not included and thus cannot be 'passported' in its own right. However, providing MiFID authorisation is held for a **'core service'** (i.e. dealing, arranging the receipt and transmission of orders, advising or managing), the firm's involvement in **'ancillary services'** such as analysis can be passported. If the firm only undertakes ancillary services, authorisation would be required in each Member State.

As a result of these differences, certain authorised firms under FSMA will not be covered by MiFID.

MiFID Activities	MiFID Activities	Non-MiFID
Core	**Ancillary**	
These require authorisation and will benefit from the passport regime enabling them to conduct business across the EEA.	These may be passported providing the firm also conducts a core activity. However, if conducted on their own they will not be able to seek the passport. They are covered by MiFID and require authorisation.	Services not covered within MiFID may need to seek authorisation if domestic rules require it. Even if authorised in their own home state they will be unable to passport their activities to other Member States.

Core	Ancillary	Non-MiFID
<ul><li>Firms executing orders or dealing on own account (**dealing**) in investments (e.g. shares, derivatives, repos, units in collective investment schemes).</li><li>Firms **arranging** the receipt and transmission of orders.</li><li>Firms **managing** investments.</li><li>Investment **advice**</li><li>Operating a Multi-lateral Trading Facility</li><li>Underwriting issues and/or placing issues.</li></ul>	<ul><li>Corporate finance advice.</li><li>Loans to faciliate MiFID transactions.</li><li>Safekeeping and administration.</li><li>Safe custody services.</li><li>Services relating to underwriting.</li><li>Foreign exchange services.</li></ul>	<ul><li>Deposit taking</li><li>Depositories and operators of Collective Investment Schemes</li><li>Corporate finance professionals providing incidental services to their professional business</li><li>Service companies</li><li>Non-financial spread betting</li><li>Lloyds insurance</li><li>Occupational pension schemes</li></ul>

3 THE FINANCIAL SERVICES AUTHORITY

Prior to FSMA, a patchwork quilt of legislation existed. There were a number of different regulators for each section of the financial services industry. Under FSMA and its related legislation, all of these functions are undertaken by a single statutory regulator – the Financial Services Authority (FSA).

3.1 Functions of the FSA

The FSA is an unusually large and powerful regulator. It regulates investment banking and insurance businesses and is the sole authorising body. The FSA is not, however, regarded as acting on behalf of the Crown or being part of the government. Its members, officers and staff are, therefore, not Crown servants nor civil servants. In fact, the FSA is a private company limited by guarantee and given powers by FSMA.

The FSA's main line of **accountability** is to **HM Treasury**, which appoints the Board and Chairman. HM Treasury will judge the FSA against the requirements laid down in S2 of FSMA. This includes a requirement to ensure that the burdens imposed on the regulated community are **proportionate** to the benefits it will provide. In delivering against this, the FSA has done a cost/benefit analysis whenever it has increased the burden of a rule.

HM Treasury also requires that the FSA submit an **annual report** covering such matters as the discharge of its functions and the extent to which the four regulatory objectives have been met. HM Treasury also has powers to commission and publish an independent review of the FSA's use of resources and commission official enquiries into serious regulatory failures.

Its principal powers include the following.

- Granting **authorisation** and permission to firms to undertake regulated activities.
- **Approving** individuals to perform controlled functions.
- The right to issue under **S138**
    - General rules (such as **COBS**) for authorised firms which appear to be necessary or expedient to protect the interests of consumers.
    - Principles (such as the **Principles for Businesses**).
    - Codes of conduct (such as the **Code of Practice for Approved Persons**).
    - Evidential provisions and guidance.
- The right to **investigate** authorised firms or approved persons.
- The right to take **enforcement** action against authorised firms and approved persons.
- The right to **discipline** authorised firms and approved persons.
- The power to take action against any person for **market abuse**.
- The power to **recognise** investment exchanges and clearing houses.

3.2 Approved persons

Section 59 of FSMA and the *Supervision Manual* (SUP) states that a person cannot carry out a controlled function in a firm unless that individual has been **approved** by the FSA. Note that we are now referring to the individual members of staff of an authorised firm. So a firm is 'authorised' while its key staff are 'approved'. The FSA may specify a function as a **controlled function** if the individual performing it is

- Exerting a significant influence on the conduct of the firm's affairs.
- Dealing directly with customers.
- Dealing with the property of clients.

The *FSA Handbook* (specifically, the *Supervision Manual* – SUP 10) has identified specific controlled functions which can be split into the following groups.

Group	Function
Governing Functions	Director Non-Executive director Chief Executive Partner Director of an unincorporated association Small Friendly Society
Required Functions	Apportionment and oversight EEA investment business oversight Compliance oversight Money Laundering Reporting Officer Actuarial
Systems and Control Functions	Systems and control function
Significant Management Functions	Significant management function
Customer Functions	Customer function

Significant Influence Functions

Individuals who fall within any of the above categories **except** customer functions would be considered to be exerting a **significant influence** on the conduct of the firm's affairs.

3.3 Procedure for obtaining approval

To obtain approval, a person must satisfy the FSA that they are **fit and proper** to carry out the controlled function. The suitability of a member of staff who performs a controlled function is covered in the 'Fit and Proper Test for Approved Persons'. The most important considerations are as set out below.

- **Honesty, integrity and reputation**

  The FSA will look at whether the person's reputation might have an adverse impact on the firm for which it is carrying out a controlled function. This will include looking at a number of factors including whether they have had any criminal convictions, civil claims, previous disciplinary proceedings, censure or investigations by any regulator, exchange, governing body or court; any other previous contraventions of regulations; any complaints which have been upheld; any connection with any body which has previously been refused a registration, authorisation or licence or had such registrations, authorisations or licences revoked or been expelled by a regulatory or governmental body; whether they have had any management role within any entities which have gone into liquidation; whether they have been dismissed or asked to resign from a similar position or position of trust; any disqualifications as a director, and finally whether they have been candid and truthful in their dealings with all regulatory bodies and demonstrated a willingness to comply with the regulatory and legal standards applicable to them. When looking at previous convictions, even old (i.e. spent) convictions, as defined in the Rehabilitation of Offenders Act 1974, can be taken into account.

- **Competency and capability**

  The FSA will look at whether the Training and Competence requirements in the *FSA Handbook* have been complied with and whether they have demonstrated by training and/or experience that they are able to perform the controlled function. If a person has been convicted of, or dismissed or suspended from employment due to drug or alcohol abuse, this will be considered in relation only to their continuing ability to perform that function. In addition, S61 of FSMA emphasises that the fit and proper test for approved persons includes assessing qualifications, training and competence. It is **not** a requirement that a person has experience in order to be approved.

- **Financial soundness**

  The FSA will look at whether the applicant has any outstanding judgement debts, has filed for bankruptcy or been involved in any similar proceedings. The fact that a person is of limited financial resources will not in itself affect their suitability to perform a controlled function.

These criteria must be met on a continuing basis. Individuals performing a controlled function must obtain approval **before** they take up the role and a firm must take reasonable care to ensure that a member of staff does not perform a controlled function unless he has prior approval from the FSA. Approved persons must adhere to the seven **Statements of Principle** which are discussed later.

3.4 Procedure for removing approval

The firm has a duty to send a notice to withdraw approval on **Form C** within **seven** business days to the FSA if an approved person ceases to perform a controlled function.

If this is just because a person has left the firm (or no longer performs that function within the firm) then this will be a 'clean' deregistration. If however, the person is dismissed on grounds that may mean they are no longer considered fit and proper, then the firm should inform the FSA via a 'dirty' deregistration (known as a qualified Form C). A qualified form is completed for one of the following three reasons:

- The firm submitting Form C reasonably believes that the information it contains may affect the FSA's assessment of an approved person's fitness and propriety; or

- A firm dismisses, or suspends, an approved person from its employment; or

- An approved person resigns whilst under investigation by the firm, the FSA or any other regulatory body.

4 HIGH LEVEL STANDARDS OF THE FSA HANDBOOK

The first block of the *FSA Handbook* is called **High Level Standards** and its main focus is on overarching principles, which provide ethical codes for the authorised business and its approved persons.

4.1 Principles for Businesses

The **Principles for Businesses** form the bedrock of the regulatory system. Whilst it is easy to criticise them as being little more than 'statements of the blindingly obvious', they are useful in that they help to clarify our thoughts about what may constitute unethical behaviour.

The Principles for Businesses apply to every **authorised firm** carrying out a regulated activity (approved persons are not covered by these principles, but are instead subject to a separate set of principles, **known as Statements of Principle**, which we shall look at later). Whilst the Principles for Businesses apply with respect to regulated activities generally, they apply only in a 'prudential context' with respect to the activities of accepting deposits, general insurance and long-term pure protection policies (i.e. that have no surrender value and are payable upon death). This means the FSA will only take action where the contravention is a serious or persistent violation of a principle that has an impact on confidence in the financial system, the fitness and propriety of the firm or the adequacy of the firm's financial resources.

The Principles for Businesses are drafted by the FSA and derive their authority from the FSA's rule making powers under FSMA and the **statutory objectives**. Note that the consequence of breaching a principle makes the firm liable to enforcement or disciplinary sanctions. The FSA may bring these sanctions where it can show that the firm has been at fault in some way. The definition of 'fault' will depend upon the principle referred to.

The FSA's **principle based approach** to regulation has earned it a reputation as a world class regulator. This has led the FSA to pursue an agenda of yet more principles based regulations and removal of detailed rules from the FSA handbook.

The 'principles-based' approach implies that, rather than formulate detailed rules to cover the varied circumstances firms are involved in, the Authority would expect firms to carry more responsibility in making their own judgement about how to apply the regulatory Principles and Statements of Principle to their business. The FSA's initiative on **'Treating Customers Fairly' (TCF)** is an example of the Authority's emphasis on principles.

The impact of principles-based regulation has also been seen in **enforcement cases**, where the FSA has relied on its expectation that firms would follow higher-level principles, even where there might not have been breaches of detailed rules. The FSA is deliberately shifting responsibility on to the **senior management** of firms to decide what higher level principles mean for them.

Below are listed the **11 Principles for Businesses** with a brief description of the activity to which each relates.

Principles for Businesses

1.	**Integrity**
	A firm must conduct its business with integrity.
2.	**Skill, Care and Diligence**
	A firm must conduct its business with due skill, care and diligence.
3.	**Management and Control**
	A firm must take reasonable care to organise and control its affairs responsibly and effectively, with adequate risk management systems. Note: it would not be a breach of this principle if the firm failed to prevent unforeseeable risks.
4.	**Financial Prudence**
	A firm must maintain adequate financial resources.
5.	**Market Conduct**
	A firm must observe proper standards of market conduct.
6.	**Customers' Interests**
	A firm must pay due regard to the interests of its customers and treat them fairly.
7.	**Communications with Clients**
	For customers – A firm must pay due regard to their information needs and communicate information to them in a way that is clear, fair and not misleading.
	For market counterparties – A firm must communicate information in a way that is not misleading.
8.	**Conflicts of Interest**
	A firm must manage conflicts of interest fairly, both between itself and its customers and between one customer and another client.
9.	**Customers: Relationships of Trust**
	A firm must take reasonable care to ensure the suitability of its advice and discretionary decisions for any customer who is entitled to rely upon its judgement.
10.	**Clients' Assets**
	A firm must arrange adequate protection for clients' assets when it is responsible for those assets.
11.	**Relations with Regulators**
	A firm must deal with its regulators in an open and co-operative way and must promptly tell the FSA anything relating to the firm of which the FSA would reasonably expect prompt notice.

It should be noted that some principles refer to **clients** (such as Principle 10), whilst others refer to **customers** (such as Principle 9). This affects the scope of the relevant principle.

- **Client**

  Client is an all-encompassing term that includes everyone from the smallest retail client through to the largest investment firm. It therefore includes eligible counterparties, professional clients and retail clients.

- **Customer**

  'Customer' is a more restricted term that excludes 'eligible counterparties'. Principle 7 applies in whole to a firm's customers and only in part to eligible counterparties.

4.2 Systems and controls

The FSA has drafted a large amount of guidance on **Principle 3**. This emphasis comes from a desire to avoid a repetition of the collapse of Barings Bank, where it was clear that management methods and the control environment were deficient.

The FSA suggests that, in order to comply with its obligation to maintain appropriate systems, a firm should carry out a regular review of the above factors.

Probably the most significant requirement is the need for the Chief Executive to apportion duties amongst senior management and to monitor their performance. Beyond this, the main issues that a firm is expected to consider in establishing compliance with Principle 3 are as follows.

- Organisation and reporting lines.
- Compliance.
- Risk assessment.
- Suitable employees and agents.
- Audit Committee.
- Remuneration policies.
- Anti-money laundering procedures

There is a section of the *FSA Handbook* called **'Senior Management Arrangements, Systems and Controls'** (the examiner may refer to it as **SYSC**). As the name suggests, the main purpose of this section of the *FSA Handbook* is to encourage directors and senior managers of authorised firms to take appropriate responsibility for their firm's arrangements and ensure they know what those obligations are.

There is a rule regarding apportionment of significant responsibilities, which requires firms to make clear how particular responsibilities are allocated within the firm and to ensure that the business of the firm can be adequately monitored and controlled by the directors, senior management and the firm's governing body. Details of apportionment and allocation of responsibilities must be recorded and kept up to date. Records must be kept for six years from the date it is replaced by a more up-to-date record.

Under **SYSC 3.1.1**, the firm has a general obligation to take reasonable care to establish and maintain systems and controls that are **appropriate** to its business.

Furthermore, the compliance function must be designed for the purpose of complying with regulatory requirements and to counter the risk that the firm may be used to further financial crime.

Depending on the nature, scale and complexity of the business it may be appropriate for the firm to have a separate **compliance department** although this is not an absolute requirement. The organisation and responsibilities of the compliance department should be properly recorded and documented and it should be staffed by an **appropriate number of persons** who are sufficiently **independent** to perform their duties objectively. The compliance function should have unfettered access to records and to the governing body of the firm.

4.3 Statements of Principle and Code of Practice for Approved Persons

The **Statements of Principle** apply to all **approved persons** (i.e. relevant employees of FSA firms) when they are performing a **controlled function**.

There are **seven Statements of Principle**. The first four principles apply to all approved persons (which includes those doing a significant influence function as well as those not doing a significant influence function). The final three principles only apply to approved persons undertaking a significant influence function.

Statements of Principle

1. Integrity
2. Skill, care and diligence   } Apply to all
3. Proper standard of market conduct   approved persons
4. Deal with the regulator in an open way

5. Proper organisation of business   } Apply only to those
6. Skill, care and diligence in management   doing a significant
7. Comply with regulatory requirements   influence function

Section 64 of FSMA requires the FSA to issue a code of practice to help approved persons to determine whether or not their conduct complies with the *Statements of Principle*. The FSA has complied with this obligation by issuing the **Code of Practice for Approved Persons (The Code)**. This sets out descriptions of conduct which, in the FSA's opinion, does not comply with one of the statements, and factors which will be taken into account in determining whether or not an approved person's conduct does comply with the **Statements of Principle**. These descriptions have the status of **evidential provisions**, meaning non-compliance with them will tend to establish a breach of the principle.

The Code is not conclusive – it is only evidential towards indicating that a Statement of Principle has been breached. Account will be taken of the context in which the course of conduct was undertaken. In determining whether there has been a breach of Principles 5-7, account will be taken of the nature and complexity of the business, the role and responsibilities of the approved person, and the knowledge that the approved person had (or should have had) of the regulatory concerns arising in the business under their control. The examples in the Code of actions that would breach a principle are not exhaustive.

In addition, the Code may be amended from time to time and the current published version at the time of the approved person's conduct will be the relevant Code that the FSA will look to in determining whether or not there has been a breach. The FSA will look at all the circumstances of a particular matter and will only determine that there has been a breach where the individual is **'personally culpable'**, i.e. deliberate conduct or conduct below the reasonable standard expected of that person in the circumstances.

We shall now look at the **seven Statements of Principle** in detail, taking into account the treatment of each by the Code.

Statement of Principle 1

An approved person must act with integrity in carrying out his controlled functions.

The Code provides examples of behaviour that would not comply with this Statement of Principle. These include an approved person

- **Deliberately misleading clients**, his firm or the FSA; or

- Deliberately failing to inform a customer, his firm or the FSA, that their understanding of a material issue is incorrect.

BPP
LEARNING MEDIA

Statement of Principle 2

An approved person must act with skill, care and diligence in carrying out his controlled functions.

Examples of non-compliant behaviour under Statement of Principle 2 include failing to inform a **customer**, or his firm, of material information or failing to control client assets.

The coverage of Statement of Principle 2 is similar to Principle 1. The difference is that Principle 1 states that each act needs to be **deliberate**. Principle 2 may be breached by acts which, whilst not deliberate wrongdoing, are **negligent**.

Statement of Principle 3

An approved person must observe proper standards of market conduct in carrying out his controlled functions.

Examples of non-compliant behaviour under Statement of Principle 3 include

- A breach of market codes and exchange rules.
- A breach of the Inter-Professional Conduct Rules or the Code of Market Conduct.

The FSA expects all approved persons to meet proper standards whether they are participating in organised markets such as exchanges, or trading in less formal over-the-counter markets.

Statement of Principle 4

An approved person must deal with the FSA and with other regulators in an open and co-operative way and must disclose appropriately any information of which the FSA would reasonably expect notice.

This Statement of Principle concerns the requirement to co-operate, not only with the FSA, but also with other bodies such as an overseas regulator or an exchange.

Approved persons do not have a duty to report concerns directly to the FSA unless they are responsible for such reports. The obligation on most approved persons is to report concerns of **'material significance'** in accordance with the firm's **internal procedures**. If no such procedures exist, the report should be made direct to the FSA.

It would also be a breach of this Statement of Principle if an approved person did not attend an interview or meeting with the FSA, answer questions or produce documents when requested to do so and within the time limit specified.

Statement of Principle 5

An approved person performing a significant influence function must take reasonable steps to ensure that the business of the firm for which he is responsible in his controlled function is organised so that it can be controlled effectively.

As stated above, Principles 5-7 relate only to those approved persons performing a significant influence function. This principle requires those performing a significant influence function to **delegate** responsibilities responsibly and effectively. Paramount to this is a requirement that they should delegate only where it is to a suitable person. In addition, they must provide those persons with proper reporting lines, authorisation levels and job descriptions. Clearly, all of these factors (and in particular the suitability requirement) should be regularly reviewed. Principle 5 will be particularly relevant to the person whose responsibility it is to ensure appropriate apportionment of responsibilities under the Senior Management Arrangements, Systems and Controls (SYSC) section of the *FSA Handbook*.

Statement of Principle 6

An approved person performing a significant influence function must exercise due skill, care and diligence in managing the business of the firm for which he is responsible in his controlled function.

This principle requires those performing a significant influence function to inform themselves about the affairs of the business for which they are responsible. They should not permit transactions or an expansion of the business unless they fully **understand the risks** involved. They must also take care when monitoring highly profitable or unusual transactions and in those or other cases, must never accept implausible or unsatisfactory explanations from subordinates.

This principle links to Principle 5 as it makes it clear that **delegation is not an abdication** of responsibility. Therefore, where delegation has been made, a person must still monitor and control that part of the business and, therefore, should require progress reports and question those reports where appropriate.

Statement of Principle 7

An approved person performing a significant influence function must take reasonable steps to ensure that the business of the firm for which he is responsible in his controlled function complies with the regulatory requirements imposed on that business.

This has a clear link to **Principle 3** of the Principles for Businesses – Management and Control. Those exerting a significant influence on the firm must take reasonable steps to ensure that the requirements set out therein are implemented within their firm. They should also review the improvement of such systems and controls, especially where there has been a breach of the regulatory requirements. Principle 7 will be particularly relevant to the person whose responsibility it is to ensure appropriate apportionment of responsibilities under the Senior Management Arrangements, Systems and Controls section of the *FSA Handbook*.

5 FSA SUPERVISION AND ENFORCEMENT POWERS

5.1 Risk-based supervision

The FSA's approach to supervision is designed to reflect a number of important concepts.

- The FSA's four regulatory objectives.
- The responsibility of senior management to ensure that it takes reasonable care to organise and control the affairs of the firm effectively and develops and maintains adequate risk management systems. It is the responsibility of the management to ensure the firm complies with its regulatory requirements.
- The principle that the burden or restriction on firms should be proportionate to the benefits to be provided.

The FSA's overall approach, therefore, is one of risk-based supervision. The aim of this is to focus the FSA's resources in the most efficient and economic way.

The Authority has developed a system known as the Advanced Risk Responsive Operating Framework ('ARROW'), which involves the FSA looking at particular risks posed by individual firms and also risks to consumers and to the industry as a whole.

The FSA will therefore undertake an impact and probability assessment on each firm to determine the risks that the firm poses to the four regulatory objectives. In terms of impact, this looks primarily at the impact on the four regulatory objectives. In terms of probability, this is assessed in terms of 'risk groups' arising from the firm's strategy, business risks, financial soundness, type of customers, systems and controls and organisation of the firm. The FSA will place firms into risk categories and communicate with them the outcome of the assessment.

The usual procedure for this categorisation is as follows.

- Preliminary assessment of the firm's impact on the regulatory objectives
- Probability assessment – the detail will depend on the impact rating and complexity of the firm
- A sample of various firm's categorisations are then reviewed by a validation panel
- A letter is sent to the firm outlining category
- The FSA ensures ongoing review of risk assessment

In terms of the supervisory process, the FSA will use a broad range of tools, including:

- Desk-based reviews
- Meetings with the firm
- On-site inspections
- Issuing public statements
- Imposing requirements on the firm

The FSA's policy on supervision is grouped under the following headings.

- Diagnostic
- Monitoring
- Preventative
- Remedial

5.2 Information gathering and investigatory powers

Under **S165** of FSMA, the FSA may, by written notice, require an authorised firm (or any person connected with it) or certain other persons (e.g. RIEs) to produce specified information or documents which it reasonably requires. The FSA can require the information or documents to be provided within a specified, reasonable timescale and at a specified place. The FSA may also require that the information provided is verified and documents are authenticated.

The FSA may seek access to an authorised firm's premises on demand (i.e. **no notice** is required).

The FSA may also commission a report from a skilled person (e.g. an accountant).

Finally, the FSA may launch an investigation on a number of grounds.

- Where it has good reason to do so.

- Where any person has contravened specific provisions of the regulatory regime (such as market abuse).

- At the request of an overseas regulator.

Whilst the FSA will normally give the subject written notice of the investigation, it can commence an investigation without doing this if it feels that the provision of the notice may result in the investigation being frustrated.

During the course of an investigation, there is no automatic requirement that the firm or an approved person cease trading.

FSMA gives sweeping powers to investigators. Generally, the FSA can also require a person under investigation or any connected person to attend at a specified time and place for questioning. The FSA may also require a person to **produce documents** (of which the investigator may take copies only).

Failure to co-operate with an investigator without reasonable excuse is a criminal offence. The FSA may also take action themselves, such as increasing the severity of the sanction for the original breach. This effectively removes a person's right to silence. In order to ensure that the regime is compliant with human rights legislation, such answers will not be admissible in criminal or market abuse proceedings.

The FSA will not normally make public the fact that it is or is not investigating a particular matter or the outcome of any investigation.

5.3 Disciplinary process and the role of the RDC

Disciplinary measures are one of the regulatory tools available to the FSA. The FSA must be proportionate in its use of disciplinary measures, i.e. the punishment must fit the crime. The disciplinary process has been designed to ensure that it is compliant with human rights legislation. Therefore, whilst FSA staff will investigate the matter and decide whether they feel enforcement action is appropriate, they will not take the final decision on matters of regulatory significance. However, the FSA can take decisions themselves under their own **executive procedures** for matters of lesser regulatory impact to the firms, such as imposing a requirement on a firm to submit regular reports covering activities such as trading, complaints or management accounts.

For more significant disciplinary decisions (called statutory notice decisions) the FSA pass the case to another body, the **Regulatory Decisions Committee (RDC)** which will look at the case and decide whether or not to take action. This would cover the giving of fines, censures, restitution orders, and withdrawing, varying or refusing authorisation or approval. For less serious disciplinary actions, e.g. requesting the firm to provide reports, the FSA may act itself under its 'executive procedures'.

The RDC is appointed by the FSA to exercise certain regulatory powers on its behalf and is accountable to the board of the FSA. However, the RDC is outside the FSA management structure and apart from the Chairman of the RDC, none of the RDC's members are FSA employees. The RDC members comprise practitioners and suitable individuals representing the public interest.

If the RDC decides to take action, a Warning Notice will be sent, containing details of the proposed action. The person concerned then has access to the material upon which the FSA is relying and may make **oral or written representations** to the RDC. The RDC will then issue a Decision Notice detailing the reasons for the decision, proposed sanction and a notice of the right to refer the matter to the Financial Services and Markets Tribunal which undertakes a complete rehearing of the case. When a Decision Notice is accepted, or appeals finalised, a Final Notice is sent to the person. Note that a Final Notice only contains FSA/RDC/Tribunal discipline, not any disciplinary action the firm has taken itself internally. This is summarised in the following table. A Warning Notice, Decision Notice and Supervisory Notice comprise the three statutory notices of the FSA.

Alternatively, after receiving a warning notice, the accused person can discuss the proposed action with FSA staff on an informal basis to try and reach **settlement**. Decisions are made by two decision makers from the FSA of at least Director status (the Director of Enforcement will usually be one of the decision makers). This means settlement decisions are made entirely separately from the RDC and so the integrity of the RDC can be maintained for contested cases. To ensure that the FSA is consistent in its approach to penalties between RDC decisions in contested cases and settlement decisions, the FSA will have regular liaison at policy level to ensure consistency of approach and ensure the RDC is fully briefed on the factors the FSA considers important for penalty setting.

```
                                    ┌─────────────────────────────────┐
                                    │ FSA may issue a Supervisory Notice │
                                    └─────────────────────────────────┘
                              ↗
                    Immediate            ┌─────────────────────────┐
                     action              │      Passed to          │
                                         │ Regulatory Decisions Committee │
        ┌──────────────┐                 │                         │
        │  FSA staff   │                 │ 1. RDC issues a warning notice │
        │ review and   │   Normal        │    setting out proposed action │
        │ decide to    │ ─ action ─→     │ 2. Person concerned has access │
        │  proceed     │                 │    to FSA material and makes oral/ │
        └──────────────┘                 │    written representations │
                                         │                         │
                                         │ 3. Decision notice issued │
                                         │    with proposed sanction │
                                         └─────────────────────────┘

          "Not guilty"          Accept              Challenge

    ┌──────────────┐     ┌────────────────────┐   ┌──────────────────────────┐
    │  Notice of   │     │ Sanction implemented │   │ May refer to Financial Services │
    │discontinuance│     └────────────────────┘   │ and Markets Tribunal within 28 │
    └──────────────┘              ⇓                │          days            │
                            Final notice           └──────────────────────────┘
```

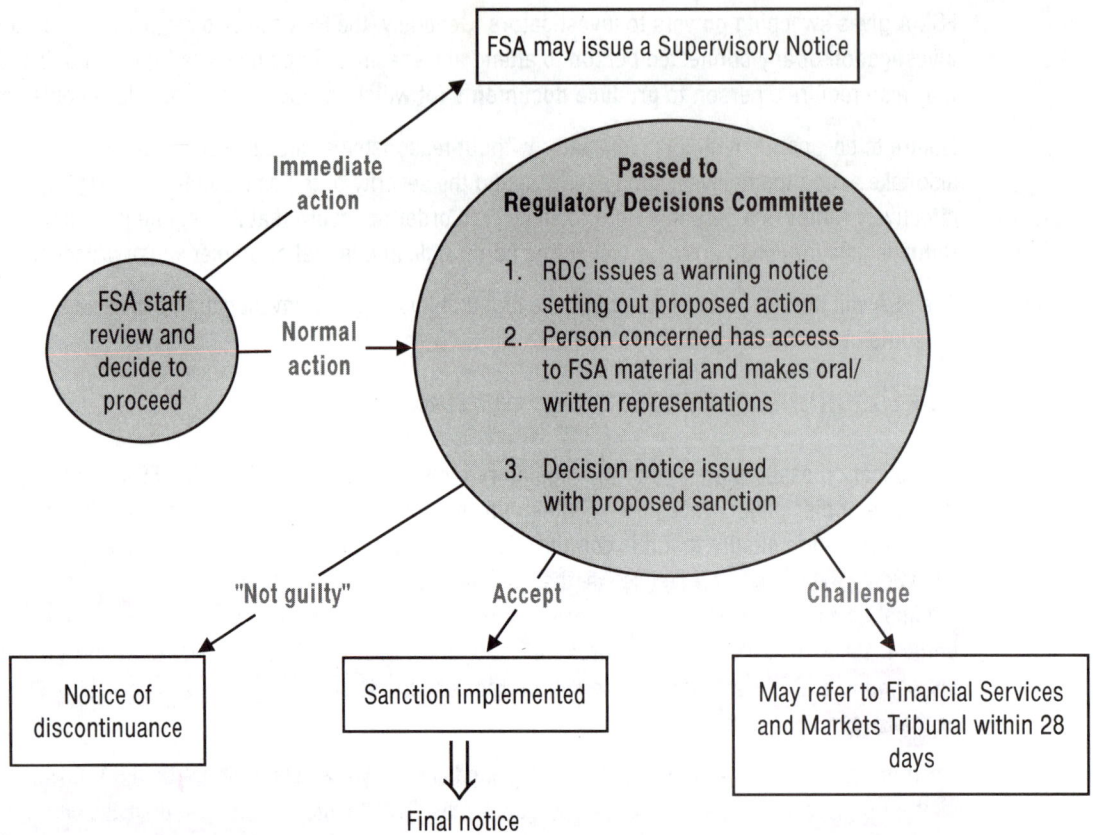

Under Part V of FSMA 2000, the FSA must commence disciplinary action within **two years** of first being aware of the misconduct.

It should be noted that S391 of FSMA states that the FSA may not publish information if it would be unfair to the person to whom it relates. The effect of this is that no Warning Notice or Decision Notice may be published by the FSA or the person to whom it is given until reference to the Tribunal has been dealt with and it is clear of further appeals. Therefore, it will be the details of the Final Decision Notice which will be published by the FSA, not the original Decision or Warning Notice.

5.4 Financial Services and Markets Tribunal

FSMA makes provision for an independent body (known as the **Financial Services and Markets Tribunal**) accountable to the Ministry of Justice which is established under the Financial Services and Markets Tribunal Rules 2001. This provides for a complete rehearing of FSA enforcement and authorisation cases where the firm or individual and the FSA have not been able to agree the outcome. Therefore, if a firm or individual receives a decision notice or supervisory notice or is refused authorisation or approval it may refer this to the Tribunal. The Tribunal will determine what appropriate action the FSA should take and in doing so can consider any new evidence that has come to light since the original decision was made.

CHAPTER ROUNDUP

- Four statutory objectives of the FSA regulatory system are set out in FSMA 2000.

- The FSA has wide powers, including approval of individuals to perform controlled functions, and authorisation of firms. The Authority can issue rules and codes of conduct, can investigate authorised firms or approved persons, and can take discipline and enforcement action.

- The Principles for Businesses (PRIN) state firms' fundamental obligations under the regulatory system, and require honest, fair and professional conduct from firms.

- FSA Statements of Principle apply generally to all approved persons (i.e. relevant employees of FSA firms) when they are performing a controlled function.

- The SYSC manual in the FSA Handbook encourages directors and senior managers of authorised firms to take appropriate responsibility for their firm's arrangements and to ensure they know what those obligations are.

- The FSA's 'principles-based' approach to regulation implies that, rather than rely on detailed FSA rules, the Authority expects firms to carry more responsibility in making their own judgement about how to apply regulatory principles to their business.

- No-one may carry on a regulated activity, unless either authorised, or exempt from authorisation. Some activities (e.g. media coverage, but not tipsheets) are excluded from the authorisation requirement.

- Disciplinary measures include public censure, unlimited fines, restitution orders and cancellation of authorisation or approval. Various Statutory Notices may be issued in cases involving the Regulatory Decisions Committee.

- The Financial Services and Markets Tribunal can re-hear FSA enforcement and authorisation cases.

- The FSA has wide powers to visit firms' premises without notice and to require documents to be produced.

- A firm may be authorised through obtaining 'Part IV permission' or, for EEA firms, through passporting under MiFID. Five threshold conditions must be met for authorisation, which is specific to the types of activities the firm carries out.

- Those carrying out a controlled function need to meet a 'fit and proper' test to be approved persons. This test covers honesty, integrity and reputation; competence and capability; and financial soundness.

- Controlled functions include exerting significant influence on the firm, and dealing with customers or their property.

TEST YOUR KNOWLEDGE

Check your knowledge of the chapter here, without referring back to the text.

1.	What are the four regulatory/statutory objectives of the FSA?	▪ ▪ ▪ ▪	
2.	What are the penalties for breaching the general prohibition?		
3.	What is the RDC and what is its role?		
4.	Can you name three excluded activities?	▪ ▪ ▪	
5.	What is the term applying to a crossing network operated by an investment firm to enable investors to buy and sell financial instruments?		
6.	What rights does the FSA have under S138 FSMA 2000?		
7.	Which Statements of Principle apply to all approved persons?		
8.	What is the difference between authorisation and approval?		
9.	List six of the FSA Principles for Businesses.	▪ ▪ ▪ ▪ ▪ ▪	
10.	Can you name three types of exempt persons?	▪ ▪ ▪	

TEST YOUR KNOWLEDGE: ANSWERS

1. Maintaining confidence, promoting public understanding, protecting consumers, reduction of financial crime.

    (See Section 2.2)

2. Penalties for breach of S19 FSMA 2000 include criminal and civil sanctions. The maximum criminal penalty is two years in prison and/or an unlimited fine (in the Crown Court). Civil penalties include contracts being unenforceable, compensation, injunctions and restitution orders.

    (See Section 2.3)

3. The RDC is the Regulatory Decisions Committee. The RDC is outside the FSA's management structure and is used to decide on action in disciplinary cases and also withdrawing, varying or refusing authorisation or approval.

    (See Section 5.3)

4. Recall the word **Demote**: **D**ealing as principal where the person is not holding themselves out to the market as willing to deal, **E**mployee share schemes, **M**edia, **O**verseas persons, **T**rustees, nomin**E**es and personal representatives. You could have mentioned any three.

    (See Section 2.5)

5. Multilateral Trading Facility (MTF).

    (See Section 2.6.4)

6. The right to issue general rules, principles, codes of conduct and guidance.

    (See Section 3.1)

7. The first four Statements of Principle apply to all approved persons. These are: Integrity; Skill, care and diligence; Proper standards of market conduct; Deal with the regulator in an open way.

    (See Section 4.3)

8. A firm needs to be authorised under S19 FSMA 2000 if it is carrying out regulated activities by way of business in the UK. An individual requires approval under S59 FSMA 2000 if he/she is undertaking one of the FSA's controlled functions e.g. as director, or compliance oversight.

    (See Section 3.2)

9. You could have listed any six of the following: Integrity, Skill, Care & Diligence, Management and Control, Financial Prudence, Market Conduct, Customers' Interests, Communications with Clients, Conflicts of Interest, Customers: Relationships of Trust, Clients' Assets, Relations with Regulators.

    (See Section 4.1)

10. You could have mentioned any three of the following (mnemonic: **April**): **A**ppointed Representatives, **P**rofessional people, **R**IEs, **R**OIEs, **R**CHs, **I**nstitutions, e.g. the Bank of England and **L**loyd's members.

    (See Section 2.6)

2

The Conduct of Business Sourcebook

INTRODUCTION

The FSA Principles for Businesses are central to the 'principles-based' approach to regulation. Recall that protection of consumers is one of the FSA's four statutory objectives. The FSA has made detailed rules in the 'Conduct of Business Sourcebook' (COBS) which are aimed largely at providing such protection.

The COBS rules cover a wide range of operational areas, and have been substantially revised in 2007 following the implementation of the Markets in Financial Instruments Directive (MiFID). This underlines the fact that regulation is increasingly being determined at the European level.

CHAPTER CONTENTS

CHAPTER LEARNING OBJECTIVES

The Application and General Provisions of the FSA Conduct of Business Sourcebook to Corporate Finance Business

- **Know** the application of Conduct of Business Rules to corporate finance business.

Rules Applying to all Firms Conducting Designated Investment Business

- **Know** the application and purpose of the rule on prohibition of inducements.

- **Know** the rules, guidance and evidential provisions regarding reliance on others.

- **Know** the requirement always to act honestly, fairly and professionally in accordance with the best interest of the client.

The Requirements of the Financial Promotion Rules

- **Know** the application of the rules on communication to clients, including financial promotions and firms' responsibilities for appointed representatives.

- **Know** the implications of S21 of FSMA 2000, the purpose and application of the financial promotion rules and the relationship with Principles for Businesses 6 and 7.

- **Know** the rule on fair, clear and not misleading communications and the guidance on fair, clear and not misleading financial promotions.

- **Know** the rule on identifying promotions as such.

- **Know** the main exceptions to the financial promotions rules in COBS, the limitations in connection to MiFID business and the existence of the Financial Promotions Order.

- **Know** the rules on prospectus advertisements and their interaction with the rules on communicating with retail clients, including financial promotions.

- **Know** the general rule in connection with communicating with retail clients; the rules on past, simulated past and future performance; and the rule on financial promotions containing offers or invitations.

- **Know** the rules on unwritten promotions, the restriction on cold calling and financial promotions for overseas persons.

- **Know** the requirement for approving financial promotions and the circumstances of relying on another firm's confirmation of compliance.

Client Categorisation

- **Understand** client status

    - The application of the rules on client classification
    - Definition of client
    - Retail client, professional client and eligible counterparty
    - When a person is acting as agent for another person

- – The rule on classifying elective professional clients
- – The rule on elective eligible counterparties
- – Providing clients with a higher level of protection
- – The requirement to provide notifications of client categorisation

Conflict of Interest

- **Understand** the concept of conflicts of interest and the application and purpose of the rules and procedures on conflicts or interest.

- **Know** the circumstances in which conflicts of interest can arise and types of conflicts particularly relevant to corporate finance.

- **Know** the rules on managing, disclosing and recording conflicts of interest.

- **Know** the rule on disclosure of conflicts.

- **Understand** the rule that requires a conflicts policy and the contents of the policy.

- **Understand** the particular conflicts of interest that relate to securities offerings.

- **Understand** how to manage conflicts of interest to ensure the fair treatment of clients including:
  - – Information barriers such as Chinese walls
  - – Reporting lines
  - – Remuneration structures
  - – Segregation of duties
  - – Policy of independence

- **Understand** the rules on managing conflicts of interest in the context of investment research and research recommendations.

Personal Account Dealing

- **Understand** the application and purpose of the personal account dealing rules and the restrictions on personal account dealing.

- **Know** the rules and personal transactions; notifications, successive personal transactions; and exception as regard the personal account dealing rules.

Advising and Dealing

- **Understand** the requirement to provide suitable advice.

- **Understand** the requirement to provide best execution and the rules on client order handling.

1 CONDUCT OF BUSINESS SOURCEBOOK (COBS)

APPLICATION TO CORPORATE FINANCE BUSINESS

1.1 Designated investment business

The COBS generally applies to all **authorised firms** carrying out the following activities from an establishment or by its appointed representatives in the **UK**:

- Accepting deposits
- Designated investment business
- Long-term life insurance business

However, the majority of the rules (except the financial promotion rules) only apply when the firm is carrying out **designated investment business** .

As we saw in Chapter 1, the term 'designated investment business' has a narrower meaning than the concept of 'regulated activities'.

1.2 Eligible counterparty business

The *Conduct of Business Sourcebook* recognises that many of its detailed rules are aimed at protecting retail clients. Therefore, only some of the COBS rules apply to **eligible counterparty business** which is MiFID or equivalent third country (that is, **non-EEA**) business.

The following main COBS rules need NOT be applied when conducting corporate finance business with eligible counterparty business (eg other banks or professionals):

- Conduct of business obligations (COBS 2), except 'Agent as client' and 'Reliance on others' rules (COBS 2.4)

- Communicating with clients (including financial promotions rules) (COBS 4)

- Rules on information about the firm and its services (COBS 6)

- Client agreements (COBS 8)

- Appropriateness rules (for non-advised sales) (COBS 10)

- Best execution, client order handling and use of dealing commission (included in COBS 11)

- Labelling of non-independent research (included in COBS 12)

- Information about designated investments (included in COBS 14)

- Reporting information to clients (COBS 16)

1.3 Further general provisions

The **territorial scope** of COBS is modified to ensure compatibility with European law: this is called the **'EEA territorial scope rule'**. One of the effects of the EEA territorial scope rule is to override the application of COBS to the overseas establishments of EEA firms in a number of cases, including circumstances covered by MiFID, the Distance Marketing Directive or the Electronic Commerce Directive. In some circumstances, the rules in COBS 4 on financial promotions and other communications will apply to communications made by UK firms to persons located outside the United Kingdom and will not apply to communications made to persons inside the United Kingdom by non-UK EEA firms.

For a UK **MiFID investment firm**, COBS rules within the scope of MiFID generally apply to its MiFID business carried on from a **UK branch or establishment**. COBS also applies to EEA MiFID investment firms carrying out business from a UK establishment. However, certain provisions (on investment research, non-independent research and on personal transactions) apply on a **'Home State' basis**: those rules will apply to all establishments in the EEA for the UK firm, and will not apply to a non-UK EEA firm.

2 ACCEPTING CUSTOMERS

2.1 Client classification

Within any cost-effective regulatory system, protection provided ought to be **proportionate** to the need for protection. This is because there is not only a cost element to protection but also an inverse relationship with freedom. It is desirable that those who do not require high protection are given more freedom to trade without the restrictions that the rules inevitably bring.

The **size** and **financial awareness** of **clients** will determine the level of protection. As the size/knowledge increases, protection will decrease. A system of categorising clients can help determine the level of protection that is appropriate to the client.

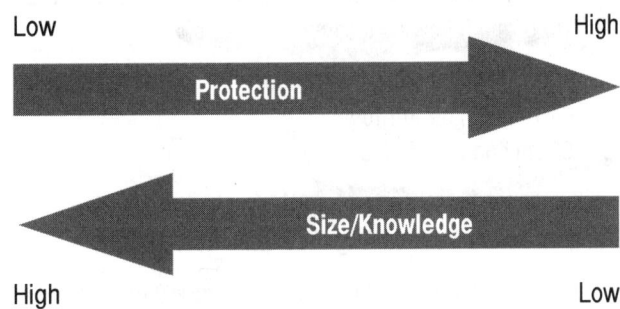

While this would ideally be a continuous process, gradually moving from full protection to no protection, in practical terms this is an impossibility.

2.2 Client categories

Firms (unless they are providing only the special level of **basic advice** on a **stakeholder product**) are obliged to classify all clients who are undertaking **designated investment business,** before doing such business.

MiFID creates three client categories:

- **Eligible counterparties** – who are either *per se* (**automatic**) or **elective** eligible counterparties
- **Professional clients** – who are either *per se* or **elective** professional clients
- **Retail clients**

As well as setting up criteria to classify clients into these categories, MiFID provides for clients to **change** their initial classification, on request.

2.2.1 Clients

A **client** is a person to whom an authorised **firm** provides a service in the course of carrying on a **regulated activity** or, in the case of MiFID or equivalent third country business, a person to whom a firm provides an **ancillary service**.

2.2.2 Retail clients

Retail clients are defined as those clients who are not professional clients or eligible counterparties.

2.2.3 Professional clients

Some undertakings are **automatically** recognised as **professionals**. Accordingly, these entities may be referred to as **per se** professional clients. (An undertaking is a company, partnership or unincorporated association).

Clients who are **per se professionals** are as follows.

- Entities that **require authorisation or regulation** to operate in the financial markets, including: credit institutions, investment firms, other financial institutions, insurance companies, collective investment schemes and pension funds and their management companies, commodity and commodity derivatives dealers, 'local' derivatives dealing firms, and other institutional investors.

- In relation to **MiFID** or equivalent third country business, a **large undertaking** – meaning one that meets two of the following size requirements:

  - €20 million balance sheet total
  - €40 million net turnover
  - €2 million own funds

- In relation to business that is not **MiFID** or equivalent third country business, a **large undertaking** meeting **either** of the following requirements:

  (a) Called up share capital of at least £10 million or equivalent, or
  (b) Two of the three following size tests:

    - €12.5 million balance sheet total
    - €25 million net turnover
    - 250 Average number of employees in the year

- Central banks, international institutions, and national and regional government bodies.

- Institutional investors whose main activity is to invest in financial instruments.

A firm may treat a retail client as an **elective professional client** if the following tests are met.

- **Qualitative test.** The firm assesses adequately the client's **expertise**, **experience** and **knowledge** and thereby gains reasonable assurance that, for the transactions or services envisaged, the client is capable of making his own investment decisions and understanding the risks involved.

- **Quantitative test.** In the case of **MiFID** or equivalent third country business, at least **two** of the following three criteria must apply:

  - The client has carried out at least 10 'significant' transactions per quarter on the relevant market, over the last four quarters

  - The client's portfolio, including cash deposits, exceeds €500,000

  - The client has knowledge of the transactions envisaged from at least one year's professional work in the financial sector

Additionally, for professional client status to apply:

- The client must agree in writing to be treated as a professional client.

- The firm must give written warning of the protections and compensation rights which may be lost.

- The client must state in writing, separately from the contract, that it is aware of the consequences of losing protections.

It is the responsibility of the professional client to keep the firm informed about changes (eg in portfolio size or company size) which could affect their categorisation.

COBS states that an elective professional client should not be presumed to have market knowledge and experience comparable to a *per se* professional client.

2.3 Eligible counterparties

The following, and their non-EEA equivalents, are *per se* **eligible counterparties** (i.e. they are automatically recognised as eligible counterparties). However, this automatic classification will only be in relation to Eligible Counterparty (ECP) Business. That is why most of these are also in the list of per se professional clients as if the transaction is not ECP business, they will default to a professional client.

- Investment firms
- Credit institutions
- Insurance companies
- UCITS collective investment schemes, and their management companies
- Pension funds, and their management companies
- Other financial institutions authorised or regulated under the law of the EU or an EEA State
- Certain own-account commodity derivatives dealers and 'local' derivatives firms
- National governments
- Central banks
- Supranational organisations

A firm may treat an undertaking as an **elective eligible counterparty** if the client:

- Is a *per se* professional client (unless it is such by virtue of being an institutional investor), or

- Is an elective professional client and requests the categorisation, but only in respect of the transactions and services for which it counts as a professional client, and

- In the case of MiFID or equivalent third country business, provides 'express confirmation' of their agreement (which may be for a specific transaction or may be general) to be treated as **an eligible counterparty**.

If the prospective counterparty is established in another EEA State, for MiFID business the firm should defer to the status determined by the law of that other State.

2.4 Agent as client

One area that has proved complicated in the past is where a firm is dealing with an **agent**. For example, suppose that a solicitor is acting for his client and approaches a firm to sell bonds on his client's behalf. Clearly, it is important that the firm establish whether it owes duties to the solicitor or to the solicitor's client.

The agent is the client of the firm, unless an agreement in writing treats the other person as the client.

The relevant COBS rule applies for designated investment business and ancillary services. The rule states that the firm may treat the agent as its client if

- The agent is another authorised firm or an overseas financial services institution, or

- If the agent is another person, provided that the arrangement is not to avoid duties which the firm would otherwise owe to the agent's clients.

An agreement may however be made, in writing, to treat the other person (in the above example, the solicitor's client) as the firm's client.

2.5 Providing a higher level of protection to clients

Firms must allow **professional clients** and **eligible counterparties** to re-categorise in order to get more protection. Such clients are themselves responsible for asking for higher protection if they deem themselves to be **unable** to assess properly or manage the risks involved.

Either on a firm's own initiative or following a client request or written agreement:

A **per se** **eligible counterparty** may be re-categorised as a **professional client** or **retail client**
A **per se** **professional client** may be re-categorised as a **retail client**

The **higher level of protection** may be provided through re-categorisation:

- On a general basis
- Trade by trade
- In respect of specified rules
- In respect of particular services, transactions, transaction types or product types

The client should (of course) be notified of a re-categorisation.

Firms must have written internal policies and procedures to recategorise clients.

3   RULES APPLICABLE TO ALL FIRMS

3.1 Clients best interest rule

A firm must act honestly, fairly and professionally in accordance with the best interests of its clients. This is know as the 'client best interest rule'. This always applies for retail clients. For MiFID business it applies to all clients.

3.2 Inducements

A firm must **not** pay or accept any fee or commission, or provide or receive any non-monetary benefit, in relation to designated investment business, or an ancillary service in the case of MiFID or equivalent third country business, other than:

- Fees, commissions and non-monetary benefits paid or provided to or by the client or a person on their behalf

- Fees, commissions and non-monetary benefits paid or provided to or by a third party or a person acting on their behalf, if the firm's duty to **act in the best interests of the client** is not impaired. Furthermore, (for MiFID and equivalent business, and where there is a personal recommendation of a packaged product, but not for 'basic advice') the firm must ensure that clear, comprehensive, accurate, understandable **disclosure** (except of 'reasonable non-monetary benefits' such as reasonable gifts and hospitality) is made to the client before the service is provided. Thus, the rule on inducements does not apply to disclosable commissions.

This rule supplements Principles 1 and 6 of the *Principles for Businesses*. It deals with the delicate area of inducements and seeks to ensure that firms do not conduct business under arrangements that may give rise to conflicts of interest.

Inducements could mean anything from gifts to entertainment to bribery. The rules provide a test to help judge whether or not something is acceptable.

Most firms deliver against the inducements requirements by drafting detailed '**gifts policies**' (although the rule does **not** explicitly require firms to have a gifts policy). These contain internal rules regarding disclosure, limits and clearance procedures for gifts.

3.3 Reliance on others

Suppose that a firm (**F1**) carrying out MiFID or equivalent third country business receives an instruction from an investment firm (**F2**) to perform an investment or ancillary service on behalf of a client (**C**).

F1 may rely on:

- Information about the client **C** which firm **F2** provides
- Recommendations about the service provided to **C** by **F2**

F2 remains responsible for the completeness and accuracy of information provided and the appropriateness of its advice.

More generally, a firm is taken to be in **compliance with COBS** rules which require it to obtain information, if it can show it was **reasonable** for it to rely on information provided by others in writing. It is reasonable to rely on written information provided by another where that person is **competent** and **not connected** with the firm.

It will generally be reasonable for a firm to rely on information provided to it in writing by an **unconnected authorised person** or a **professional firm** (eg legal due diligence from a law firm).

This rule links with Principle 2 *Skill, Care and Diligence*. Note that this rule has no impact on the requirements laid down in the Money Laundering Regulations, which require a firm to identify its clients for money laundering purposes.

4 FINANCIAL PROMOTION RULES

A **financial promotion** is an **invitation** or **inducement** to engage in investment activity. The term therefore describes most forms and methods of marketing financial services. It covers traditional advertising, most website content, telephone sales campaigns and face-to-face meetings.

The purpose of regulation in this area is to create a regime where the quality of financial promotions is scrutinised by an authorised firm who must then comply with lengthy rules to ensure that their promotions are **clear**, **fair and not misleading** (Principle 7) and that customers are treated **fairly** (Principle 6).

4.1 Application of the financial promotions rules

The **financial promotions rules** within COBS apply to a firm:

- Communicating with a **client** in relation to **designated investment business** other than a third party prospectus

- **Communicating** or **approving** a **financial promotion** (with some exceptions in respect of: credit promotions, home purchase plans, home reversion schemes, non-investment insurance contracts and unregulated collective investment schemes)

Firms must also apply the rules to promotions issued by their **appointed representatives**.

4.2 Territorial scope

For financial promotions, the **general application rule** applies. This indicates that the rules apply to a firm in respect of designated investment business carried out from an establishment maintained by the firm or its appointed representative in the UK. Additionally, in general the rules apply to firms carrying on business with a client in the UK from an establishment overseas.

The financial promotions rules also apply to:

- Promotions communicated to a person in the UK

- Cold calling (where the call is not requested) to someone outside the UK, if the call is from within the UK or is in respect of UK business

4.3 Fair, clear and not misleading

A firm must ensure that a communication or financial promotion is **fair, clear and not misleading**, as is **appropriate** and **proportionate** considering the means of communication and the information to be conveyed.

Note that additionally **Section 397 FSMA 2000** creates a criminal offence relating to **market manipulation**, as explained in Chapter 3 of this Study Book.

The **fair, clear and not misleading rule** is specifically interpreted in COBS as it applies to financial promotions in some aspects, as follows.

- If a product or service places a client's capital at risk, this should be made clear

- Any yield figure quoted should give a balanced impression of both short term and long term prospects for the investment

- Sufficient information must be provided to explain any complex charging arrangements, taking into account recipients' needs

- The regulator (FSA) should be named, and any non-regulated aspects made clear

- A fair, clear and not misleading impression should be given of the producer for any packaged or stakeholder products not produced by the firm

The British Bankers' Association / Building Societies Association **Code of Conduct for the Advertising of Interest Bearing Accounts** is also relevant in the case of financial promotions relating to deposits.

4.4 Identifying promotions as such

A firm must ensure that a **financial promotion** addressed to a **client** is clearly **identifiable as such**.

- This rule does not apply to a third party prospectus in respect of **MiFID** (or equivalent third country) business.

- There are also some exceptions in respect of **non-MiFID** business, including prospectus advertisements, image advertising, non-retail communications, deposits and pure protection long-term care insurance (LTCI) products.

4.5 Exceptions

As mentioned earlier, the **financial promotions rules** in **COBS 4** do **not apply** to promotions of qualifying credit, home purchase plans, home reversion schemes, non-investment insurance contracts, and certain unregulated collective investment schemes whose promotions firms may not communicate or approve.

Except in regard to disclosure of compensation arrangements, **COBS 4** does **not** apply when a firm communicates with an **eligible counterparty**.

The financial promotions rules do **not** apply to incoming communications in relation to **MiFID business** of an investment firm **from another EEA State** that are, in its home State, regulated under MiFID.

4.6 Excluded communications

A firm may rely on one or more of the following aspects which make a communication into an **excluded communication** for the purposes of the rules.

- A financial promotion that would benefit from an exemption in the Financial Promotion Order (see below) if it were communicated by an unauthorised person, or which originates outside the UK and has no effect in the UK

- A financial promotion from outside the UK that would be exempt under articles 30, 31, 32 or 33 of the Financial Promotion Order (Overseas communicators) if the office from which the financial promotion is communicated were a separate unauthorised person

- A financial promotion that is subject to, or exempted from, the Takeover Code or to the requirements relating to takeovers or related operations in another EEA State

- A personal quotation or illustration form

- A 'one-off' financial promotion that is not a cold call. The following conditions indicate that the promotion is a 'one-off', but they need not necessarily be present for a promotion to be considered as 'one-off'.

    (i) The financial promotion is communicated only to one recipient or only to one group of recipients in the expectation that they would engage in any investment activity jointly

    (ii) The identity of the product or service to which the financial promotion relates has been determined having regard to the particular circumstances of the recipient

    (iii) The financial promotion is not part of an organised marketing campaign

4.7 Financial Promotions Order

S21 FSMA 2000 makes it criminal for someone to undertake a financial promotion, i.e. invite or induce another to engage in investment activity, unless they are either:

- An **authorised firm** (i.e. **issuing the financial promotion**), or
- The content of the communication is **approved** by an authorised firm

Contravention of section 21 is punishable by up to **two** years in jail and an **unlimited** fine.

There are a number of exemptions from s21 set out in the **Financial Promotions Order**. The effect of being an **exemption** is that the promotion would **not** need to be issued or approved by an authorised firm. It would therefore not have to comply with the detailed financial promotion rules.

The main examples are as follows. (Other exemptions cover certain one-off and purely factual promotions.)

Exemption	Comments
1. Investment professional	A communication to an authorised or exempt person.
2. Deposits and insurance	Very limited application of COBS.
3. Certified high net worth individuals	Anyone may promote **unlisted securities** to persons who hold certificates of high net worth (normally signed by their accountant or employer, however, these can be self-certified by an individual) and who have agreed to be classified as such. Requirements for a certificate are that a person must have a net income of £100,000 or more, or net assets (excluding principal property) of £250,000 or more.
4. Associations of high net worth individuals	Anyone can promote non-derivative products to associations of high net worth investors.
5. Sophisticated investors	Anyone can promote products to a person who holds a certificate indicating that they are knowledgeable in a particular stock (signed by a firm or self-certified) and who have signed a statement agreeing to be such.
6. Takeover Code	Promotions subject to the Takeover Code.

4.8 Types of communication

Two types of communication are distinguished in the Financial Promotion Order: **real-time** and **non-real time**.

4.8.1 Real-time financial promotions

A **real-time financial promotion** is a promotion communicated in the course of a personal visit, telephone conversation or other interactive dialogue.

4.8.2 Non-real time financial promotions

A **non-real time financial promotion** is a promotion that is not real-time and **includes** promotions communicated by letter, email or included in publications disseminated in paper format, in material displayed on a website or in a sound and television broadcast.

Factors **indicating** that a promotion is non-real time:

- It is communicated to more than one person in an identical form
- It is communicated in a way that creates a record
- It is made in a way that does not require immediate response

4.9 Prospectus advertisements

Where a **prospectus** is issued on an offer or an admission of transferable securities to trading, there are rules governing advertisements relating to it.

The **advertisement**:

- Must state that a prospectus has been or will be published, and indicate where it can be obtained
- Must be clearly recognisable as an advertisement
- Must not contain inaccurate or misleading information
- Must be consistent with information in the prospectus

A written advertisement should contain a **bold and prominent statement** indicating that it is not a prospectus but an advertisement and that investors should not subscribe for transferable securities mentioned except on the basis of information in the prospectus.

All information issued – oral or written, even if not for advertising purposes – must be **consistent** with the prospectus.

4.10 Communicating with retail clients

4.10.1 General rule

The general rule on **communicating with retail clients** in relation to **designated investment business** states that firms must ensure that the information:

- Includes the **name of the firm** (which may be the **trading name** or **shortened name**, provided the firm is identifiable).

- Is accurate and does not emphasise potential benefits of investment without also giving a **fair and prominent indication of relevant risks.**

- Is **sufficient** for and presented so as to be **likely to be understood** by the **average member** of the group to whom it is directed or by whom it is likely to be received.

- Does **not disguise, diminish** or **obscure** important **items, statements** or **warnings.**

In deciding whether and how to communicate to a target audience, the firm should **consider**: the nature of the product/business, risks, the client's commitment, the average recipient's information needs and the role of the information in the sales process.

The firm should consider whether omission of a relevant fact will result in information being **insufficient, unclear, unfair** or **misleading**.

4.10.2 Comparative information

Information comparing business / investments / persons must:

- Present **comparisons** in a meaningful, fair and balanced way

- In relation to MiFID or equivalent third country business, specify **information sources**, key facts and assumptions

4.10.3 Tax treatment

If **tax treatment** is referred to, it should be stated prominently that the tax treatment depends on the individual circumstances of the client and may be subject to change in future.

4.10.4 Consistency

The firm should ensure that information in a financial promotion is **consistent** with other information provided to the retail client.

4.11 Past, simulated past and future information

Rules on **performance information** apply to information disseminated to retail clients, and to financial promotions. In the case of non-MiFID business, the rules do not apply to deposits generally nor to pure protection long-term care insurance (LTCI) contracts.

4.11.1 Past performance

Past performance information must

- **Not** be the most prominent feature of the communication.

- Include appropriate information covering at least the **five preceding years**, or the whole period the investment/service has been offered/provided or the whole period the financial index has been established, if less than **five** years.

- Be based on and must show complete **12-month periods.**

- State the **reference period** and **source of the information.**

- Contain a **prominent warning** that the figures refer to the past and that past performance is not a reliable indicator of future results.

- If denominated in a foreign **currency**, state the currency clearly, with a warning that the return may increase or decrease as a result of currency fluctuations.

- If based on gross performance, disclose the effect of **commissions**, fees or other charges.

The above provisions are to be interpreted in a way that is '**appropriate and proportionate**' to the communication. For example, in a periodic statement issued for investments managed, past performance may be the most prominent feature, in spite of the first bullet point immediately above.

For a **packaged product** (except a unitised with-profits life policy or a stakeholder pension scheme), information should be given on

- An **offer to bid** basis (which should be stated) for an actual return or comparison with other investments, or

- An **offer to offer**, **bid to bid** or **offer to bid** basis (which should be stated) if there is a comparison with an index or with movements in the price of units, or

- A **single pricing** basis with allowance for charges.

4.11.2 Simulated past performance

Simulated past performance information must

- Relate to an investment or a financial index.

- Be based on actual past performance of investments/indices which are the same as, or underlie, the investment concerned.

- Contain a **prominent warning** that figures refer to simulated past performance and that past performance is not a reliable indicator of future performance.

4.11.3 Future performance

Future performance information must

- **Not** be based on nor refer to simulated past performance.
- Be based on **reasonable assumptions** supported by **objective data.**
- If based on gross performance, disclose the effect of **commissions**, fees or other charges.
- Contain a **prominent warning** that such forecasts are not a reliable indicator of future performance.
- Only be provided if **objective data** can be obtained.

4.12 Financial promotions containing offers or invitations

A **direct offer financial promotion** is a form of non-real time financial promotion which enables investors to purchase investments directly 'off the page' without receiving further information.

A direct offer financial promotion to retail clients must contain whatever **disclosures** are relevant to that offer or invitation (as outlined earlier, such as information about the firm and its services, and costs and charges). For non-MiFID business, additional appropriate information about the relevant business and investments must be stated so that the client is reasonably able to understand their nature and risks, and consequently to take investment decisions on an informed basis. This information may be contained in a separate document to which the client must refer in responding to the offer or invitation. Alternatively, information disclosures may be omitted if the firm can demonstrate that the client referred to the required information before making or accepting the offer.

A firm may wish to include in a direct offer financial promotion a summary of **tax** consequences, and a statement that the recipient should seek a **personal recommendation** if he has any doubt about the suitability of the investments or services.

4.13 Unwritten promotions and cold calling

An **unwritten financial promotion** outside the firm's premises may only be initiated if the person communicating it

- Does so at an appropriate time of day.

- Identifies himself and his firm, and makes his purpose clear.

- Clarifies if the client wants to continue or terminate the communication, and terminates it on request at any time.

- If an appointment is arranged, gives a contact point to a client.

Firms may only make **cold (unsolicited) calls** if

- The recipient has an established client relationship with the firm, such that the recipient envisages receiving them, or

- The call is about a generally marketed packaged product (not based on a high volatility fund), or

- The call relates to controlled activities by an authorised person or exempt person, involving only readily realisable securities (not warrants).

4.14 Financial promotions for the business of overseas persons

An 'overseas person' here means a firm carrying on regulated activities who does not do so within the UK.

Any financial promotion for the business of such an **overseas person** must

- Make clear which firm has approved or communicated it.

- Explain that rules for protection of retail clients do not apply.

- Explain the extent and level of any available compensation scheme (or state that no scheme applies).

If the firm has any reason to doubt that the overseas person will fail in its obligations to deal with UK retail clients in an honest and reliable way, then the firm must not approve or communicate the promotion.

4.15 Approving financial promotions

The rules in SYSC require that a firm which communicates with a client regarding designated investment business, or communicates or approves a financial promotion, puts in place **systems and controls** or **policies and procedures** in order to comply with the rules in COBS.

Section 21(1) FSMA 2000 prohibits an unauthorised person from communicating a financial promotion, unless either an exemption applies or the financial promotion is approved by an authorised firm.

Approval of a financial promotion by an **authorised firm** enables it to be communicated by an **unauthorised firm**.

A firm **approving** a financial promotion must confirm that it **complies** with the **financial promotion rules**. The firm must withdraw its approval, and notify anyone it knows to be relying on its approval, if it becomes aware that it no longer complies with the financial promotion rules.

A promotion made during a personal visit, telephone conversation or other interactive dialogue cannot be approved.

Approval given by the firm may be '**limited**', e. g. limited to communication to **professional clients** or **eligible counterparties**.

In communicating a financial promotion, a firm is permitted to **rely on another firm's confirmation of compliance** with the financial promotions rules. The firm must take reasonable care to ensure that the promotion is only communicated to types of recipients for whom it was intended.

5 SUITABILITY

5.1 Assessing suitability

Suitability rules apply when a firm makes a **personal recommendation** in relation to a **designated investment** (but not if the firm makes use of the rules on basic scripted advice for stakeholder products).

The firm has obligations regarding the assessment of **suitability**: the firm must take reasonable steps to ensure that, in respect of designated investments, a personal recommendation or a decision to trade is **suitable for its client**.

To meet this obligation, the firm must **obtain necessary information** regarding the client's:

- **Knowledge and experience** in the relevant investment field This will include: types of investment or service with which the client is familiar; transactions experience; level of education and profession or former profession; understanding of risks

- **Investment objectives** including: length of time he wishes to hold the investment; risk preferences; risk profile; purposes of the investment

- **Financial situation** including: extent and source of regular income; assets including liquid assets; investments and real property; regular financial commitments and ability to bear any investment risks consistent with their investment objectives

The firm is entitled to **rely** on **information provided by the client**, unless it is aware that the information is out of date, inaccurate or incomplete.

6 DEALING AND MANAGING

6.1 Application

COBS 11 covers rules on **dealing and managing**. These rules (except for the COBS rules on personal account dealing – see below) apply to **MiFID business** carried out by a **MiFID investment firm**, and to equivalent third country business.

The provisions on **personal account dealing** apply to designated investment business carried on from a UK establishment. It also applies to passported activities carried on by a UK MiFID investment firm from a branch in another EEA State, but not to the UK branch of an EEA MiFID investment firm in relation to its MiFID business. In other words, incoming EEA firms passporting into the UK require their UK staff to follow the **home state** personal accounting dealing rules.

6.2 Conflicts of interest

Inevitably, authorised firms, particularly where they act in dual capacity (both broker and dealing for the firm itself), are faced with **conflicts** between the firm and customers or between one customer and another.

6.2.1 Principle 8

Principle 8 of the *Principles for Businesses* states: 'A firm must manage conflicts of interest fairly, both between itself and its customers and between a customer and another client'.

Principle 8 thus requires that authorised firms should seek to ensure that when **conflicts of interest** do arise, the firm **manages** the conflicts to ensure that customers are treated **fairly**.

6.2.2 Senior Management Arrangements, Systems and Controls (SYSC)

SYSC 10 applies to **common platform firms** carrying on regulated activities and ancillary activities or providing MiFID ancillary services, where a service is provided, to any category of client.

The common platform firm must take all **reasonable steps** to **identify conflicts of interest** between the firm, its managers, employees and appointed representatives or tied agents, or between clients, which may arise in providing a service.

The firm must take into account, as a minimum:

- Likely financial gains, or avoidance of losses, at the expense of a client

- Interests in the outcome of a service which are different from the client's interest

- Financial incentives to favour some clients or groups of client

- Whether the firm carries on the same business as the client, or receives inducements in the form of monies, goods and services other than the standard commission or fee for that service

Regularly updated records must be kept of where conflicts of interest have or may arise.

The firm must maintain and operate effective **organisational and administrative arrangements** to prevent conflicts of interest from giving rise to material risk of damage to clients' interests.

Where conflicts are not preventable, the firm must disclose them to clients – in a durable medium, in sufficient detail for the client to take an informed decision – before undertaking business.

Common platform firms should aim to **identify** and **manage** conflicts under a **comprehensive conflicts of interest policy**. That firms actively manage conflicts is important: 'over-reliance of disclosure' without adequate consideration of how to manage conflicts is not permitted.

6.3 Conflicts policy

A **common platform firm** must maintain an effective **conflicts of interest policy**, in **writing** and appropriate to the size and type of firm and its business.

The conflicts of interest policy must:

- Identify circumstances constituting or potentially giving rise to conflicts materially affecting clients
- Specify procedures and measures to manage the conflicts

The procedures and measures must:

- Be designed to ensure that activities are carried on an appropriate **level of independence**

- As and where necessary, include procedures to **prevent and control exchange of information** between persons involved, to **supervise persons separately**, to remove **links in remuneration** producing possible conflicts, to prevent exercise of **inappropriate influence**, and to **prevent and control simultaneous and sequential involvement** of persons in separate services or activities

In drawing up its conflicts policy, the firm must pay **special attention** to the following **activities** (in particular, where persons perform a combination of activities):

- Investment research and advice

- Proprietary trading

- Portfolio management

- Corporate finance business (including underwriting or selling in an offer of securities, and advising on mergers and acquisitions)

In management of an **offering of securities**, the firm might wish to consider:

- Agreeing relevant aspects of the offering process with the corporate finance client at an early stage

- Agreeing allocation and pricing objectives with the corporate finance client, inviting the client to participate actively in the allocation process, making the initial recommendation for allocation to retail clients as a single block and not on a named basis and disclosing to the issuer the allocations actually made

6.4 'Chinese walls'

Chinese walls are administrative and physical barriers and other internal arrangements, designed to contain **sensitive information**. Most commonly, they are used around the corporate finance departments of firms that often have confidential, sometimes inside, information.

Chinese walls **do not have to be used** by firms, but if they are, this rule becomes relevant.

Where a common platform firm establishes and maintains a Chinese wall, it allows the persons on one side of the wall, e.g. corporate finance, to withhold information from persons on the other side of the wall, e.g. equity research, but only to the extent that one of the parts involves carrying on **regulated activities, ancillary activities** or **MiFID ancillary services**.

A firm will not be guilty of the offences of **Market Manipulation** (S397 FSMA), **Market Abuse** (S118 FSMA) or be liable to a lawsuit under **S150** (FSMA) where the failure arises from the operation of a Chinese wall.

The **effect** of the Chinese walls rule above is that a corporate finance department may have plans for a company that will change the valuation of that company's shares. The equity salesman on the other side of the 'wall' should have no knowledge of these plans; consequently his inability to pass this knowledge on to clients is not seen as a failure of his duty to them.

6.5 Investment research

COBS 12 deals with **non-independent investment research** prepared for publication or distribution to clients. There have been concerns that analysts have been encouraged to write favourable research on companies in order to attract lucrative investment banking work.

COBS 12 applies to MiFID business carried on by a MiFID investment firm. Rules on disclosure of research recommendations apply to all firms.

Non-independent research must

- Be clearly identified as such.

- Contain a clear and prominent statement that it does not follow the requirements of independent research and is not subject to prohibitions on dealing ahead of dissemination of research.

Financial promotions rules apply to non-independent research as if it were a marketing communication.

In managing conflicts of interest in line with SYSC 10, **situations where conflicts can arise** include

- Employees trading in financial instruments which they know the firm has or intends to publish non-independent research about, before clients have had a reasonable opportunity to act on the research (other than where the firm is acting as a market maker in good faith, or in the execution of an unsolicited client order).

- Non-independent research intended first for internal use and for later publication to clients.

Firms must take **reasonable care** to ensure that research recommendations are fairly presented, and to disclose its interests or indicate conflicts of interest.

The **identity** (name, job title, name of firm, competent authority) of the person responsible for the research should be disclosed clearly and prominently.

The research should meet certain **general standards** for example to ensure that facts are distinguished from interpretations or opinions. Projections should be labelled as such. Reliable sources should be used, and any doubts about reliability clearly indicated. The substance of the recommendations should be possible to be substantiated by the FSA on request.

Additionally, the firm must take reasonable care to ensure **fair presentation**, broadly covering the following aspects.

- Indication of material sources, including the issuer (if appropriate)
- Disclosure of whether the recommendation was disclosed to the issuer and then amended
- Summary of valuation basis or methodology
- Explanation of the meaning of any recommendation (e. g. 'buy', 'sell', 'hold')
- Risk warning if appropriate
- Planned frequency of updates
- Date of release of research, and date and time of prices mentioned
- Details of change over any previous recommendation in the last year

Firms must make **disclosures** in research recommendations broadly covering the following areas.

- All **relationships and circumstances** (including those of affiliated companies) that may reasonably be expected to impair the objectivity of the recommendation (especially, financial interests in any relevant investment, and a conflict of interest regarding the issuer).

- Whether employees involved have **remuneration** tied to investment banking transactions.

- **Shareholdings** held by the firm (or an affiliated company) of over **5%** of the share capital of the issuer.

- **Shareholdings** held by the issuer of over **5%** of the share capital of the firm (or an affiliated company).

- Other **significant financial interests**.

- Statements about the **role of the firm** as market maker, lead manager of previous offers of the issuer in the last year, or provider of investment banking services.

- Statements about **arrangements** to prevent and avoid conflicts of interest, prices and dates at which employees involved acquired shares.

- **Data** on the proportions of the firm's **recommendations** in different categories (e. g. 'buy', 'sell', 'hold'), on a quarterly basis, with the proportions of relevant investments issued by issuers who were investment banking clients of the firm during the last year.

- Identification of a **third party** who produced the research, if applicable, describing also any alteration of third party recommendations and ensuring that any summary of third party research is fair, clear and not misleading.

For shorter recommendations, firms can just make reference to many of the relevant disclosures, e. g. by providing a website link.

6.6 Best execution

The basic COBS rule of **best execution** is as follows.

A firm must take all reasonable steps to obtain, when executing orders, the best possible result for its clients taking into account the execution factors.

When a firm is **dealing on own account with clients**, this is considered to be execution of client orders, and is therefore subject to the best execution rule.

If a firm provides a best quote to a client, it is acceptable for the quote to be executed after the client accepts it, provided the quote is not manifestly out of date.

The obligation to obtain best execution needs to be interpreted according to the particular type of financial instrument involved, but the rule applies to **all types of financial instrument**.

The **best execution criteria** are that the firm must take into account **characteristics of**

- The client, including categorisation as retail or professional.
- The client order.
- The financial instruments.
- The execution venues.

The **'best possible result'** must be determined in terms of **total consideration** – taking into account any costs, including the firm's own commissions in the case of competing execution venues, and not just quoted prices. (However, the firm is not expected to compare the result with that of clients of other firms.) Commissions structure must not discriminate between execution venues.

6.7 Order execution policy

6.7.1 Policy requirements

The firm must establish and implement an **order execution policy**, and it must monitor its effectiveness regularly.

The policy must include, for each class of financial instruments, information on different execution venues used by the firm, and the factors affecting choice of execution venue.

The firm should choose venues that enable it to obtain on a consistent basis the **best possible result** for execution of client orders. For each client order, the firm should apply its execution policy with a view to achieving the best possible result for the client.

If orders may be executed outside a regulated market or multilateral trading facility, this must be disclosed, and clients must give prior express consent.

A firm must be able to demonstrate to clients, on request, that it has followed its execution policy.

6.7.2 Client consent and clients' specific instructions

The firm must provide a **retail client** with details on its execution policy before providing the service, covering the relative importance the firm assigns to execution factors, a list of execution venues on which the firm relies, and a clear and prominent warning that **specific instructions** by the client could prevent the firm from following its execution policy steps fully.

If the client gives **specific instructions**, the firm has met its best execution obligation if it obtains the best result in following those instructions. The firm should not induce a client to gives such instructions, if they could prevent best execution from being obtained. However, the firm may invite the client to choose between execution venues.

The firm must obtain the **prior consent** of clients to its execution policy, and the policy must be **reviewed annually** and whenever there is a material change in the firm's ability to achieve the best possible result consistently from execution venues.

6.7.3 Portfolio management and order reception and transmission services

Firms who act as **portfolio managers** must comply with the **clients' best interests rule** when placing orders with other entities. Firms who provide a service of **receiving and transmitting orders** must do the same when transmitting orders to other entities for execution. Such firms must:

- Take all reasonable steps to obtain the best possible result for clients
- Establish and maintain a policy to enable it to do so, and monitor its effectiveness
- Provide appropriate information to clients on the policy
- Review the policy annually or whenever there is a material change affecting the firm's ability to continue to obtain the best possible result for clients

6.8 Client order handling

The general rule on **client order handling** is that firms must implement procedures and arrangements which provide for the **prompt, fair and expeditious** execution of client orders, relative to other orders or the trading interests of the firm.

These procedures and arrangements must allow for the execution of otherwise comparable orders in accordance with the time of their reception by the firm.

When carrying out **client orders**, firms must:

- Ensure that orders are promptly and accurately recorded and allocated
- Carry out otherwise comparable orders **sequentially** and **promptly**, unless this is impracticable or not in clients' interests
- Inform a retail client about any material difficulty in carrying out orders promptly, on becoming aware of it

Where it is not practicable to treat orders sequentially e.g. because they are received by different media, they should not be treated as 'otherwise comparable'.

Firms must not allow the **misuse of information** relating to pending client orders. Any use of such information to deal on own account should be considered a misuse of the information.

When overseeing or arranging **settlement**, a firm must take reasonable steps to ensure that instruments or funds due are delivered to the client account promptly and correctly.

6.9 Personal account dealing

Personal account dealing relates to trades undertaken by the staff of a regulated business for themselves. Such trades can create **conflicts of interest** between staff and customers.

A firm conducting **designated investment business** must establish, implement and maintain adequate **arrangements** aimed at preventing employees who are involved in activities where a conflict of interest could occur, or who has access to inside information, from:

- Entering into a transaction which is prohibited under the **Market Abuse Directive**, or which involves misuse or improper disclosure of confidential information, or conflicts with an obligation of the firm to a customer under the regulatory system

- Except in the course of his job, advising or procuring anyone else to enter into such a transaction

- Except in the course of his job, disclosing any information or opinion to another person if the person disclosing it should know that, as a result, the other person would be likely to enter into such a transaction or advise or procure another to enter into such a transaction

The **firm's arrangements** under these provisions must be designed to ensure that:

- All relevant persons (staff involved) are aware of the personal dealing restrictions

- The firm is informed promptly of any personal transaction

- A service provider to whom activities are outsourced maintain a record of personal transactions and provides it to the firm promptly on request

- A record is kept of personal transactions notified to the firm or identified by it, including any related authorisation or prohibition

The rule on personal account dealing is **disapplied** for personal transactions:

- Under a discretionary portfolio management service where there has been no prior communication between the portfolio manager and the person for whom the transaction is executed

- In UCITS collective undertakings (e.g. OEICs and unit trusts) where the person is not involved in its management

- In life policies

- For successive personal transactions where there were prior instructions in force, nor to the termination of the instruction provided that no financial instruments are sold at the same time

CHAPTER ROUNDUP

- The Conduct of Business Sourcebook (COBS) generally applies to authorised firms engaged in designated investment business carried out from their (or their appointed representatives') UK establishments. Some COB rules do not apply to eligible counterparty business.

- The level of protection given to clients by the regulatory system depends on their classification, with retail clients being protected the most. Professional clients and eligible counterparties may both be either *per se* or elective. Both professional clients and eligible counterparties can re-categorise to get more protection.

- It is generally acceptable for a firm to rely on information provided by others if the other firm is competent and not connected with the firm placing the reliance.

- A financial promotion inviting someone to engage in investment activity must be issued by or approved by an authorised firm. Communications must be fair, clear and not misleading. Prospectus advertisements must clearly indicate that they are not a prospectus. Communications with retail clients must balance information about benefits of investments with information about risks.

- Unwritten financial promotions rules cover cold calling, which must be limited to an 'appropriate time of day'.

- Firms must seek to ensure fair treatment if there could be a conflict of interest. Common platform firms must maintain an effective conflicts of interest policy. Conflicts of interest policies must cover financial analysts producing investment research.

- Inducements must not be given if they conflict with acting in the best interests of clients, and there are controls on the use of dealing commission.

- Firms must establish arrangements designed to prevent employees entering into personal transactions which are prohibited forms of market abuse. Staff must be made aware of the personal dealing restrictions.

TEST YOUR KNOWLEDGE

Check your knowledge of the chapter here, without referring back to the text.

1.	Name the three main categories of client.	▪ ▪ ▪
2.	Name three types of *per se* eligible counterparty.	▪ ▪ ▪
3.	A firm's communications and financial promotions must be '....., ... and not ...'. *Fill in the blanks.*	▪ ▪ ▪
4.	What is the FPO?	
5.	What is the name for administrative and physical barriers and other internal arrangements, designed to contain sensitive information?	

TEST YOUR KNOWLEDGE: ANSWERS

1.   Eligible counterparties, professional clients and retail clients.

     (See Section 2.2)

2.   Investment firms, national governments and central banks are all examples.

     (See Section 2.3)

3.   Fair, clear and not misleading.

     (See Section 4.3)

4.   The FPO is the Financial Promotions Order. It contains a number of exemptions from S21 FSMA and the FSA's rules on financial promotions.

     (See Section 4.7)

5.   'Chinese walls'.

     (See Section 6.4)

BPP LEARNING MEDIA

3

Financial Crime

INTRODUCTION

There are various measures designed to deal with crimes relating to the financial services sector as well as to financial transactions generally. Crimes could be committed by persons within the industry or outside it. In the case of the laundering of proceeds of crime, a criminal may make use of accounts and transactions in ways that financial services employees become aware of.

Measures against financial crime have been stepped up in recent years. It is important to know the law so that one does not inadvertently breach it, as ignorance of the law is not a defence. It is also important to know how legislation and regulations require those working in the financial sector to contribute to the detection and investigation of crime.

CHAPTER LEARNING OBJECTIVES

Insider Dealing

- **Understand** the meaning of 'inside information' and 'insider' in CJA 1993.
- **Understand** the offences described in the legislation and the instruments covered.
- **Know** that insider dealing is a criminal offence and the penalties.
- **Know** the general defences available with regard to insider dealing.

FSMA 2000 S397

- **Know** the purpose, provisions, offences and defences of S397 FSMA 2000.

Market Abuse

- **Understand** the statutory offence of market abuse.
- **Know** the concept of effect rather than intention.
- **Know** the due diligence defence.
- **Know** the territorial scope of the legislation and regulation.
- **Know** the penalties for contravention of the legislation on market abuse.
- **Understand** the enforcement regime for market abuse.
- **Know** the safe harbours: Takeover Code, FSA Rules, buy-back and stabilisation.
- **Know** the status of FSA's Code of Market Conduct.
- **Understand** when price stabilisation is used.
- **Know** the obligation to make suspicious transaction reports.

Money Laundering

- **Understand** the terms 'money laundering', 'criminal conduct' and 'criminal property' and the application of money laundering to all crimes.

- **Know** that the UK legislation on money laundering is found in the Proceeds of Crime Act 2002 (POCA), the Money Laundering Regulations 2003, and the guidance to these provisions is found in the Joint Money Laundering Steering Group Guidance Notes.

- **Know** the obligations placed on senior management in relation to anti-money laundering, including the obligation to arrange regular money laundering training for individuals.

- **Understand** the three stages of money laundering.

- **Understand** the main offences set out in POCA Part 7 Sections 327, 328, 329, 330, 333 (Assistance, i.e. concealing, arrangements, acquisition use and possession; Failure to Report; Tipping off) and the implications of Part 7 regarding the objective test in relation to reporting suspicious transactions; that appropriate disclosure (internal for staff and to SOCA) for the firm is a defence.

- **Know** the penalties in a Crown Court for committing the offences set out in POCA.

- **Understand** the necessity to obtain documentation proving the identity of new clients and to record the KYC process; the types of documents that would be appropriate and the consequences of failure to obtain such documentation.

BPP
LEARNING MEDIA

- **Understand** the requirements to identify both source of funds and source of wealth.

- **Understand** the importance of being able to recognise a suspicious transaction and the requirement for staff to report to the MLRO and for the firm to report to SOCA.

- **Understand** the differences between laundering the proceeds of crime and the financing of terrorist acts.

- **Understand** the purpose of the Bank of England ~~the Bank of England~~ *H M Treasury &* sanctions list.

1 INSIDER DEALING

1.1 Introduction

Insider dealing is the offence of acting with information that is not freely and openly available to all other participants in the market place. This is an offence under **Part V** of the **Criminal Justice Act 1993**.

The Act makes it a **criminal offence** for connected persons who receive inside information to act on that information.

The legislation (Schedule 2) covers the following instruments.

- Shares.
- Debt securities issued by the private or public sector.
- Warrants.
- Depository receipts.
- Options, futures or contracts for a difference on any of the above.

1.2 Insider

An insider is defined as an **individual** (not a company) who has **information** in his possession that he **knows** is **inside information** and **knows** is from an **inside source**.

Inside information in this context refers to **unpublished price-sensitive information** that is **specific or precise** and **relates to a security or its issuer**.

For the purposes of determining what is **published** information the following information is deemed to be published.

- Information published via a regulated market, e.g. an RIE.

- Information contained in public records.

- Information that can otherwise be readily acquired by market users, e.g. in the financial press.

- Information derived from public information.

- Information that can only be acquired by expertise or by the payment of a fee.

- Information that is published only to a section of the public, rather than the public in general, or published outside the UK.

- Information that can be acquired by observation, e.g. a factory burning down.

An inside source is **an individual** and would include a **director, employee** or **shareholder** of an issuer of securities or a person who has access to the information by virtue of their employment, office or profession. A person will also be an inside source if he receives the information directly or indirectly from one of the above and in addition satisfies the general definition above.

1.3 Offences

If a person satisfies the definition of an insider it is an offence to

- **Deal** in the affected securities either on a regulated market or through a professional intermediary.

- **Encourage another** person to deal with reasonable cause to believe that dealing would take place on a regulated market or through a professional intermediary.

- **Disclose the information** to another person other than in the proper performance of their duties.

1.4 Defences

An individual is not guilty of insider **dealing** if he can show

- That he did not, at the time, expect the dealing to result in a profit attributable to the fact that the information was price sensitive.

- That, at the time, he believed on reasonable grounds that the information had been disclosed widely enough to ensure that none of those taking part in the dealing would be prejudiced by not having the information.

- That he would have done what he did even if he had not had the information.

A similar series of defences are available to the charge of **encouraging** another to deal in price-affected securities.

An individual is not guilty of insider dealing by virtue of a **disclosure** of information if he shows

- That he did not, at the time, expect any person, because of the disclosure, to deal in securities either through a regulated market or via a professional intermediary.

- That although he had such an expectation at the time, he did not expect the dealing to result in a profit attributable to the fact that the information was price sensitive in relation to the securities.

1.5 Penalties

The case may be brought through the Magistrates' Court and then committed for trial by jury in a Crown Court should it be considered to be of appropriate magnitude.

The maximum penalty the Magistrates' Court can impose is, once again, limited to six months' imprisonment and/or a £5,000 fine. The Crown Court can impose a harsher sentence – imprisonment for a maximum of **seven years** and/or an unlimited fine.

2 MARKET MANIPULATION (FSMA S397)

Under S397 of Financial Services and Markets Act 2000 (FSMA) Market Manipulation, it is an offence to

- Mislead the market through a **statement, promise or forecast.** Misleading statements that are intended to make individuals or the market move in a particular direction will constitute an offence if they are made recklessly or with dishonest intent. It is a defence if the statement was made in accordance with the price stabilisation rules, or as a result of the operation of a Chinese wall.

- Engage in a **course of conduct** which creates a false or misleading impression as to the market, price or value of investments and that is intended to make individuals or the market move in a particular direction. It is a defence if the statement was made in accordance with the price stabilisation rules or the offender reasonably believed a false or misleading impression would not be created by their conduct.

- Dishonestly **conceal** material facts, which may make individuals or the market move in a particular direction.

This is a criminal offence, which applies to all persons and can be brought to justice either through a Magistrates' Court or through a Crown Court. The sentencing powers of the Magistrates' Court are limited, as before, to a maximum of six months' imprisonment and/or a £5,000 fine. The Crown Court, trial by jury, has wider sentencing powers for this offence, and the maximum penalty is **seven years'** imprisonment and/or an unlimited fine. The fine is often referred to as the 'statutory fine'.

3 MARKET ABUSE

3.1 Introduction

Market abuse is a civil offence under S118 of FSMA which provides an alternative civil regime for enforcing the criminal prohibitions on insider dealing and market manipulation.

The UK market abuse rules implement the EU Market Abuse Directive.

The **territorial scope** of market abuse is very wide. It covers everyone, not just authorised firms and approved persons. Furthermore, firms or persons outside the UK are also covered by the offence.

As market abuse is a **civil offence**, the FSA must prove, on the balance of probabilities, that a person

- Engaged in market abuse; or
- By taking or refraining from action required or encouraged another person to engage in market abuse.

The table below gives a high level summary of the market abuse offence. You will see that there are seven types of behaviour which can amount to market abuse.

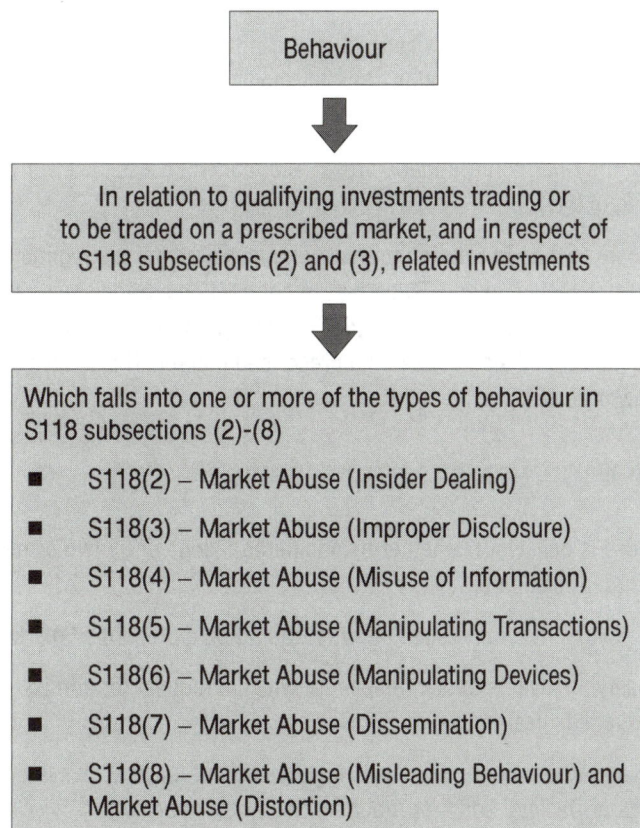

```
Behaviour
   ↓
In relation to qualifying investments trading or
to be traded on a prescribed market, and in respect of
S118 subsections (2) and (3), related investments
   ↓
Which falls into one or more of the types of behaviour in
S118 subsections (2)-(8)
- S118(2) – Market Abuse (Insider Dealing)
- S118(3) – Market Abuse (Improper Disclosure)
- S118(4) – Market Abuse (Misuse of Information)
- S118(5) – Market Abuse (Manipulating Transactions)
- S118(6) – Market Abuse (Manipulating Devices)
- S118(7) – Market Abuse (Dissemination)
- S118(8) – Market Abuse (Misleading Behaviour) and
  Market Abuse (Distortion)
```

Before we look at the seven heads of market abuse in detail, we need to be familiar with the following terms.

3.2 Insider

An insider is someone who **has** inside information as a result of

- Membership of the administration, management or supervisory body of an issuer.
- Holding capital in an issuer.
- Their employment, profession or duties.
- Criminal activities.

The definition also covers inside information **obtained by any other means** and where the person knows or could reasonably be expected to know the information is inside information.

3.3 Intention

The market abuse regime is **'effects based'** rather than 'intent based'. Thus, whether the perpetrator intended to abuse the market is largely irrelevant – the key question is whether the action did abuse the market.

3.4 Qualifying investments and prescribed markets

Behaviour will only constitute market abuse if it occurs in the UK or in relation to qualifying investments traded on a prescribed market. The term 'behaviour' is specifically mentioned as the offence of market abuse can cover both action and inaction.

A prescribed market means any UK RIE and any regulated market as defined in MiFID. Qualifying investment thus means any investment traded on a UK RIE or a regulated market. Regulated markets cover the main EEA exchanges.

The definition of prescribed market and qualifying investment are amended slightly with reference to the offences of 'Misuse of Information' and 'Misleading Behaviour' and 'Distortion'. Here, a prescribed market means any UK RIE. Thus these offences are only relevant to the UK markets.

In addition, the rules confirm that a prescribed market accessible electronically in the UK would be treated as operating in the UK.

As behaviour must be **in relation to** qualifying investments, the regime is not limited to on-market dealings. A transaction in an OTC derivative contract on a traded security or commodity would be covered by the regime. In addition, abusive trades on foreign exchanges could constitute market abuse if the underlying instrument also trades on a prescribed market. This makes the regime much wider than the criminal law offences.

3.5 The definition of market abuse

Market abuse is behaviour, whether by one person alone or by two or more persons jointly or in concert, which occurs in relation to

- Qualifying investments admitted to trading on a prescribed market; or
- Qualifying investments in respect of which a request for admission to trading on a prescribed market has been made; or
- Related investments of a qualifying investment (strictly, this is only relevant to the offences of 'Insider Dealing' and 'Improper Disclosure', see below).

And falls within one or more of the offences below.

3.6 The seven 'offences' of market abuse

The seven types of behaviour which can constitute market abuse are

- 'Insider Dealing'. This is where an insider deals, or attempts to deal, in a qualifying investment or related investment on the basis of inside information.

- 'Improper Disclosure'. This is where an insider discloses inside information to another person otherwise than in the proper course of the exercise of his employment, profession or duties.

- 'Misuse of Information'. This fills gaps in '1' or '2' above and is where the behaviour

    – Is based on information which is not generally available to those using the market but which, if available to a regular user of the market, would be regarded by him as relevant when deciding the terms on which transactions in qualifying investments should be effected; and

    – Is likely to be regarded by a regular user of the market as a failure on the part of the person concerned to observe the standard of behaviour reasonably expected of a person in his position.

- 'Manipulating Transactions'. This consists of effecting transactions or orders to trade (otherwise than for legitimate reasons and in conformity with accepted market practices) which

    – Give, or are likely to give a false or misleading impression as to the supply, demand or price of one or more qualifying investment; or

    – Secure the price of one or more such investment at an abnormal or artificial level.

- 'Manipulating Devices'. This consists of effecting transactions or orders to trade which employ fictitious devices or any other form of deception.

- 'Dissemination'. This consists of the dissemination of information by any means which gives, or is likely to give, a false or misleading impression as to a qualifying investment by a person who knew or could reasonably be expected to have known that the information was false or misleading.

- 'Misleading Behaviour' and 'Distortion'. This fills any gaps in '4', '5' and '6' above is where the behaviour

    – Is likely to give, a regular user of the market a false or misleading impression as to the supply of, demand for or price or value of, qualifying investments; or

    – Would be regarded by a regular user of the market as behaviour that would distort the market in such an investment and is likely to be regarded by a regular user of the market as a failure on the part of the person concerned to observe the standard of behaviour reasonably expected of a person in his position.

3.7 Due diligence defence

Under S123 of FSMA, the FSA may not impose a financial penalty in relation to market abuse where it is satisfied that the person believed, on reasonable grounds, that his behaviour did not amount to market abuse or he took all reasonable precautions and exercised all due diligence to avoid engaging in market abuse.

3.8 Code of Market Conduct

Whilst the law is set out in FSMA, the FSA also has a duty to draft a Code of Market Conduct. The main provisions of the Code of Market Conduct are that it sets out

- Descriptions of behaviour that, in the opinion of the FSA, do or do not amount to market abuse. Descriptions of behaviour which do not amount to market abuse are called 'safe harbours'.

- Descriptions of behaviour that are or are not accepted market practices in relation to one or more identified markets.

- Factors that, in the opinion of the FSA, are to be taken into account in determining whether or not behaviour amounts to market abuse.

The Code does not exhaustively describe all types of behaviour that may or may not amount to market abuse.

3.9 Enforcement and penalties

The FSA may impose one or more of the following penalties on those found to have committed market abuse

- An unlimited fine.

- Issue a public statement.

- Apply to the court to seek an injunction or restitution order.

- Where an authorised/approved person is guilty of market abuse, they will also be guilty of a breach of the FSA's Principles and they could, in addition to the above penalties, have disciplinary proceedings brought against them, which may result in withdrawal of authorisation/approval.

Note that as market abuse is a civil offence, offenders cannot be sent to prison unlike the criminal laws of insider dealing and S397. Civil offences are also easier to prosecute.

In addition to being able to impose penalties for market abuse, the FSA is given criminal prosecution powers to enforce insider dealing and S397. The FSA has indicated that it will not pursue both the civil and criminal regime. In terms of the enforcement process for market abuse, this is the same as the FSA's disciplinary process.

3.10 Reporting suspicious transactions (market abuse)

A firm which has reasonable grounds to suspect that a transaction might constitute market abuse must notify the FSA without delay. The notification must include a description of the transaction and reasons for the suspicion. The firm must not inform any other persons of this notification, in particular the person on behalf of whom the transaction has been carried out.

3.11 Safe harbours

If a person is within one of the safe harbours set out in the Code of Market Conduct they are not committing market abuse. These are indicated by the letter C in the Handbook.

Generally, there are no rules in the Takeover Code which permit or require a person to behave in a way which amounts to market abuse.

However, the following rules provide safe harbour meaning that behaviour conforming with that rule does not amount to market abuse.

3.11.1 FSA rules

Behaviour caused by the proper operation of a Chinese wall or behaviour which relates to the timing, dissemination or content to a disclosure under the Listing Rules will not amount to market abuse.

3.11.2 Takeover Code

Behaviour conforming with any of the rules of the Takeover Code about the timing, dissemination or content of a disclosure does not, of itself, amount to market abuse. This is subject to the behaviour being expressly required or permitted by a rule and provided it conforms to the General Principles of the Takeover Code.

3.11.3 Behaviour that does not amount to market abuse (general): buyback programmes and stabilisation

Behaviour which conforms with the Buyback and Stabilisation Regulation (in the Market Conduct Sourcebook of the FSA's Handbook) will not amount to market abuse.

However, buyback programmes which do not follow the Buyback and Stabilisation Regulation are not automatically seen as market abuse, but do not have an automatic safe harbour.

3.12 Price stabilising rules

The Market Conduct section of the FSA Handbook sets out how and when a lead manager in an initial public offering may purchase securities to stabilise a price without abusing the market.

- Where the offer is for cash.

- Where the offer is public on a qualifying exchange.

- When it is for a limited period.

- When adequate prior disclosure is given to the market in the prospectus.

- When information on stabilising activity is given to the issuer, although this would not include identifying individual clients.

3.12.1 Greenshoe options

Price stabilisation is often achieved through a process of over-allotment, backed up by a greenshoe option over further shares for the stabilising manager.

By allotting to new investors more than 100% of the shares actually created by the issuing company, the stabilising manager has left itself 'short' of these extra shares it has sold but does not yet have. This means the manager will go into the market and buy these extra securities from any new shareholders willing to sell their allocation. This creates an artificial demand to support the price.

Of course, this leaves the stabilisation manager exposed to having to buy the extra shares needed at above the issue price, incurring a loss. To protect against this risk, the manager will hold 'greenshoe' options to buy more shares from the issuing company at the issue price.

Greenshoe options may be used for other purposes besides stabilisation, but the reason must be disclosed to the issuer.

4 MONEY LAUNDERING

Money laundering is the process by which money from illegal sources is made to appear legally derived. By a variety of methods, the nature, source and ownership of those criminal proceeds are concealed.

The three stages of money laundering can be broken down as follows.

- **Placement** – the investment of the proceeds of criminal activity.

- **Layering** – the mingling of the money from an illegal source with that from a legitimate source. This is the stage at which the money will be **separated** from its illegal source.

- **Integration** – the withdrawal and usage of the now undetectable proceeds of criminal activity.

The consequence is that the origin of and entitlement to the money are disguised and the money can again be used to benefit the criminal and/or his associates.

In recognition of the scale and impact of money laundering internationally various national governments have in recent years collaborated on an international scale to combat money laundering. Action taken has concentrated not only on the law enforcement process but also on recommendations to banks and financial institutions to put in place practices and procedures which will assist in the detection of money laundering activity.

4.1 Money Laundering Directive

The **European Union Money Laundering Directive** stipulates that EU member states should ensure that all financial and credit institutions located within the national member states should implement certain **internal procedures** and controls and also ensure that it is a **criminal offence** for individuals to assist money laundering. In the UK, the internal procedures requirement are implemented by the Money Laundering Regulations 2003.

The aims of those internal procedures are threefold.

- **Deterrence** – to prevent credit and financial institutions being used for money laundering purposes.

- **Co-operation** – to ensure that there is co-operation between credit and financial institutions and law enforcement agencies.

- **Detection** – to establish customer identification and record-keeping procedures within all financial and credit institutions that will assist the law enforcement agencies in detecting, tracing and prosecuting money launderers.

Not only is the Money Laundering Directive the source of the Money Laundering Regulations 2003, it is also the source of the **Proceeds of Crime Act 2002 (POCA)**. The POCA consolidates and updates the money laundering requirements which apply to individuals and is the main legislation covering individual liability.

4.2 Individual liability

The main offences are set out in Part 7 of POCA.

4.2.1 Assistance (S327, S328 and S239)

The offence

If any person knowingly helps another person to launder the proceeds of criminal conduct, he will be committing a criminal offence. This covers obtaining, concealing, disguising, transferring, acquiring, possessing, investing or using the proceeds of crime. The legislation historically covered the laundering of the proceeds of **serious crime**. However, as a result of the POCA it now covers the proceeds of **all crimes**, no matter how small.

The possible defence

It is a defence to the above offence that a person **disclosed** his knowledge or belief concerning the origins of the property either to the police or to the appropriate officer in his firm.

The penalty

The maximum penalties for any offence of assisting a money launderer are 14 years' imprisonment and/or an unlimited fine.

4.2.2 Failure to report (S330)

The offence

If a person discovers information during the course of his employment that makes him **believe or suspect** money laundering is occurring, he must inform the police or the appropriate officer (usually the MLRO) of the firm as soon as possible. If he fails to make the report as soon as is reasonably practicable, he commits a criminal offence.

For those working in the **regulated sector** (for an authorised firm) this offence covers not only where the person had actual suspicion of laundering (i.e. subjective suspicions) but also where there were **reasonable grounds for being suspicious**. The grounds are when a hypothetical reasonable person would in the circumstances have been suspicious (i.e. **objective suspicions**).

The possible defence

The only defences to this charge are if a person charged can prove

- He had a **reasonable excuse** for failing to disclose this information. Whether an excuse is reasonable will depend on the circumstances of the case, but it is noteworthy that the person charged has the burden of proving that he had a reasonable excuse for his failure to disclose.

- Where the person had no subjective suspicion but is deemed to have objective suspicions, they had not been provided by their employer with appropriate **training** to recognise and report suspicions.

The relevant legislation specifically provides that any person making a disclosure of this kind will not be in breach of any duty of confidentiality owed to a customer.

The penalty

This offence is punishable with a maximum of five years imprisonment and/or an unlimited fine.

4.2.3 Tipping off (S333)

The offence

If a person either knows or believes that the police are or will be investigating the laundering of the proceeds of criminal conduct that person **must not disclose to any third party** any information which might prejudice such an investigation. If he does, he will commit the offence of tipping off. This covers the proceeds of **all** crimes no matter how small.

The possible defence

It is a defence to this offence if the person charged can prove that he neither knew nor suspected that the disclosure would prejudice an investigation.

Once again, the burden of proving the defence rests upon the person who has been charged with an offence.

The penalty

Tipping off is punishable with a maximum of five years' imprisonment and/or an unlimited fine.

4.3 Institutional liability

The **Money Laundering Regulations** require internal procedures to be implemented to deter criminals from using financial institutions to launder money. This should also enable money laundering to be more easily detected and prosecuted by the law enforcement agencies. The Money Laundering Regulations apply to all firms and individuals authorised to conduct regulated activities under FSMA, as well as to other **financial institutions**, such as Bureaux de Change.

The following internal systems must therefore be established.

- **Internal reporting procedures** involving the appointment of an officer of the firm to act as money laundering reporting officer (MLRO).

- **Identification procedures** (unless an exception applies) and know your customer requirements.

- **Record-keeping procedures** whereby relevant records of transactions must be kept for a minimum of **five years**. (Note that this is different to the general FSA rule of three years.)

- **Regular appropriate training programmes** for all relevant employees.

- RISK-BASED APPROACH to anti-money laundering systems and controles.

4.3.1 Identification of clients

There is a requirement to obtain satisfactory identification of all applicants for business as soon as is reasonably practical after initial contact and before doing business with them. If a client does not supply sufficient identification as soon as is reasonably practicable, unless a report has been made to the Serious Organised Crime Agency (SOCA) (formerly called the National Criminal Intelligence Service (NCIS)), the firm must discontinue any regulated activity it is conducting for the client and end any understanding it has reached with the client.

It is important that these identification checks are maintained for existing clients. The financial institution must also check the source of the wealth of a client, as well as sources of funds.

Where a client appears to be acting on behalf of another person the obligation is to identify and know **both** parties. For clients who are not individuals, different checks would be appropriate and guidance would be found on what would be appropriate in the **Joint Money Laundering Steering Group's Guidance Notes**.

Individual clients

The following evidence of identity is required for an individual.

- **Evidence of identity**, e.g. a passport.
- **Evidence of address**, e.g. a utility bill.

Corporate clients

Care should be taken to verify the legal existence of corporate clients from official documents because these are the most likely vehicles to be used for money laundering.

Firms are required to identify the owners and managers of companies by using a risk-based approach. This approach will depend on the nature and location of the company and the product/service that the company requires. In all cases the firm should obtain and record information about the normal business activities the client expects to undertake to enable the firm to build up sufficient know your customer information.

The types of documentation that would be appropriate include the following.

- A copy of the certificate of incorporation and evidence of the company's registered address.
- A copy of the latest report and accounts (audited if applicable).

Firms should not establish a business relationship until all relevant parties to the relationship have been identified. Satisfactory identification evidence must be obtained as soon as is reasonably practicable, and if satisfactory evidence is not forthcoming, the relationship must not proceed any further.

In addition to the identification requirements, a firm needs to ensure that it **knows its customer**. This means obtaining an understanding of a client's proposed patterns of trading which will enable the firm to identify any suspicious changes in a client's activities. The types of information a firm may obtain include details regarding the **nature and level of business** to be conducted and the expected **origin of funds** the client is using. What information is required will depend upon the application of commercial judgement by the firm in the circumstances. Any information obtained must be kept up to date by the firm.

Failure to implement these measures is a criminal offence, punishable with a maximum sentence of **two years**' imprisonment for any senior officer of the firm and/or an unlimited fine, irrespective of whether money laundering has taken place.

4.4 Internal reporting procedures

All institutions must appoint an 'appropriate person' within the organisation, generally known as the **Money Laundering Reporting Officer (MLRO)**.

The functions of the MLRO are as follows.

- To receive reports of transactions giving rise to knowledge or suspicion of money laundering activities from employees of the institution.

- To determine whether the report of a suspicious transaction from the employee, considered together with all other relevant information, does actually give rise to knowledge or suspicion of money laundering.

- If, after consideration, he knows or suspects that money laundering is taking place, to report those suspicions to the appropriate law enforcement agency, e.g. SOCA.

For the purpose of each individual employee, it is important to note that a report made to the money laundering reporting officer concerning a transaction means that the employee has fulfilled his statutory obligations and will have **no criminal liability** in relation to any money laundering offence in respect of the reported transaction.

4.5 Senior management responsibilities

With the passing of FSMA, the FSA became a prosecuting authority in this area and signalled its intention to take this responsibility seriously. The FSA has high level rules regarding senior management money laundering that operates alongside the existing regime.

Under the Senior Management Arrangements, Systems and Controls (SYSC) sourcebook in the FSA's Handbook, firms must take reasonable care to establish and maintain effective systems and controls for compliance with applicable requirements and standards under the regulatory system and for countering the risk that the firm might be used to further financial crime.

Firms must ensure that these systems and controls enable it to identify, assess, monitor and manage **money laundering risk** and that these are **comprehensive and proportionate to the nature, scale and complexity of its activities**. Money laundering risk is the risk that a firm may be used to further money laundering.

In identifying its money laundering risk and in establishing the nature of these systems and controls a firm should consider a range of factors, including:

- Its customer, product and activity profiles
- Its distribution channels
- The complexity and volume of its transactions
- Its processes and systems
- Its operating environment

Failure by a firm to manage this risk effectively will increase the risk to society of crime and terrorism. The FSA, when considering whether a breach of its rules on systems and controls have occurred will have regard to the firm's compliance with the Joint Money Laundering Steering Group Guidance Notes. Firms must carry out regular assessments of the adequacy of these systems and controls and ensure compliance with relevant legal requirements, including the Terrorism Act 2000, the Proceeds of Crime Act 2002 and the Money Laundering Regulations 2003.

Firms should ensure that the systems and controls include:

- **Appropriate training** for its employees

- Appropriate provision of information to its governing body and senior management, including a **report at least annually** by that firm's money laundering reporting officer (MLRO) on the operation and effectiveness of those systems and controls.

- Appropriate documentation of its risk management policies and risk profile in relation to money laundering

- Appropriate measures to ensure that money laundering risk is taken into account in its day-to-day operation, including in relation to the development of new products, the taking on of new customers and changes in its business profile

- Appropriate measures to ensure that procedures for identification of new customers do not unreasonably deny access to its services to potential customers who cannot reasonably be expected to produce detailed evidence of identity

- The requirement that a firm must allocate to a director or senior manager (who may also be the MLRO) overall responsibility within the firm for the establishment and maintenance of effective anti-money laundering systems and controls

4.6 Financing terrorist acts

4.6.1 Terrorist activities

The acts of terrorism committed against the USA in September 2001 have increased the international efforts to locate and cut off funding for terrorists and their organisations. Terrorists are using increasingly sophisticated methods to transfer terrorist funds and often require the services of bankers, accountants and lawyers.

There is a considerable overlap between the movement of terrorist funds and the laundering of criminal assets. Terrorist groups are also known to have well-established links with organised criminal activity. However, there are two major differences between terrorist and criminal funds.

- Often only **small amounts** are required to commit a terrorist atrocity, therefore increasing the difficulty of tracking the funds.

- Whereas money laundering relates to the **proceeds** of crime, terrorists can be funded from legitimately obtained income and it is the **purpose** for which the funds will be used that is important.

The Terrorism Act 2000 defines terrorism in the UK as the use or threat of action wherever it occurs, designed to influence a government or to intimidate the public for the purpose of advancing a political, religious or ideological cause where the action

- Involves serious violence against a person; or

- Involves serious damage to property; or

- Endangers a person's life; or

- Creates a serious risk to the health or safety of the public; or

- Is designed seriously to interfere with, or seriously to disrupt an electronic system, e.g. a computer virus.

4.6.2 ~~Bank of England~~ sanctions list

[handwritten: HM Treasury]

In terms of identifying clients who may potentially be involved in the financing of terrorism, institutions should refer to the sanctions list maintained by the ~~Bank of England~~ *[handwritten: HM. TREASURY]*

The ~~Bank of England~~ *[handwritten: HM Treasury]* maintains the UK version of the financial sanctions list that consolidates the lists of known terrorist suspects of the United Nations, EU and UK Government.

Financial institutions are requested to check whether they maintain any accounts or otherwise hold any funds or economic resources for, or provide financial services to, the individual named on the financial sanctions list and, if so, they should freeze the accounts or other funds or economic resources, suspend the provision of any financial services (unless licensed by HM Treasury) and report their findings to the ~~Bank of England~~ *[handwritten: HM Treasury]*.

CHAPTER ROUNDUP

- To act on information not freely available to the market is to commit the criminal offence of insider dealing.

- Various types of behaviour, including insider dealing and manipulation of transactions, can constitute market abuse.

- The FSA's Code of Market Conduct describes behaviours that amount to market abuse, but not exhaustively.

- Money laundering has three stages: placement, layering, integration. Those in the financial services industry must keep alert to possible offences relating to the proceeds of any crime.

- Joint Money Laundering Steering Group guidance emphasises the need for firms to assess risks when implementing money laundering precautions. The 'Know Your Customer' principle implies that firms should, where appropriate, take steps to find out about the customer's circumstances and business.

- It is a criminal offence to assist laundering the proceeds of crime, to fail to report it satisfactorily, or to tip off someone laundering the proceeds of crime.

- The Money Laundering Regulations apply to all authorised firms and individuals. Each firm must have a Money Laundering Reporting Officer, who will decide whether to report suspicions to the Serious Organised Crime Agency.

- Fund raising, use and possession, funding arrangements and money laundering are offences under the Terrorism Act 2000.

- There is a duty to report suspected terrorism to the police.

BPP
LEARNING MEDIA

TEST YOUR KNOWLEDGE

Check your knowledge of the chapter here, without referring back to the text.

1.	What criminal legislation covers insider dealing?	
2.	What is the definition of an insider under criminal law?	
3.	What is the maximum penalty for market abuse?	
4.	What are the three stages of money laundering?	▪ ▪ ▪
5.	What legislation makes it a criminal offence for an individual to assist a money launderer?	
6.	What is the maximum penalty for assisting a money launderer?	

BPP LEARNING MEDIA

1.   The Criminal Justice Act 1993.

   (See Section 1.1)

2.   Under CJA 1993, an insider is an individual who knowingly has inside information and knows it is from an inside source.

   (See Section 1.2)

3.   An unlimited fine. Other sanctions also include a public statement, an injunction or restitution order.

   (See Section 3.9)

4.   Placement, layering and integration.

   (See Section 4)

5.   The Proceeds of Crime Act 2002.

   (See Section 4.1)

6.   Fourteen years in prison and/or an unlimited fine.

   (See Section 4.2.1)

4

The Takeover Code

INTRODUCTION

In this chapter we examine the role of the Takeover Panel in ensuring mergers and acquisitions in the UK are fair and orderly. There is a great deal of detail in the bid timetable and you should ensure you have memorised all the key dates.

The ultimate decision as to whether a takeover should go ahead or not will, however, belong to the competition commission within the UK, or European Commission on an EU-wide basis.

BPP
LEARNING MEDIA

CHAPTER LEARNING OBJECTIVES

Relevant Bodies

- **Know** the role of the Takeover Panel in takeovers and mergers.

- **Know** the role and responsibilities of:
    - The Office of Fair Trading (OFT)
    - The Competition Commission (CC)
    - The Secretary of State for Trade and Industry
    - The relevant industry regulators (eg telecommunications and utilities)
    - The European Commission

- **Understand** the responsibilities of pension fund trustees in takeovers and mergers

- **Understand** the role of the Pensions Regulator in takeovers and mergers

The Takeover Code

- **Know** the legal nature and purpose of the Takeover Code.

- **Know** companies and transactions and persons subject to the Takeover Code.

- **Know** the six General Principles.

- **Know** the definitions of 'acting in concert' dealings, 'interest shorts' and 'relevant securities'.

- **Know** Rules 2, 7.1 and 17.1 – Announcements

- **Know** Rule 3 –Independent Advice

- **Know** Rule 4 – Prohibited Dealings

- **Know** Rule 5 – Timing Restrictions on Acquisitions

- **Know** Rules 6 and 11 – Minimum Level and Nature of Consideration to be Offered

- **Know** Rules 8, 24.3, 25.3 and 38.5 – Disclosure of Dealings and Interests

- **Know** Rules 9 and 37 and Appendix 1 – The Mandatory Offer, Redemption or Purchase by a Company of its Own Securities and "Whitewashes"

- **Know** Rule 13 – Conditions and Pre-Conditions

- **Know** Rules 19 and 20 – Information

- **Know** Rule 21 –Restrictions on Frustrating Action

- **Know** Rule 28 – Profit Forecasts

- **Know** Rules 30 to 35 – Timing and Revision

KNOW – SCHEMES of arrangement – APP. 7

1 TAKEOVERS AND MERGERS

Until recently, the regulation of takeovers and mergers was the last aspect of the UK regulatory environment which was left almost exclusively to practitioner self-regulation.

From May 2006, the Takeover Directive has been implemented. Whilst maintaining the significant practitioner involvement, the Directive gives statutory powers for the first time to the Panel.

1.1 The Panel

The Takeover Panel is a grouping of all the important organisations in the City of London. Backing the Panel is the Bank of England, which appoints the Chairman and Deputy Chairman, together with representatives of key City institutions.

The Panel's duty is to monitor adherence to the general principles laid down in the Takeover Code ('the Blue Book'). Its main weapon is to withdraw the facilities of the market from anybody who breaks those rules. This is referred to within the Takeover Code as 'cold shouldering' and is such a powerful weapon that it seldom has to be used – the mere threat of it tends to bring people into line with the rules and regulations. The Takeover Directive has given the Panel statutory powers to write rules and to seek compensation orders in the courts for investors of a target company where its rules have been breached.

The basic concept behind the Panel and the Takeover Code is to ensure that there is a level playing field in takeover activity in the UK. In other words, each party has an equal chance to state its case and make its point of view clear to the target's shareholders. The principles and rules contained in the Takeover Code ensure that this takes place.

The Panel comprises two main units.

- The Panel itself (split into a Code Committee and a Hearing Committee).
- The Executive.

The Panel meets on both a regular and ad hoc basis. Members are senior executives of major City institutions who are not full-time Panel employees. The Panel is split into two subgroups, the Code Committee (who write the rules) and the Hearings Committee (who implement them). The day-to-day work of the Panel is carried out by the Executive, which is staffed on a full-time basis by a mixture of permanent staff and professionals who have been seconded from the leading investment banks, securities houses, accountants and legal firms. The Executive monitors actual and potential transactions, provides advice, investigates potential breaches and makes decisions promptly. Any unresolved disputes are referred to the Panel's Hearing Committee, which if required can meet at short notice. The Panel has the power to waive or alter any rules should the circumstances indicate that this is desirable. Any party who does not accept decisions of the Panel may take these decisions to the Takeover Appeal Board.

The combination of experienced staff, flexibility, promptness and power makes the Panel an effective regulator of the UK takeover and mergers market.

1.2 The purpose of the Takeover Code

The purpose of the Takeover Code is set out in its Introduction

> The Code is designed principally to ensure that shareholders are treated fairly and are not denied an opportunity to decide on the merits of a takeover and that shareholders of the same class are afforded equivalent treatment by an offeror. The Code also provides an orderly framework within which takeovers are conducted. In addition, it is designed to promote, in conjunction with other regulatory regimes, the integrity of the financial markets.
>
> *The Introduction to the Takeover Code*

The Takeover Code goes on to clarify that it is not responsible for

- The financial or commercial advantages or disadvantages of a takeover. These are matters for the company and its shareholders.

- Competition policy, which is the responsibility of government and other bodies.

Following the implementation of the Takeover Directive in May 2006, the Code now has **statutory** powers. This means the Panel may apply to the courts for enforcement of its rules and also requires, bidding companies to pay compensation if they breach the Code.

1.3 Application of the Code to companies, transactions and people

1.3.1 Companies

The Code regulates mergers, offers and potential offers for **all companies,** whether listed or unlisted, which are registered in the UK, Channel Island or Isle of Man **and** they have securities trading on a UK Regulated Market or Stock Exchange in Channel Islands or Isle of Man). The Code also applies to private companies which have, in the past ten years, had their shares traded on an exchange or have offered shares to the public. The Code does not apply to Open Ended Investment Companies (OEICs).

1.3.2 Transactions

The Code applies to any form of offer to acquire the voting equity shares of a company, whether through a 'takeover bid', a 'scheme of arrangement' or any other method that would transfer full or partial control of the company. Therefore it does not apply to the acquisition of non-voting non-equity shares.

1.3.3 People

The Code applies to anyone who participates in the takeover or is any way connected.

This will include

- Advisers.
- Directors or Partners.
- Employees.
- Any other Representatives.

1.4 The six general principles of the Takeover Code

In very much the same way as the FSA rulebook has been written, the Takeover Code begins with six general principles governing the conduct of takeover activity in the UK. This is then followed by a series of detailed rules which add guidance on the application of the principles, as well as provisions on specific aspects of takeover procedure.

1.4.1 The general principles

The six general principles are as follows.

1. All holders of the securities of an offeree company of the same class must be afforded **equivalent treatment**; moreover, if a person acquires control of a company, the other holders of securities must be protected.

2. The holders of the securities of an offeree company must have **sufficient time and information** to enable them to reach a properly informed decision on the bid; where it advises the holders of securities, the board of the offeree company must give its views on the effects of implementation of the bid on employment, conditions of employment and the locations of the company's places of business.

BPP
LEARNING MEDIA

3.   The board of an offeree company must act in the **interests of the company as a whole** and must not deny the holders of securities the opportunity to decide on the merits of the bid.

4.   **False markets** must not be created in the securities of the offeree company, of the offeror company or of any other company concerned by the bid in such a way that the rise or fall of the prices of the securities becomes artificial and the normal functioning of the markets is distorted.

5.   An offeror must announce a bid only after ensuring that he/she can **fulfil in full** any cash consideration, if such is offered, and after taking all reasonable measures to secure the implementation of any other type of consideration.

6.   An offeree company must **not be hindered** in the conduct of its affairs for **longer than is reasonable** by a bid for its securities.

These are the guiding principles of the Code. Where there is doubt as to the application of a rule then reference should always be made to the principles. A breach of a principle, even when in strict accordance with the rules, is deemed to be a breach of the Code itself. The Panel will apply the General Principles in accordance with their spirit to achieve their underlying purposes.

1.5 Announcements

The most important rules governing the pre-bid environment relate to the **secrecy** of negotiations. The Panel is concerned to prevent leaks about potential bids, which could result in the development of a false market in the securities of both the bidder and target companies.

An announcement will, however, be required in the following circumstances.

- A firm intention to make an offer has been reached.

- A mandatory bid under Rule 9 has been triggered.

- There is volatility in the target or bidder's share price (broadly speaking, a 5% price increase in one day, or a 10% increase since the start of talks).

- There is rumour and speculation surrounding a possible offer.

- Talks are extended beyond a small number of parties (so that a leak becomes more likely).

It is within the Panel's powers to force potential bidders into the open rather than to allow a **false market** to continue.

The Panel has the power to impose a time limit on a potential bidder to "put up or shut up". This will require the potential bidder to either announce a formal offer or confirm they are not making an offer and they will be unable to launch a bid for **six months**.

Under Principle 5, a bid must only be announced after the most careful and responsible consideration in the belief that the offeror can fulfil the bid terms. The following details must be included in the announcement.

- Terms of the bid including any conditions applied to the bid.
- Identity of the offeror.
- Holdings by offeror in the target company (including derivatives and stock loans).
- Irrevocable letters of intent to sell target company shares to the bidder.
- Any break fees or inducements offered.
- Confirmation from financial adviser that cash offer can be fulfilled.

The announcement is made to the Panel and the shareholders of the target company. Following the introduction of the Takeover Directive, there is now also a requirement to circulate the announcement to the employees of both the target and the bidder.

Rule 13 requires that an offer must not be subject to conditions that are subjective or can only be fulfilled by the bidder. The main acceptable condition is clearance of the takeover by the Competition Commission. If new securities are to be issued to finance the takeover, a condition that shareholder and exchange permissions are obtained can be a condition.

Under Rule 19, it is the directors' duty to ensure that information is prepared with the highest standards of care and accuracy and must be adequately and fairly presented. Directors must take care not to omit important information nor to give misleading impressions to the market to create uncertainty.

1.6 Bid timings

The Bid Timetable
(all calendar days)

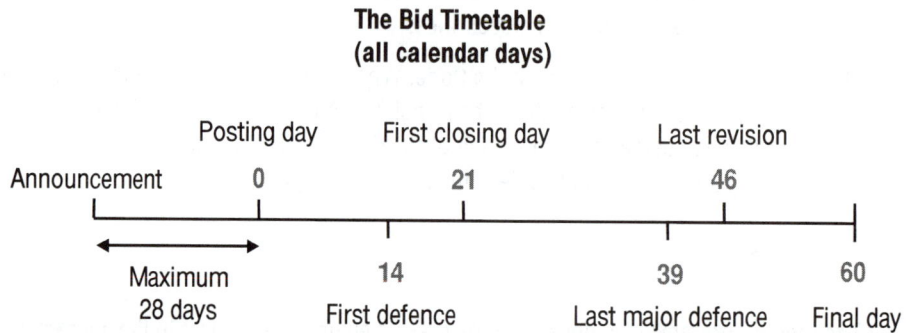

Once a bid has been announced, takeovers in the UK fit into a detailed and fixed time-frame. The time limits refer to calendar days throughout.

Announcement day

Once a bid has been publicly announced, the offeror has **28 days** in which to post the offer document, giving full details of its offer to the target's shareholders. If the bid is hostile, it is unlikely that the offeror will take the full 28-day allowance. The offer to acquire the target shares must be conditional on, *inter alia*, a minimum level of shareholder acceptance. The minimum level of acceptances allowed in the Takeover Code is the amount that would bring the offeror's total shareholding to over 50%, but any higher level is permitted. If this level of acceptances is not reached, the offer cannot proceed.

If, following an announcement of a bid, the offeror buys any of the target's shares in the market, this transaction must be disclosed to the market by **noon the next business day**. If the price of these acquired shares is higher than the offer price, then the offer price must be increased to at least match this price. If the offer was not originally a cash offer, it must be amended to include a full cash alternative. This rule arises from the first general principle of the Takeover Code.

Whenever a party to a transaction is required to make a public disclosure or announcement, this must be done through a Regulatory Information Service (RIS), authorised by FSA to act for companies in disseminating news to the markets.

Posting day

The posting day is the day on which the offer document is posted to the target's shareholders. This counts as Day 0 for all other reference points. If the offer is a recommended offer, the target's directors will include in the offer document a letter to their own shareholders explaining why they recommend acceptance of the offer for their shares. In a hostile offer, they are required to send a defence document to their shareholders.

The offer document must state the holdings of the offeror and connected parties in the target company at the latest practicable date to the posting day and any trades they have conducted in those securities in the last 12 months.

4: THE TAKEOVER CODE

Day 14 – the first defence document

In a hostile bid, the target company's directors must post defence documents to all shareholders by Day 14. Typically, defence documents will contain the directors' response to the offer document, recommending that shareholders reject the offer. Under General Principle 3, the directors must act in the best interests of their shareholders. Under Rule 3, they must take competent independent advice on the merits or otherwise of the bid before making their recommendation. The substance of this advice must also be made known to shareholders.

They are also required to disclose all holdings by directors and any connected parties in their own shares and any transactions by them since the start of the offer.

The target Board must not take any actions to frustrate the takeover without shareholders approval at a general meeting. This will prohibit the target Board from

- Issuing any more of its own shares or selling treasury shares (own shares held by the company).
- Issuing options over own shares.
- Issuing any convertible securities.
- Selling or buying any material assets.
- Entering into contracts other than in the normal course of business.

A similar provision concerns any inducements such as a 'break fee' that the offeree agrees to pay to a recommended bidder if the bid fails for certain reasons (usually the later recommendation of a another bidder by the offeree). This must not exceed 1% of the target's total value based on the offer price.

Day 21 – the first closing day

The first day that the bid can close is Day 21. At this point, the offeror company will review the number of acceptances they have received from the target's shareholders.

- If the company has reached its specified acceptance level, it must declare that the offer is now 'unconditional with regard to acceptances'. Any offer will then remain open for a further **14 days** to the remaining shareholders to accept the offer.

- If the minimum acceptance condition has not been accepted by Day 21, the offeror company may, at its discretion, increase the level of the bid and extend the offer period. If at any time during the takeover timetable, the offeror states that this is the final bid, or that no extension will be made, the offeror must abide by that decision unless another bidder declares itself.

- If the bidder improves their offer at any time the bid must remain open for a minimum 14 days following posting of the revised offer.

Day 39 – last defence documents

Day 39 is the last day for the announcement of any new information by the target's board – for example, dividend or profit forecasts or trading statements.

Day 42 – right of withdrawal

If the offer has not been declared unconditional with regard to acceptances by Day 42 (21 days after the first closing day) then any shareholder who had accepted the original bid may now withdraw their acceptance.

Day 46 – last offer amendment

Day 46 is the final day on which the offeror company may **amend its offer in any way**. From this point on, it is therefore also not able to buy shares in the market at above the offer price. However, in the case of a **competitive bid**, i.e. two or more bidders, the Panel may, in some cases, allow bids to be revised after this date.

Day 60 – the final day

A bid can remain open for 60 days. By Day 60, it must be unconditional with regard to acceptances or the bid will lapse. By 08:00 on Day 61, the offeror must state the total number of acceptances, together with its own holdings and irrevocable commitments held. If a bid lapses, the offeror may not launch another offer for the target for **12 months** from that date.

If, during the course of a bid, a new bid emerges, the original offeror will automatically move back to the start of the new bidder's timetable, so that the two offers progress in tandem.

The bid may be delayed if it is subject to an investigation by the Office of Fair Trading (OFT). If this investigation (discussed further below) takes longer than allowed for in the bid timetable, the Panel will generally 'freeze' the timetable, starting It again at Day 37 if the bid is cleared by the OFT. If, however, it is referred to the Competition Commission for a detailed investigation, the bid must lapse (i.e. end). If it is subsequently cleared by the Competition Commission, the bidder has 21 days to choose whether to launch a new offer.

1.7 Share stake disclosures (Rule 8)

During the offer period, the following dealings must be disclosed either publicly (through an RIS, with a copy to the Panel) or privately (to the Panel). These rules relate to dealings in **relevant securities**, which are

- The voting shares of the target.

- Where the offer is a securities offer, securities of the bidder of the type being offered as consideration.

- Any instruments convertible into those securities.

The definition of dealings is very wide and includes any action which may result in the number of securities in which a person is interested, including short positions. This will therefore include:

- Options on securities.

- Conversion or subscription rights on securities.

- Derivatives on securities (unless the securities concerned are only a small fraction (less than 20%) of a basket of securities to which the derivative relates).

- Agreements to buy or sell securities.

The disclosures to be made are as follows.

- Public disclosure.

  - Any dealings in the relevant securities by the offeror, offeree or their associates, on their own account or on behalf of discretionary investment clients.

  - Any dealings by direct or indirect holders of 1% or more of the offeror or offeree.

  - Any dealing by a connected exempt fund manager.

  - Summary of total acquisitions and disposals with highest and lowest prices by exempt principal traders with recognised intermediary status (market makers).

- Private disclosure.

  - Any dealings in relevant securities for discretionary investment clients by an exempt fund manager associated with the offeror/offeree.

  - Dealings by the parties and their associates for non-discretionary clients.

All disclosures must be made without delay, and at the latest by **12 noon on the next business day** (T+1). (15:30 for 1% shareholders not connected to the offeror of offeree).

1.8 Restrictions on acquisitions of shares (Rule 5)

Rule 5 aims to prevent a person obtaining control, or consolidating control, over a company except in a number of acceptable circumstances. The basic rule states that a person (including people acting in concert with him) may not acquire any shares or rights over shares which would mean that he would hold 30% or more of the voting rights in the company. Moreover, when he already holds between 30% and 50% of the company's voting securities, he may not **consolidate control**, i.e. acquire any further shares in that company. If he breaches this rule, he is subject to Rule 9 and must make a mandatory offer (see below).

There are a number of exceptions where the above basic rule does not apply, allowing a stake of over 30% to be acquired. These are as follows.

- Where a person already holds shares with more than 50% of the voting rights, since they already have legal control.

- Where there is a vote of independent shareholders, excluding the acquirer, which approves the acquisition – a 'whitewash'.

- Where the purchase of shares or rights over shares is from a single shareholder and it is the only purchase in a seven-day period. Where such a purchase is made, then no subsequent purchases will be permitted unless the situations given below apply.

- Where the purchase is immediately before, or at any time after, a firm announcement to make an offer or during an offer and either the offer itself or a competing offer will be/has been recommended by the offeree board. Where the purchase is immediately before the announcement, it must be conditional on the offer being made.

- Where an offer has been announced, the first closing date of the offer has passed and it is not to be referred to the Competition Commission.

- Where the first closing date of a competing offer has passed and that offer is not to be referred to the Competition Commission.

- During an offer that is unconditional in all respects.

- Where the acquisition is by way of a shareholder accepting an offer, as opposed to selling in the market.

1.9 Mandatory offers (Rules 9, 37 and Appendix 1)

Under the Takeover Code, if a shareholder, or persons acting in concert with them, takes their stake to an aggregate **30%** level or more, known as **'effective control'**, then they will be required to make a **mandatory offer** under Rule 9. If a shareholder already has a stake of between 30% and 50%, and acquires any further shares at all, this shareholder would also be required to make a mandatory offer. As noted above, under Rule 5 there are only very limited circumstances in which a person is permitted to acquire 30% or more of a company.

Rule 37 considers the position if the holding of an bidder goes over 30% not as a result of their own transactions, but because the target company has done a share buy-back or other redemption of shares. The Panel will consider waiving a mandatory bid under Rule 9 if a majority of independent shareholders approve (referred to as a 'whitewash'). Appendix 1 sets out the requirements for consultations with the Panel and circulars to independent shareholders that are required.

Under a voluntary offer, the offeror may impose a number of conditions which must be met before they are required to proceed with the offer. These include the acceptance condition mentioned earlier, which must be set at a minimum of 50%, but may be at up to 90% of total shares and voting rights. Further conditions could include the need for the offeror's shareholders' approval, or regulatory approval. However, under the terms of a mandatory offer, much of the offeror's discretion to impose conditions is removed and the following rules apply.

- A mandatory bid must be at least at the **best price** at which the offeror has purchased shares in the target **within the last 12 months**. Remember that in a voluntary offer, the bid need only be at the best price the offeror has paid for any target shares in the last three months and need not have any cash element (subject to Rule 11 above).

- The offer must be for cash or have a full cash alternative available.

- Once the bidder acquires a holding in excess of 50% of total shares and voting rights, the bid must be declared unconditional with regard to acceptances, and the only other condition allowed relates to the need for regulatory approval.

1.10 Other Takeover Code rules

1.10.1 Concert parties

Under the Takeover Code, shareholdings of parties acting in concert are aggregated. The definition of acting in concert is 'persons who, pursuant to an agreement or understanding, co-operate through the acquisition of shares to obtain or consolidate control'. Certain relationships are presumed to create a concert party; these include a company and its parent, fellow associates and subsidiaries, its own subsidiaries and associates (a holding of 20% or more in the shares of a company is assumed to make it an associate). Accordingly when considering whether a share stake requires disclosure or gives rise to a mandatory offer, the aggregated holding of all these parties must be taken into account.

1.10.2 Exempt market makers and fund managers

As stated above, certain relationships are presumed to create a concert party, so that share stakes are aggregated. Within an investment bank, **market makers, discretionary fund managers** and corporate finance advisers may each separately and independently deal in shares in a company subject to the Code. In principle, all of these shareholdings must be aggregated with those of all their clients in establishing any obligations under the Code.

This imposes significant restrictions on market makers and fund managers, who must be able to perform their functions of making markets in shares and acting for discretionary clients. They may therefore apply to the Panel for exempt status, which grants them exemption from the requirement to aggregate their share transactions with those of the offeror or offeree company and their advisers.

1.10.3 Requirement for a minimum price (Rule 6) or a cash alternative (Rule 11)

The offer consideration may consist of cash only; shares or loan stock (a paper offer); a mixture of cash and shares; or a choice offering a number of alternatives. In any case the minimum price to be offered is the highest the offeror has paid in the last **three months** for any target shares.

However, where the offeror has purchased **10%** or more of the voting shares in the target **for cash** in the 12 months prior to the announcement, the offer must be for cash or have a cash alternative. In this case the price must be set at not less than the **highest price paid** by the offeror in the **last 12 months**. If the shares were acquired for consideration other than cash (e.g. off-exchange share-for-share transactions), then an equivalent form of consideration must be offered.

Furthermore, where the offeror purchases any target shares for cash during the offer period at a price higher than the offer price, the offer must be increased to the highest price paid, and a full cash alternative must be offered to all shareholders.

1.10.4 The post-bid environment (Rule 31)

Any offer declared unconditional as to acceptances must remain open for acceptance by the remaining shareholders for at least a further **14 days** after the date on which it goes unconditional. The offeror has a maximum of 21 days from the date the offer goes unconditional to acceptances to fulfil any other outstanding conditions.

The consideration (cash or shares) for a successful bid must be settled within 14 days of going unconditional.

As we have seen above, should the bid fail (i.e. not go unconditional as regards acceptances), the offeror is prohibited from bidding for the target again for 12 months (unless a rival bidder emerges, or the target's board recommends the new offer).

If the successful bidder did not acquire all the target's shares, they cannot pay a higher price than the final offer to acquire any more shares for at least six months after the bid.

1.10.5 Prohibited dealings (Rule 4)

The Panel is concerned to avoid the creation of a false market in the shares of either the bidder or the target, and in particular to avoid price manipulation. Accordingly the bidder is not permitted to dispose of any shares in the target, except after announcing his intention 24 hours in advance, and with the Panel's consent.

Moreover, the target's financial advisers are not allowed to deal in the shares of their client, or encourage anyone else to deal in these shares. Dealing in the shares of the bidder is only permitted if the offer is not price-sensitive to those securities, e.g. in an all-cash offer. There is also a general prohibition on dealing while in possession of unpublished price-sensitive information, which echoes the insider dealing and market abuse rules.

1.10.6 Equality of information (Rule 20)

The bidder and target boards are required to make all disclosures to their shareholders and to competing bidders at the same time and in the same format. There are very specific rules which apply.

- Any information provided in confidence to one actual or potential bidder must be provided on request to any other bona fide potential bidder.

- No new information or opinions must be disclosed selectively to shareholders or analysts and the company's advisers must attend meetings with shareholders and analysts and confirm the company's compliance with this rule.

- All disclosures must be made through an RIS.

1.10.7 Profit forecasts (Rule 28)

One particularly problematic area for regulators arises where the target wishes to include profit forecasts in its defence document. Given the difficulties of verification there is considerable scope for misuse and accordingly the Code contains provisions on profit forecasts.

Firstly, it defines a profit forecast as any statement which sets an upper or lower limit on expected profits for the current or any subsequent year. Secondly, it states that where a profit forecast is provided, it must be reported on by both the auditors to the company making the statement, and by their financial advisers, and these reports shown in the document concerned. There must be full disclosure of the assumptions underlying the profit forecast.

2 THE COMPETITION AUTHORITIES AND THE PENSIONS REGULATOR

The role of the Takeover Panel was to ensure that the process of the bid was fair to all. It is the role of the competition authorities to decide whether the takeover should be blocked.

Most takeovers in the UK are subject to the UK merger control regime under the **Enterprise Act 2002**.

2.1 The Office of Fair Trading

The Office of Fair Trading (OFT) may investigate any transaction involving a UK company which may be expected to result in a **'substantial lessening of competition'**. This is deemed to be one which creates or consolidates a **25% market share**, or which involves the acquisition of a target with **UK-wide turnover of £70m** or more. Following an initial investigation of up to four months, the OFT either clears the transaction or refers it for further investigation to the Competition Commission. The Panel may freeze the timetable during an OFT investigation. However, on referral to the Competition Commission, any offer subject to the Takeover Code must lapse.

2.2 Competition Commission

The Competition Commission's investigation may last up to 24 weeks and, at the end of this time, it determines whether the bid is cleared or prohibited, or whether steps may be taken to maintain competitiveness. Any appeal may be made to the **Competition Appeals Tribunal**, an independent body.

2.3 Secretary of State for Trade and Industry

In addition, the Secretary of State for Trade and Industry may refer any merger to a Competition Commission investigation if they believe it is **against the public interest**.

If the Secretary of State has referred a public interest case, the Competition Commission will make recommendations to the Secretary of State, who will then make the final decision as to clearance.

2.4 European Commission

In addition to UK competition regulation, the European Commission investigates on its own behalf the validity of substantial pan-European mergers and acquisitions. Once the European Commission commences an investigation, the UK Competition Commission usually ceases to be involved.

EU merger regulation will apply if a merger is deemed to give rise to a 'concentration'. The European Commission will examine a transaction to ensure it is compatible with the Common Market. The Treaty of Rome prohibits, as incompatible with the Common Market, the following.

- All agreements which restrict trade and have as their object the prevention or distortion of competition (Article 85).

- The abuse of a dominant position within the Common Market (Article 86).

A transaction will fall within the European Commission's jurisdiction if the following tests are satisfied.

- The combined aggregate worldwide turnover of both parties exceeds **€5bn**.
- The aggregate EU turnover of both parties is greater than **€250m**.

However, if each party has more than two thirds of its turnover in the UK, the transaction will fall under the jurisdiction of the UK regulators.

It is also possible that, where a merger affects a distinct market in one member state, the European Commission may allow that country to conduct an investigation in parallel. In other circumstances, the member state may invite the European Commission to investigate a merger in which it would not normally become involved.

2.5 Industry regulators

In certain sectors such as telecoms and utilities, there may be an industry regulator who can also refer a merger to the Competition Authorities for further investigation. The specific sectors concerned are:

- Utilities (gas and electricity)
- Telecommunications
- Water
- Newspapers

There are specialist panel members for each sector and at least one of them must be involved in cases referred by these industry regulators.

2.6 The Pensions Regulator and the Role of Pension Fund Trustees

Another factor to consider during a takeover bid, is whether the pension rights of current and former employees will be protected during and after the merger. **'The Pensions Regulator'** is the body charged with considering whether a takeover of a UK company would be financially detrimental to a company's pension fund.

It is possible to approach The Pensions Regulator and obtain a **'clearance'** before the takeover. This would give comfort that there will not be a 'contribution notice' or 'financial support direction' given to the acquirer requiring them to contribute to the pension fund to cover a deficit.

The pension scheme trustees have the prime responsibility for safeguarding members' interests. Their powers and duties are set out in statute, trust law and the scheme's trust deed and rules. They need to be familiar with those powers and duties and act in accordance with them.

As directors of the target company are often also trustees of the company's pension fund, the guiding principles of The Pensions Regulator require such conflicted trustees to act appropriately. They are recommended to take independent advice in relation to their duties as trustees.

CHAPTER ROUNDUP

- The Takeover Directive made the Takeover Panel the statutory regulator of takeovers in the UK.

- The purpose of the Takeover Code is to ensure that the process of a bid is fair and orderly.

- The Takeover Code applies to all companies in the UK who have their securities traded on a regulated market.

- There are six general principles of the Takeover Code which can be summarised as:
  - Equivalent treatment
  - Sufficient time and information
  - Looking after the interests of the company as a whole
  - Avoid false markets
  - Ability to fulfil an offer
  - Don't hinder targets longer than is reasonable

- There is a set timetable for a bid with key dates such as:
  - Minimum offer period   – 21 calendar days after posting day
  - Maximum offer period   – 60 calendar days after posting day

    – 88 calendar days after announcement
  - Last defence – 39 calendar days after posting day
  - Last revision – 46 days after posting day

- Dealings during the offer period by 1% + shareholding must be disclosed by noon T+1.

- If a bidder acquires 30% or more of target they will be required to launch a mandatory bid.

- Initial reviews of whether a takeover would result in a substantial lessening of competition are considered by the Office of Fair Trading.

- The Secretary of State for Trade and Industry may refer a bid on public interest grounds.

- The ultimate decision as to whether to block a UK-only takeover is determined by the Competition Commission.

- Larger EU wide mergers are considered by the European Commission.

- Other industry regulators or The Pensions Regulator can also influence the clearance of a takeover.

BPP LEARNING MEDIA

TEST YOUR KNOWLEDGE

Check your knowledge of the chapter here, without referring back to the text.

1.   What is the nickname used for the Takeover Code?

2.   Name the six principles of the Takeover Code.

3.   Give the latest day for the following

     –   First closing

     –   Posting of offer document following announcement

     –   Last revision of offer

     –   Last defence

4.   Above what percentage of interest in shares must dealings in the offer period be disclosed, and by whom?

5.   What percentage holding would trigger a mandatory bid?

6.   What percentage of combined market share resulting from a takeover would indicate a risk of substantial lessening of competition for the OFT.

7.   On what grounds could the Secretary of State for Trade and Industry refer a bid to the Competition Commission?

8.   What is the single criteria for worldwide turnover of a combined entity that would trigger a referral to the European Commission?

1.   It is called the 'Blue Book' as it is contained in a blue plastic folder

(See Section 1.1)

2.   ■   Equivalent treatment
      ■   Sufficient time and information
      ■   Looking after interests of company as a whole
      ■   Avoid false markets
      ■   Ability to fulfil an offer
      ■   Don't hinder target longer than is reasonable

(See Section 1.4.1)

3.   ■   First closing – 21 calendar days after posting day
      ■   Posting of offer document – 28 days after announcement day
      ■   Last revision – 46 calendar days after posting day
      ■   Last defence – 39 calendar days after posting day

(See Section 1.6)

4.   1% or more and disclosed by noon on T+1

(See Section 1.7)

5.   30%, known as effective control

(See Section 1.9)

6.   25% or more market share

(See Section 2.1)

7.   On the grounds of public interest

(See Section 2.3)

8.   €5 billion

(See Section 2.4)

BPP LEARNING MEDIA

5

Companies Act and the Combined Code

INTRODUCTION

This chapter addresses the key regulations for companies and their directors. Companies Acts set out the rules on the formation of a company and any subsequent changes to its capital. In particular, we look at a scheme of arrangement as an alternative acquisition method in an agreed takeover.

The Combined Code on corporate governance sets out the best practice for directors in their role of managing the business.

CHAPTER CONTENTS

CHAPTER LEARNING OBJECTIVES

The Companies Acts 1985/89 and 2006

- **Know** the provisions contained in the Companies Acts 1985/89 and 2006 relating to

  - Schemes of arrangement and reconstructions (CA85 S425 to 427A).
  - Squeeze out and sell out (CA06 S974 to 985).
  - The reduction of share capital (S135 to 137).
  - Pre-emption rights (CA85 S89).
  - Investigations by inspectors (CA85 S431 to 432).
  - Financial assistance for the acquisition of a company's own shares (CA85 S151).
  - Main statutory rights of shareholders (CA85 S368, 371, 376, 459-461).
  - Company meetings (CA85 S368 to 370, 372).
  - Company requiring information about interests in its shares (CA06 S793 to 795).
  - Requirement to be a plc (CS85 S43).
  - Restrictions on public offers by a private company (CA85 S81).

Combined Code on Corporate Governance

- **Understand** the main provisions of the Combined Code in relation to

  - Companies and directors.
  - Institutional shareholders.
  - Non-executive directors.
  - Remuneration committees.
  - Audit committees.

SII Code of Conduct

- **Know** the SII Code of Conduct.
- **Be able to apply** the Code of Conduct to the provision of corporate finance advice.

1 THE COMPANIES ACTS 1985/89 AND 2006

The Companies Acts are complex pieces of legislation designed to achieve a number of ends. In particular, they look to protect shareholders from the directors and the general public from the abuse of limited liability. Companies Act 2006 will ultimately replace previous acts but is being implemented over 2007 and 2008.

1.1 Nature of a company and its constitution

1.1.1 Separate legal personality

A company is a separate legal person, distinct from its owners (the shareholders) and its managers (the directors). Thus, the company itself as an entity has legal rights and duties. For example, as we saw earlier, a company can become an authorised firm under FSMA 2000.

The Companies Act 1985 specified two types of company, specifically public limited companies and private companies.

1.1.2 Public Limited Companies (plc)

Under section 43 of Companies Act 1985, a public limited company is one

- That has a minimum of two shareholders.

- That has a minimum issued share capital of **£50,000** on which all the share premium and **at least 25%** of the nominal value have been paid up.

- Whose Memorandum of Association states that it is a public company.

- Which is correctly registered as public.

Such companies must have either 'plc' or 'Public Limited Company' at the end of their names and require a minimum of two members or shareholders.

Public companies are allowed to sell their shares to the public and are able to obtain a listing from the UK Listing Authority, however, they do not have to be listed. The terminology here is sometimes confusing, as obtaining a listing is frequently referred to as 'going public'.

1.1.3 Private companies

All other companies are private companies and must have 'Limited' at the end of their names.

Private companies may place restrictions on who may be a shareholder, reducing the opportunity of any shareholder to sell his shares. They require a minimum of only one member or shareholder.

Under Section 81 of the Companies Act 1985 it is an offence for a private company to offer securities to the public. The company and any of its officers would be liable to unlimited fines for a breach of this section. *refer to handout.*

1.1.4 Company constitution

Since a company as an entity has a relationship with the outside world, it needs a constitution. This is provided by two documents – the Memorandum and Articles of Association.

1.1.5 The Memorandum of Association

This is the **external** rulebook of the company governing its relationship with the outside world. The Memorandum must state

- The company's name.

- The location of the company's registered office (England and Wales or Scotland).

- That the company's liability is limited.

- If the company is to be a plc, then the Memorandum must state this.

- The **authorised** share capital of the company. Note that this will be the maximum that the company may issue and not necessarily the amount they currently have issued.

- The objects of the company – in other words, the main trading objectives and permitted activities of the company.

1.1.6 The Articles of Association

The Articles are the **internal** rulebook of the company governing the relationship between the company and its members (shareholders). There are standard terms contained within Table A of the Companies Act, but each company can create its own rules.

Once established, the provisions are binding on the shareholders in their relationships with the company and with each other.

1.2 Requiring Information About Interest in Own Shares CA06 S793

In the UK, all shares are issued in registered form. However, the use of nominee names and delays in the settlement process may result in companies being unaware of the ultimate owner of particular shares. Section 793 gives a **public company** the power to require shareholders to give information regarding their shareholding. The investigation notice can be sent to existing shareholders asking them to reveal the ultimate owner of any shares held in their names. It may also be sent to a particular individual asking whether he has, in the **last three years**, been an owner of shares in the company, either directly or through concert parties. Generally, the **Company Secretary** is responsible for dealing with these requirements. In addition, a shareholder with at least **10%** of the voting capital can request a S793 investigation.

In the absence of a response, companies may remove the voting/dividend rights of defaulting shareholders during the course of an investigation.

Refer to handout for more

1.3 Company meetings

Whilst directors are responsible for making decisions regarding the day-to-day running of the business, decisions which affect the structure of a company or the rights of members are decided upon in a meeting of the shareholders.

1.3.1 Companies Act 1985 Provisions

The Companies Act provides general provisions as to the conduct and structure of company meetings which will apply in the absence of any provisions to the contrary in the company's Memorandum and Articles.

1.3.2 Types of meetings

The two varieties of meeting are Annual General Meetings (AGMs) and Extraordinary General Meetings (EGMs). AGMs must be held once a year with a maximum time between AGMs of 15 months. An EGM may be held at any other time as required.

1.3.3 Notice

All members must be informed in writing in advance of the meeting and of the nature of the business to be transacted. This notice differs according to the type of meeting. An AGM requires **21 calendar days'** notice, whereas an EGM requires **14 calendar days**. The notice may be reduced, and an AGM held on short notice, if 100% of members entitled to attend a meeting vote in favour. This figure becomes 95% of members in the case of reduced notice for an EGM. *Refer to handout*

1.3.4 Resolutions

Decisions made at company meetings are known as resolutions. **Ordinary resolutions** require only a **simple majority** (>50%) of votes cast at the meeting to be carried. **Special resolutions** cover more unusual matters, such as changes to a company's constitution or structure. Any meeting voting on special resolutions must have 21 calendar days' notice and requires a **75%** majority of votes cast to be passed. Unless specified to the contrary in the company's constitution, each member will be entitled to one vote in respect of each share held. *refer to handout*

1.3.5 Meeting conduct

Directors normally call the meeting and send out the required notice. However, members holding **at least 10%** of a company's voting shares may requisition that the directors call an EGM. Directors must send out notice within 21 days of such a request, thereby convening a meeting. In exceptional circumstances, the courts may order that a meeting be held.

A meeting can only validly pass resolutions if it is quorate, a **quorum** is two members. Any member so elected may act as Chairman at any meeting.

1.3.6 Proxies

Any member entitled to attend and vote at a company's meeting is entitled to appoint another person (who may not be a member) as his proxy to attend and vote in his place. In a public company, a proxy may attend and vote, but may not exercise the member's right to speak.

1.4 Alterations to capital structure

1.4.1 Capital maintenance

The funds which a company raises from the issue of shares are generally maintained within the company as a permanent source of finance rather than being returned to shareholders. This concept of capital maintenance is of great importance within the Companies Act. However, there are various exceptions contained within the Companies Act, whereby capital may be reduced.

1.4.2 Reduction of capital

A company may reduce its share capital, provided the Articles of Association permit it; a **special resolution** is passed in favour of the reduction and (in some cases) if the courts confirm the action. It can be done for any reason, but the Act specifically mentions three instances.

(a)   Extinguish or reduce the liability of shareholders or shares which are not fully paid up.

(b)   Cancellation of share capital which has been permanently lost, and is thus no longer represented by assets.

(c)   Return of capital to shareholders which is in excess of the company's needs.

In relation to (a) and (c) above, any creditor of the company is entitled to object to the court, unless their claim is in some way secured or guaranteed by the company.

The court has the power to add 'and reduced' to the company name for a specified period.

1.5 Reconstructions and amalgamations – schemes of arrangement

A scheme of arrangement is a statutory procedure allowed for under S425-427 of the Companies Act 1985, whereby a company makes a compromise arrangement with its shareholders or creditors, allowing it to restructure itself. The company (through its directors) proposes a new corporate structure for itself; shareholders and/or creditors approve the structure; the courts then approve the structure; and the new structure is immediately in effect.

Under a reconstruction, a business is preserved and is carried on by substantially the same people, subsequent to the reorganisation. Typically, such a procedure may be used to rescue a company that is in financial difficulties to give the company a fresh start. Often, it is a case of altering the capital structure to reflect the true state of affairs in the company.

For example, a company may wish to transfer the business to a new company; in return for their shares in the old company, shareholders will receive shares in the new company. This is represented in the diagram below.

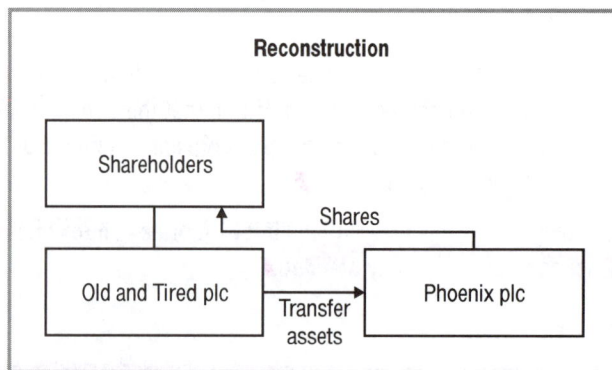

Reconstruction

Shareholders

Shares

Old and Tired plc → Transfer assets → Phoenix plc

Thus, the shareholders in Old and Tired plc become shareholders in Phoenix plc; the original company Old and Tired plc would then be wound up.

An amalgamation is a situation where two companies combine, either by forming a new company encompassing both the original businesses or by one company owning the other.

Therefore, a scheme of arrangement can be used for the following purposes.

- To acquire a company.
- To merge two or more companies.
- To acquire shares owned by minority investors.
- To restructure a business (e.g. create a new holding company etc.).
- To effect a management buy-out of a company.
- To demerge a company into separate entities.
- To reconstruct a group into two or more separate companies under the provisions of the 1986 Insolvency Act.
- To effect a moratorium amongst a company's creditors (e.g., an agreement to postpone payments to them).

BPP LEARNING MEDIA

1.5.1 Required procedures for amalgamations and reconstructions

There are three main stages: *ref to handout.*

- **Explanatory statement**. This is dispatched to shareholders and creditors at the same time as a notice convening the meetings. It must explain the effect of the scheme, and must give all information reasonably necessary to enable the shareholder or creditor to decide how to vote. The statement normally takes the form of a letter from the company's financial advisers (S426).

- **Members' and creditors' meetings**. The company, a creditor, the liquidator or a shareholder must apply to the court for permission for a meeting to be held for each of the classes of the interested parties concerned (i.e. creditors or shareholders). The scheme must be approved by **75% (in value)** of the creditors or class of creditors or shareholders present, voting either in person or by proxy at each meeting.

- **Court approval**. After the proposal has been approved, an application is made to the court to sanction the scheme (S423(2)). The court will ensure that the arrangement is such that an 'intelligent and honest man', a member of the class concerned and acting in respect of his interest, might reasonably approve the arrangement. Once the scheme is sanctioned by the court, a copy of the court order must be filed with the Registrar of Companies. At this stage the scheme becomes effective and binding on all creditors of the class that voted in favour of the scheme.

1.5.2 Advantages and disadvantages of a scheme of arrangement

Advantages	Disadvantages
Once approved, the scheme is binding on all shareholders	Timing – obtaining court approval is a lengthy procedure, and must be fitted into the court's timetable
A scheme effects an immediate transfer of shares	Cost – legal counsel will need to be employed
If used in a takeover, it gives certainty of 100% of the shares	Schemes can be complex to prepare and difficult for shareholders and creditors to understand
A takeover effected by a scheme is not bound by the Takeover Code timetable, although Panel approval of the overall timetable will be required	For a takeover, it can only be used for a **recommended bid** and not for a hostile bid. The target company and directors control the timing and implementation of the scheme, and so the bidder runs the risk that the scheme may be withdrawn – for example, if a higher offer is received or anticipated
Stamp duty may be saved (in the case of a capital reduction scheme)	
Only 75% of those voting (in person or by proxy) are required to approve the scheme for it to proceed	

1.6 Financial assistance

1.6.1 Basic rule

S151 of the Companies Act 1985 provides that it is illegal for a company directly or indirectly to give financial assistance for the purchase of its own shares (or those of its holding company). The reason for this is the principle of capital maintenance. If a company provides financial assistance to allow a third party to buy its shares, it reduces its own assets without receiving compensation in exchange, and potentially reduces its ability to meet its debts as they fall due.

1.6.2 Definition of financial assistance

Financial assistance would include

- A gift.
- Provision of a guarantee, security, indemnity, release or waiver.
- Any other form of assistance, whereby the company's net assets are reduced to a material extent.

Thus, many transactions are caught under these definitions, not just direct cash payments.

1.6.3 Consequences of contravention

Any financial assistance in contradiction of these rules is void. In other words, all contracts in connection with it have no legal effect.

The company and its officers may be liable to a fine and/or two years' imprisonment.

Directors who are in breach of their duties are liable to the company for any losses.

1.6.4 Exceptions

There are various exceptions when transactions that would satisfy the definition of financial assistance are permitted.

- If the principal purpose of the transaction is not the provision of financial assistance.

- If the financial assistance is an incidental part of a larger purpose.

- When the assistance is lending in the ordinary course of business.

- Where a loan is made to employees as part of an Employee Share Scheme.

In addition, the financial assistance rules are relaxed for private companies to a significant extent, known as a '**whitewash**'. This requires the passing of a special resolution and a statement of solvency of the company by the directors and verified by the auditors. The financial assistance must then be given within 8 weeks of the passing of the special resolution.

1.7 Company investigations by inspectors

1.7.1 Introduction

The Companies Act 1985 (S431-432) gives members the right to apply to the Department for Business, Enterprise and Regulatory Reform (DBERR) for an inspector to investigate the company's affairs.

1.7.2 Criteria

An inspector may be appointed by the DBERR on application of

- At least 200 members or holders of at least 10% of issued shares.
- The company itself, if it has passed an ordinary resolution approving such an action.

Any applicant must provide £5,000 security for costs and must furnish the DBERR with evidence to support their claim.

The Companies Act also gives the DBERR the power to exercise their investigative powers at their discretion in the following three circumstances.

- The company has been conducting its affairs with intent to defraud auditors or in a manner prejudicial to members, or for unlawful or fraudulent purposes.

- The promoters or managers have been guilty of fraud or any other act of misconduct.

- The company has failed to provide proper information to the members.

The DBERR has no obligation to warn the company or reveal the circumstances which led to the investigation.

1.7.3 Inspector's powers

The inspectors have very wide powers to obtain and require disclosure of information. They may also question any person on oath, obtain a warrant to search premises and finally inform the Secretary of State for Business, Enterprise and Regulatory Reform of any matters coming to their attention during the investigation.

1.8 Minority shareholder protections, 'sell outs' and 'squeeze outs'

Sections 459–461 of the Companies Act 1985 make provisions for the protection of members against unfair prejudice. If members believe that their company or large shareholders are taking action against their interests they may seek redress through the courts. This may result in the courts ordering the majority shareholder to buy out the minority shareholders at a fair price.

Under Companies Act 2006, S985 protects a minority in giving them the right to insist that a successful bidder buys them out within three months of the end of their bid – **known** as a '**sell out**'.

In contrast, if a bidder is successful enough to secure a total of **90%** or more of the voting rights of a company, then under S974 they can compulsorily purchase ('**squeeze out**') the remaining minority shares.

2 CORPORATE GOVERNANCE

2.1 Combined Code on Corporate Governance

Corporate governance can be defined as the way in which companies are directed and controlled. Institutional shareholders have abandoned their traditional 'back seat' role and show an increasingly proactive approach to holding directors of the company to account. The change in attitude has been fuelled by some notable corporate failures and the perception that directors may be improving their own pay and conditions at the expense of the shareholders.

The principles of corporate governance are included as an appendage to the Listing Rules called the 'Combined Code'. This Code has been derived from the recommendations of the Cadbury, Greenbury and Hampel reports in the 1990s, which considered corporate accountability and directors' remuneration. Further additions were made following the Higgs report on the role of non-executive directors (those not involved in the daily operations) and the Smith report on audit committees.

The UKLA requires companies to disclose (in their annual report) how they have applied the principles of good governance and whether they have complied with the provisions of the Combined Code *(Listing Rules, LR 9.8.6)*. Any departures from the Code's provisions should be explained. This 'comply or explain' approach is widely supported by companies and investors as allowing flexibility whilst ensuring sufficient information for investors to come to their own conclusions.

2.2 Board of directors and institutional shareholders

The main provision of the Combined Code are as follows.

2.2.1 Board of directors

- Every listed company should be headed by an effective board, which should lead and control the company. The board should meet regularly. Directors should bring independent judgement to bear on issues of strategy, etc.

- No one individual should have unfettered powers of decision. The posts of chairman and chief executive officer should be separate. There should be a strong and independent non-executive element on the board.

- The board should have a balance of executive and non-executive directors, such that no small group of individuals can dominate the board's decision taking.

- There should be a formal and transparent procedure for the appointment of new directors.

- All directors should submit themselves for re-election at least every **three years**. Non-executives should serve a maximum of two terms.

- Levels of remuneration should be sufficient to attract and retain directors needed to run the company successfully. Remuneration should be structured to link rewards to corporate and individual performance.

- Remuneration committees should be responsible for this. They should consist exclusively of independent non-executive directors.

- There should be an objective to have service contracts with notice periods of a **maximum of one year**.

- The annual report should contain a statement of remuneration policy and details of the remuneration of each director.

- Companies should be ready to enter into a dialogue with institutional shareholders based on a mutual understanding of objectives. They should use the AGM to communicate with private investors and encourage their participation. One senior non-executive should serve as a 'listening post' for shareholders.

- The board should maintain a sound system of internal control to safeguard shareholders' investment and the company's assets.

2.2.2 Institutional shareholders

Institutional shareholders have a responsibility to make considered use of their votes.

Institutional shareholders should be ready, where practicable, to enter into a dialogue with companies based on a mutual understanding of objectives.

2.3 Non-executive directors

The key issues to consider in relation to non-executive directors are

- The role of non-executive directors is to

  - Contribute an independent view to the board's deliberations.
  - Help the board provide effective leadership.
  - Ensure the continuing effectiveness of executive directors.
  - Ensure high standards of financial probity.

- They should be sufficient in number and calibre for their views to carry significant weight. Major listed companies (FTSE 350) should aim to have **at least half** the board as non-executives. Smaller companies should have at least two.

- Whereas all directors have a duty to monitor the company's performance, non-executive directors also have the duty to monitor the performance of the board as a whole and to inform shareholders if they are not satisfied. The non-executive directors should meet at least once very year without the executive directors to consider corporate governance issues.

- Non-executive directors should be free from bias, involvement and partiality. Professional advisers such as merchant banks may fulfil a specialist role, but are not a substitute for non-executive directors. Independence is most likely when non-executive directors

    - Have not been employed in an executive capacity by the firm in the last five years.
    - Are not retained as a professional adviser for the company.
    - Are not a significant supplier or customer of the company.

- Non-executive directors should not participate in share option schemes or performance-related or other incentive schemes. They should not be entitled to compensation for loss of office. The purpose of this is to avoid impairing their impartiality.

- Other directorships should only be held in other companies in the same industry with the approval of the board.

2.4 Remuneration committees

There should be a remuneration committee consisting exclusively of non-executive directors to determine, on behalf of the shareholders, the company's policy on executive remuneration and the remuneration of specific executive directors.

The chairman of the committee should account directly to the shareholders for the committee's decisions. He should attend the company's AGM to answer any questions shareholders have about directors' remuneration.

The remuneration committee should make a report to shareholders each year, which should form part of, or be annexed to the company's annual report and accounts. The report should set out key details of the company's policy on executive remuneration, including levels, comparator groups of companies, performance criteria and contracts of service. The report should also contain full details of all elements of the remuneration package of each director by name, including share options and pension entitlements.

2.4.1 Remuneration policy

Packages must be provided to attract, retain and motivate directors of the quality required, but should avoid paying more than is necessary for this purpose. The remuneration committee should be sensitive to the wider scene, including pay and employment conditions elsewhere in the company. Performance-related elements of the package should be designed to align the interests of shareholders and directors and give directors keen incentives to perform at the highest levels. Executive share options should never be issued at a discount. The impact of salary increases on pension commitments for the company should be considered, especially for directors nearing retirement.

2.4.2 Service contracts and compensation

The remuneration committee should consider what compensation payments, if any, should be available on the early termination of directors' contracts of service, particularly in the case of unsatisfactory performance. There is a strong case for setting **notice or contract periods of one year**, although in some cases up to two years may be appropriate.

2.5 Audit committees

The audit committee should comprise non-executive directors who will be engaged in monitoring and reviewing the external auditors' independence, objectivity and effectiveness and making recommendations to the board on any areas for improvement. The committee is also responsible for monitoring the integrity of the company's financial statements; reviewing internal financial controls and reviewing the effectiveness of the internal audit function.

3 THE SECURITIES AND INVESTMENT INSTITUTE'S CODE OF CONDUCT

The Securities and Investment Institute (SII) is a widely respected professional body for those working in the securities and investment industry. It is therefore important to familiarise yourself with the SII's Professional Code of Conduct which is set out below.

3.1 Professional Code of Conduct

Professionals within the securities and investment industry owe important duties to their clients, to the market, the industry and to society at large. Where these duties are set out in law or in regulation, the professional must always comply with the requirements in an open and transparent manner.

Membership of the Securities and Investment Institute requires **members** to meet the standards set out within the Institute's Principles. These principles impose upon members an obligation to act in a way that moves beyond mere compliance and supports the underlying values of the Institute.

A material breach of the Principles would be incompatible with continuing membership of the Securities and Investment Institute.

Members who find themselves in a position which might require them to act in a manner contrary to the Principles are encouraged to

- Discuss their concerns with their line manager.

- Seek advice from their internal compliance department.

- Approach their firm's non-executive directors or audit committee.

- If unable to resolve their concerns and, having exhausted all internal avenues, to contact the Securities and Investment Institute for advice.

The Principles	Stakeholder
1. To act honestly and fairly at all times when dealing with clients, customers and counterparties and to be a good steward of their interests, taking into account the nature of the business relationship with each of them, the nature of the service to be provided to them and the individual mandates given by them	Client
2. To act with integrity in fulfilling the responsibilities of your appointment and seek to avoid any acts or omissions or business practices which damage the reputation of your organisation or which are deceitful, oppressive or improper and to promote high standards of conduct throughout your organisation	Firm
3. To observe applicable law, regulations and professional conduct standards when carrying out financial service activities and to interpret and apply them to the best of your ability according to principles rooted in trust, honesty and integrity	Regulator
4. When executing transactions or engaging in any form of market dealings, to observe the standards of market integrity, good practice and conduct required by, or expected of participants in that market	Market participant
5. To manage fairly and effectively and to the best of your ability any relevant conflict of interest, including making any disclosure of its existence where disclosure is required by law or regulation or by your employing organisation*	Conflict of interest
6. To obtain and actively maintain a level of professional competence appropriate to your responsibilities and commit to continued learning and the development of others	Self
7. To strive to uphold the highest personal standards including rejecting short-term profits which may jeopardize your reputation and that of your employer, the Institute and the industry	Self

CHAPTER ROUNDUP

- A plc is allowed to offer securities to the public. It must have a minimum share capital of £50,000 nominal value, at least 25% of which has been paid up.

- Section 793 of CA2006 gives a company the right to investigate an individual's holdings in their shares over the past three years.

- An AGM must be held in each calendar year with at least 21 calendar days notice.

- An EGM can be held with 14 calendar days notice (for ordinary resolutions requiring > 50% to pass) or 21 calendar days notice (for special resolutions requiring 75% or more to pass).

- Schemes of arrangement under S425 of CA85 are a means of performing an agreed takeover that only needs 75% of shareholders to vote in favour.

- The Combined Code sets out the best practice for the composition and conduct of a Board of Directors.

- The SII Code of Conduct applies to SII members and has seven principles.

TEST YOUR KNOWLEDGE

Check your knowledge of the chapter here, without referring back to the text.

1. Which two documents form the constitution of a UK company?

2. What percentage of shareholders can request the Company Secretary to perform a S793 investigation?

3. What is the minimum notice period for an EGM with special resolutions and what percentage of shareholders would have to agree to hold the meeting at short notice?

4. Who else besides 75% of shareholders must agree to a s425 CA85 scheme of enlargement?

5. Which section of CA85 makes it illegal for a firm to give financial assistance for the purchase of its own shares?

6. What percentage of total shares must an acquirer obtain in order to 'squeeze out' minority shareholders?

7. Which firms are required to 'comply or explain' with the Combined Code?

8. What are the maximum terms of office and service contract notice for directors under the Combined Code?

9. How many principles are there in the SII Code of Conduct?

TEST YOUR KNOWLEDGE: ANSWERS

1.   The Memorandum of Association and the Articles of Association.

      (See Section 1.1.4)

2.   10%

      (See Section 1.2)

3.   The normal minimum notice period for an EGM with special resolutions is 21 calendar days. However this can be waived if 15% of the shareholders agree.

      (See Section 1.3.3)

4.   75% of creditors by value and the court must approve. Although not directly under the Takeover Code, the Takeover Panel will approve the timetable.

      (See Sections 1.5.1 and 1.5.2)

5.   Section 151 of Companies Act 1985.

      (See Section 1.6.1)

6.   90%

      (See Section 1.8)

7.   Listed companies subject to the UK Listing Authority's Listing Rules.

      (See Section 2.1)

8.   Maximum term of office is three years and maximum notice is one year.

      (See Section 2.2.1)

9.   Seven principles

      (See Section 3.1)

BPP LEARNING MEDIA

6

Equity Capital Markets – The Listing Rules

INTRODUCTION

When a company wishes to issue securities to raise finance, it must consider which primary market they wish to apply to. The main market in the UK is the Full List and application is made to the UK Listing Authority. However, there is also a junior market with fewer regulations called the Alternative Investment Market operated by the the London Stock Exchange. This provides a cheaper and easier way of having securities admitted for trading on a market.

Regulation of the UK capital market

- **Understand** the FSA's role as the UK Listing Authority (UKLA) and the purpose of the Listing Rules, Disclosure Rules and Transparency Rules (DR).

- **Understand** the Listing Rules Principles.

- **Understand** the guidance on Listing Rule Principle 2 with regards to procedures, systems and controls.

- **Understand** the key requirements for listing.

- **Understand** an issuer's obligation to disclose inside information.

- **Understand** when a listed company may delay the public disclosure of inside information.

- **Understand** how a listed company must control access to inside information, including the requirement to draw up insider lists.

- **Understand** the requirement for an issuer to appoint a sponsor and the role of a sponsor generally and on transaction.

- **Understand** the main methods of bringing shares to listing and the differences between them: offer for sale, offer for subscription, placing, rights issue, open offer and vendor consideration placing.

- **Understand** the vote holder and issue notification rules.

- **Be able to calculate** the classification of transactions.

- **Understand** that AIM is an exchange-regulated market.

- **Know** that AIM companies must comply with the AIM rules and, when appropriate, the Prospectus Rules, Disclosure Rules and Transparency Rules.

- **Know** the requirement for AIM companies to appoint a nominated adviser and a broker.

- **Know** the duties of the nominated adviser.

- **Understand** when an AIM company will be required to issue a prospectus complying with the Prospectus Rules.

- **Know** the admission criteria for judging AIM.

Prospectuses

- **Understand** when a prospectus approved by the FSA in accordance with the Prospectus Rules (PR) will be required.

- **Know** which offers to the public are exempt and when an admission of shares to a regulated market is exempt.

- **Understand** the **interaction** between the Prospectus Rules and the Financial Promotion regime.

- **Understand** the requirement to prepare, have approved and publish a prospectus in connection with an IPO.

1 NEW ISSUES OF EQUITIES

When a limited company is formed, the initial shareholders have a choice as to the type of company that is created. The initial choice is between a Private Limited Company (Ltd) or a Public Limited Company (plc). The difference between these two legal forms is that only a plc may offer its shares or securities to the public. One important point to note is that even though a company may be a plc, it is in no way obliged to issue securities to the general public. In fact, over 75% of all plcs do not take this route for finance.

If the company does decide to seek further finance, the firm's management faces a second choice, namely whether or not to raise that finance through an offer of shares to the public through a Stock Exchange. A Stock Exchange operates a **primary market**, where companies offer shares to the investing public for cash. In addition, it operates a **secondary market**, where investors in the company may trade their shares with each other.

If a plc decides to issue shares to new shareholders, it is under no obligation to use any Stock Exchange. However, it is very difficult to encourage new investors to buy shares without the ability to trade on a Stock Exchange. The Exchange provides them with liquidity, i.e. the assurance that they will be able to sell their shares in a secondary market.

1.1 The role of the London Stock Exchange and the FSA

The London Stock Exchange is a listed company whose object is to run a market place in securities. It should be noted that it has no monopoly powers over the running of the market place, and other operators may compete against it.

The FSA regulates the LSE and has granted it the status of Recognised Investment Exchange (RIE). At present, the Stock Exchange operates two levels of entry into the market, namely the **Official List** and the **Alternative Investment Market (AIM)**. Of the two, the Official List (also called the Full List or the Main Market) is the senior market, and membership demands the most onerous responsibilities.

Since 1 May 2000, it is the FSA as the United Kingdom Listing Authority **(UKLA)** that determines which securities should be admitted to the Official List. This is a statutory role known as that of the **Competent Authority** and is governed by Part VI of FSMA 2000.

- The UKLA determines which companies are eligible to join the Official List, and writes and enforces the Listing Rules which apply to these companies.

- The LSE determines which companies are eligible to join AIM, and writes and enforces the AIM Rules which apply to these companies.

- The LSE's Stock Exchange Rules govern trading in the shares of Listed and AIM companies by shareholders and intermediaries.

2 APPLYING FOR A LISTING

There are various legal and regulatory requirements with which a company must comply when seeking a listing.

2.1 Prospectus Directive

The purpose of the Prospectus Directive is to introduce uniform requirements for prospectuses on public issues of securities in the European Union and to facilitate mutual recognition across stock exchanges in Europe. The Directive applies in two main circumstances.

- An offer of securities which are to be admitted to trading on an EU regulated market.

- An offer of any securities valued at more than €2.5m **and** offered to the public (broadly, more than 100 persons).

The Prospectus Directive provides EU standardised rules, regulations and guidance outlining circumstances in which a prospectus is required, and what that prospectus must contain. It thus creates a single formal and approval process for prospectuses across the EU. This should provide enhanced investor protection through enforcing common disclosure requirements. Specifically, it provides rules in relation to

- Exemptions from the obligations to publish a prospectus.
- General contents and format of the prospectus, including minimum information requirements.
- Approval and publication of the prospectus, including the filing and publication rules.
- "Passporting" of prospectuses by issuers across the EU and the use of the English language.
- Annual information update by issuers and the qualified investors register.
- These rules are contained in the Prospectus Rules, which is a sourcebook of the FSA Handbook.

2.1.1 Prospectus Directive and AIM

As stated above, the Prospectus Directive applies where securities are to be admitted to trading on an EU regulated market (such as the main market of the London Stock Exchange) or where securities are to be offered to the public.

AIM is however classified as an **Exchange-Regulated Market**, and not a regulated market. As such, the Prospectus Directive only applies for AIM flotations where securities are offered to the public. In these circumstances, an AIM prospectus would have to comply with the Prospectus Rules. In other circumstances (such as offers solely to institutions) the Prospectus Rules do not apply. Instead, AIM has adopted a set of rules in relation to the publication of admission documents, which are a scaled-down version of the Prospectus Directive, and referred to as AIM-PD. This provides certain 'carve-outs' (exemptions) from the full Prospectus Rules.

2.2 The Financial Services and Markets Act 2000

As we saw in Chapter 2, Section 21 of the Financial Services and Markets Act (FSMA) requires all financial promotions to be issued or approved by an authorised firm. However, the preparation of a prospectus issued in accordance with the Prospectus Rules or AIM Rules is specifically exempted under the Financial Promotions Order.

2.2.1 Section 80 – general duty of disclosure

FSMA has imposed a general duty on the issuer and their advisers as to the contents of prospectuses approved by the UKLA.

Section 80 states that prospectuses must give all information which investors and their advisers would reasonably require to make an informed decision whether or not to buy the securities. Specifically, they should contain sufficient information to enable investors to ascertain details of the issuer's

- Assets and liabilities.
- Financial position.
- Results and future prospects.
- Rights attaching to the securities.

Persons preparing a prospectus are required to disclose all relevant information that is known to them or which could be obtained by making reasonable enquiries.

Persons responsible for a prospectus may have to provide financial compensation to any person who has relied on the document in making an investment, and suffers a loss as a consequence of an omission. Persons responsible include the following.

- Directors of the issuer.
- Issuer of the securities.
- Any person who accepted responsibility or authorised any part of the prospectus.

2.3 UKLA listing principles

In the years prior to the introduction of the Prospectus Directive, the UKLA took the opportunity to review their Listing Rules. As a result the UKLA Rules for listed companies are now split into three separate rulebooks, which together form a block of the FSA Handbook.

- Listing Rules comprise general rules for listed companies, including the provisions for listing, overarching listing principles and continuing obligations. The format follows the FSA Handbook structure, with rules and guidance shown in a single text.

- Disclosure Rules and Transparency Rules provide rules and guidance for the dissemination of price-sensitive and other information.

- Prospectus Rules consolidate all rules on prospectuses, bringing them in line with the Prospectus Directive.

Within the Listing Rules are found six high level listing principles which underpin the Listing Rules and are enforceable by the FSA in the same way as the rules. The principles stated that an issuer of equity securities should

---

The listing principles

1. Take reasonable steps to enable its directors to understand their responsibilities and obligations as directors.

2. Take reasonable steps to establish and maintain adequate procedures, systems and controls to enable it to comply with its obligations.

3. Act with integrity towards holders and potential holders of its listed equity securities.

4. Communicate information to holders and potential holders of its listed equity securities in such a way as to avoid the creation or continuation of a false market in such listed equity securities.

5. Ensure that it treats all holders of the same class of its listed equity securities that are in the same position equally in respect of the rights attaching to such listed equity securities; and

6. Deal with the FSA in an open and co-operative manner.

Further guidance on Principle 2 states that listed companies place particular emphasis on control over significant and related party transactions and ensuring timely and accurate disclosure of information to the market.

2.4 UKLA criteria for listing on the LSE

2.4.1 The Listing Rules

The UKLA's rules for admission to the Official List are contained in the Listing Rules. These detail threshold conditions for companies and their securities, if they wish to be admitted to the Official List. The basic conditions detailed in the Listing Rules are as follows.

- The expected market value of shares issued by the company must be at least **£700,000**. If the company is to issue **debt**, the expected market value of any such debt is to be at least **£200,000**.

- All securities issued must be freely transferable and the securities will be admitted to trading on a Recognised Investment Exchange (e.g. LSE).

- The shares must be sufficiently marketable. A minimum of **25% of the company's share capital being made available for public purchase** (known as the **free float**) is seen to satisfy this requirement. The lower the free float, the fewer shares are available in the market, leading to, potentially, higher share price volatility. A lower percentage may be acceptable if the UKLA is satisfied that the shares will still be marketable.

- The issue of warrants or options over the stock of a company is limited to **20%** of the existing capital base.

- The UKLA has additional requirements for a company with a **major** shareholder. If the UKLA allows a company with this type of shareholder to come to the market, then the UKLA will need to be assured that there are measures in place to allow the listed company to **operate independently**.

- The company's Articles of Association must contain **pre-emption rights** in relation to issues of new shares for cash. The Listing Rules further provide that whilst shareholders may vote to waive their pre-emptive rights, the maximum period of such a waiver is five years. (This subject is discussed in more detail later in this chapter).

- All applicants for listing agree to be bound by the **continuing obligations** of the UKLA. These obligations are fully discussed later in this chapter.

3 METHODS OF BRINGING SECURITIES TO LISTING

3.1 Permitted methods for new applicants

There are five main methods for a new applicant for bringing their securities to listing for the first time.

- An offer for sale.
- An offer for subscription.
- An intermediaries offer.   } marketing operations
- A placing.
- An introduction.

The first four of these methods are described as **marketing operations**. A marketing operation is one in which the company offers shares for sale. The last method – the introduction – does not involve an offer of shares for sale. Instead, it merely allows the company's existing shareholders to trade their shares on the Stock Exchange.

3.2 Offer for sale

Offer for Sale

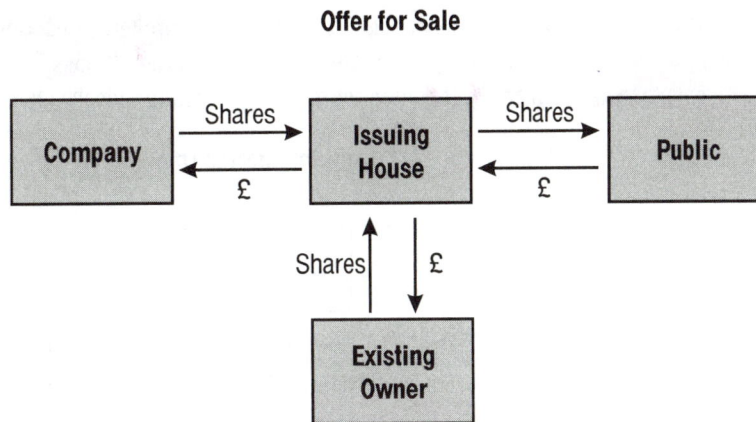

With an offer for sale, the company appoints an issuing house to offer shares to the public on its behalf. The issuing house advertises the securities, obtains acceptances from the public, processes applications, allots shares and then sends the money raised to the company after the deduction of its fee.

An offer for sale need not revolve around the issue of new securities. It can equally be used by a large shareholder selling a stake into the market place. Many of the privatisations launched by the UK Government have been offers for sale, where a broking house has acted on the Government's behalf to sell a large block of the shares in a company to the public.

3.3 Offer for subscription

Offer for Subscription

An offer for subscription involves the offer by the company of new shares directly to the public. The key difference between this and an offer for sale is that the shares themselves are not physically in existence until applications have been received from the new shareholders. They are 'subscribers' for the shares, and are the first ever holders of these shares. In an offer for sale, the shares are in existence prior to the offer, either representing the holdings of the original selling shareholders, or are created by the company and issued to the issuing house for on-sale to the general public.

An offer for subscription is most commonly used by investment companies, such as venture capital trusts.

3.4 Placing

By far the quickest and cheapest route open to a company is to elect for a placing (also known as 'selective marketing'). Under a placing, the company arranges for its corporate broker to sell the securities to its client base. This removes most of the requirement for marketing and underwriting, and is also the quickest and most efficient method of issuing shares. A placing is also used for a secondary offering.

Placing

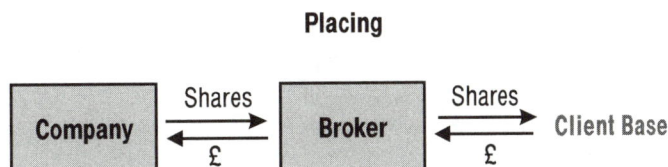

3.5 Intermediaries offer

An intermediaries offer is where intermediaries such as stockbrokers subscribe for shares on behalf of their own clients, who are not permitted to apply for shares direct. It gives more opportunity for the public to participate than with a placing. It can be represented diagrammatically as follows.

Intermediaries Offer

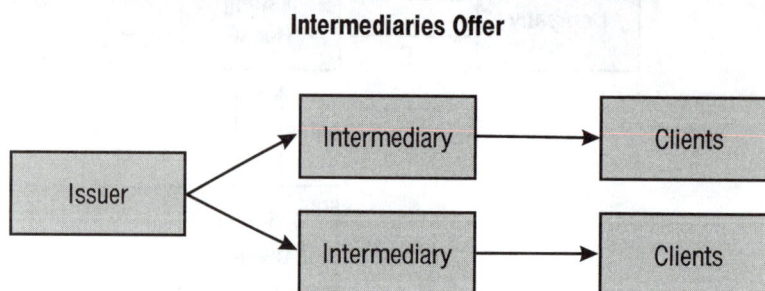

3.6 Introductions

As mentioned above, offers for subscription, offers for sales and placings are all marketing operations, in that they involve the sale of shares. An introduction, however, is not a marketing operation. It merely brings the shares already held by existing shareholders into the market place, providing them with the opportunity to realise them whenever they wish. The UKLA is likely to approve an introduction in the following circumstances.

- The shares are already listed on an overseas stock exchange and the company wishes to transfer its listing to the London Stock Exchange or arrange for a dual listing.

- The shares are already traded on AIM and the company wants to be admitted to the Full List.

- Whilst the company is not traded on an exchange as such, the shares have already achieved a reasonably wide distribution, for example, the company is employee owned.

- Where two previously listed companies have agreed to merge their operations in a new company, the new company's shares will be allocated to the shareholders of the original companies and then introduced to the market place.

- Where a listed company demerges one of its operations, it issues the shares in the demerged entity to its own shareholders, and applies for an introduction for those shares.

3.6.1 When each method can be used

A company can freely select its own issue method, the only Listing Rules requirement being that all issuers must also be admitted to trading on a Recognised Investment Exchange, e.g. the London Stock Exchange. The aim of this rule is to ensure that there will be liquidity in the secondary market in the company's shares.

4 APPLYING FOR LISTING: THE IPO PROCESS

Whichever method the company adopts when applying for a listing for its shares, there are a number of key processes which must be followed. These may be summarised as follows.

- Appointment of advisers.
- Due diligence.
- Preparation of listing particulars or prospectus.

BPP
LEARNING MEDIA

- Pricing the issue.
- Approval of listing particulars or prospectus.
- Publishing and advertising listing particulars or prospectus.
- Formal application for admission to listing.

4.1 Requirement for a sponsor

All applicants for listing must have a **sponsor**. There is no obligation for the sponsor to be an Exchange member firm, but it must be a firm approved as a sponsor by the UKLA.

The role of the sponsor is with due care and skill to

- Satisfy itself, after careful and diligent enquiry, that the issuer meets the requirements for listing.

- Provide the UKLA with all information requested by them or required under the rules.

- Ensure that the issuer is properly guided and advised as to the application or interpretation of the listing rules and disclosure rules on an ongoing basis.

- Guide them through the process of applying for a listing and liaise with the UKLA.

4.2 Pricing the issue

With all initial public offerings, the issuer has the problem of knowing how to price the issue.

There are three main solutions.

- A fixed price offer.
- A tender offer.
- Book building.

4.2.1 Fixed price offer

Under a **fixed price offer**, the issuing house establishes a fair price for the security, which is frequently based on the price of similar company securities already trading in the market. Once the price has been arrived at, the offer is made to the public on the basis that potential purchasers state the number of shares they wish to buy at the fixed price. In the event of over-subscription, allocations are dealt with on a pro rata basis in line with the terms contained in the offer document.

It is frequently the intention of the company that the offer price should be artificially low, so that potential purchasers can foresee an immediate rise in the share price. It is hoped that this will generate goodwill amongst purchasers that in future guarantees the company's access to new finance. Investors who purchase shares in a new issue in the belief that the share will rise immediately due to its underpricing, and who plan to sell as soon as this has happened, are called **stags**.

4.2.2 Tender offer

Under a **tender offer**, the potential purchasers are asked to divulge the number of shares they wish to buy and the price they are prepared to pay. The issuing house then receives their application forms, which are ranked in order of the prices purchasers are prepared to pay – highest first.

Example

A company wishes to issue 20 million shares and states that there is a minimum price of £1.00. Bids are received from potential shareholders in the following sequence.

> 1 million @ £1.50
>
> 3 million @ £1.45
>
> 7 million @ £1.40
>
> 11 million @ £1.35
>
> 10 million @ £1.30
>
> 17 million @ £1.25

Progressing down the list, the offer can be filled at the point where the price is £1.35, since there are more than 20 million applicants. However, a company will frequently establish the price at a lower value, say £1.30, as this will again encourage the market to rise on issue, ensuring both profit and investor goodwill. Note that within this structure, all the shareholders applying for shares pay the **common strike price** set by the company, be it £1.35 or £1.30. Even those applicants who entered at £1.50 will only pay the strike price.

4.2.3 Bookbuilding

Bookbuilding is an approach frequently used in the placing of larger issues. The issuing house sets a price range for the Initial Public Offer (IPO), based on its own in-house valuation and the reaction of potential investors to presentations by management. It then approaches potential institutional investors to solicit interest at this price range. The level of interest of investors, i.e. the number who wish to be on the issuing house's 'book', determines whether the final price is set at the higher or lower end of the price range.

4.3 Prospectuses

4.3.1 Introduction

A company is required to prepare a prospectus when it is issuing securities for which it is applying for a listing on a regulated market in the EU. This requirement relates to issues by companies which are coming to the market for the first time, i.e. an initial public offer. It also applies to companies that already have a listing but are issuing new securities for which they will apply for a listing, for example, through a rights issue.

The purpose of a prospectus is to give a complete view of the company, its history, finances and operations. There are three parts to the prospectus.

- **Registration document** containing general information about the issue.

- **Securities note** containing detailed information about the equity or non-equity securities being offered.

- **Summary document** containing a summary of key information.

Each part may be approved separately, or the prospectus may be prepared and approved as a single document.

An **outline document** may be prepared as part of the initial marketing of this new issue. This is known as a **pathfinder prospectus**.

4.3.2 When is a prospectus required?

The Prospectus Directive, implemented in the UKLA Prospectus Rules, require a prospectus to be issued when securities are offered to the public, or admitted to trading on a regulated exchange. This applies to both primary and secondary offerings of securities, over €2.5m. There are certain exceptions to this requirement.

4.3.3 Exemptions

A prospectus may not be required in certain circumstances, in particular

- A bonus or capitalisation issue.
- The exercise of conversion rights or warrants.
- Shares issued in place of shares already listed, so long as the nominal value in total does not increase as a result, e.g. a share split or consolidation.
- Small issues of securities, which would not increase the class of securities in issue by 10% or more, or by more than €100,000 consideration over a year.
- Where offer is made only to qualified investors, or to fewer than 100 persons per EU Member state, excluding qualified investors. This exemption is only available when securities are not being admitted to trading on a regulated market – e.g. AIM placings.
- Issues of wholesale securities – i.e. where the minimum subscription or denomination of the securities is €50,000. This would only realistically apply to corporate bond issues.

4.3.4 Responsibility for preparation of a prospectus

One of the sponsor's main obligations is co-ordinating the preparation of the prospectus in connection with the offering. However, the primary responsibility for the contents of a prospectus lies with the directors of the issuer. To this end, they are required to make a statement in the prospectus, acknowledging their responsibility. In addition, they must also confirm to the UKLA, by signed letter, that the prospectus contains all relevant information that they know or should have been aware of as the directors of the company.

4.3.5 Approval of the prospectus

A prospectus must not be published, advertised or circulated until it has been **approved by the competent authority – in the UK, this is the UKLA**. To obtain approval, the sponsor must provide the UKLA with certain stipulated information at least ten clear business days before the approval is granted (20 days for new issuers or in complicated cases); the information is known as the **ten-day documents**, and the main items include

- Draft prospectus and copies of all documents referred to within them.
- Request for authorisation to omit information normally required under the rules.
- Application forms to acquire or subscribe for shares.
- Copies of the Board resolution allotting the securities (or confirmation it will be provided within three days of approval).
- The Sponsor's Declaration on an Application for Listing.
- Contact details for questions, available 07:00 to 18:00.

4.3.6 Supplementary prospectus

It may be the case that, subsequent to approval of the prospectus, there is a significant change in the company's state of affairs. If this is the case, then a supplementary prospectus should be published giving details of the change or new matter that has arisen. This must be submitted to the FSA for approval as soon as practicable.

5 CONTINUING OBLIGATIONS

5.1 The objectives of the Continuing Obligations

The Continuing Obligations are contained in the Listing Rules and the Disclosure Rules and Transparency Rules. They govern the conduct of directors of listed companies and the disclosure of information necessary to protect investors, maintain an orderly market and ensure that investors are treated fairly. In addition, the Disclosure Rules and Transparency Rules contain over-arching requirements which relate to the timely and accurate dissemination of inside information.

5.2 Inside information

5.2.1 Announcements

The first main requirement of the Continuing Obligations is timely disclosure of all relevant information. A listed company has a **general duty to disclose** all information necessary to appraise investors of the company's position and to avoid a false market in its shares. This reinforces S397 of FSMA, which makes it a criminal offence to conceal information dishonestly in order to create a false market in the company's shares. In addition, a company should announce details of any major new developments in its activities which are not known to the public but which may, when known, significantly affect its share price and affect a reasonable investor's decision. This is referred to as Inside Information.

The second requirement is **equal treatment of all shareholders**. This is to ensure that all shareholders receive inside information in the same way at the same time. All regulatory disclosures required must be disclosed to a Regulatory Information Service as soon as possible, prior to being disclosed to third parties.

A **Regulatory Information Service (RIS)** is a firm that has been approved by the FSA to disseminate regulatory announcements to the market on behalf of listed companies. Once an announcement is sent to the RIS, the company's obligation is met. The RIS is then required to release the announcement to the markets through its links with secondary information providers such as data providers, newswires and the news media.

5.2.2 Secrecy and confidentiality

Allied to the general principle of equal treatment of all shareholders is the requirement to **prevent leaks of price-sensitive information**. This particularly relates to impending developments or matters in the course of negotiation, where (apart from to advisers) there must be no selective dissemination of information, and matters in the course of negotiation must be kept confidential.

5.2.3 Insider lists

An issuer must ensure that it and its agents and advisors draw up a list of those who have access to inside information, whether on a regular or occasional basis. The FSA can request this list at anytime.

Every insider list must contain the following information

- The identity of each person having access to inside information.
- The reason why they are on the insider list.
- The date the list was created and updated.

An insider list must be promptly updated and records kept for five years.

An issuer must take the necessary measures to ensure that its employees on the list acknowledge the legal and regulatory duties entailed (including dealing restrictions) and are aware of the sanctions attaching to the misuse or improper circulation of such information.

5.2.4 Holding announcements

If it becomes apparent that secrecy has been breached or that it is becoming increasingly difficult to maintain confidentiality, the company should make a warning announcement with outline details of the matters concerned and undertake to provide further information as soon as possible. If the issuer is unwilling or unable to make a holding announcement, trading in its shares may be suspended.

5.2.5 Dispensations from making announcements

A company may obtain permission from the UKLA not to make an announcement if the announcement would be prejudicial to the company's legitimate interests. It may also be allowed to delay an announcement of matters in the course of negotiation, provided that this can be kept confidential.

5.3 Classification of transactions

In deciding whether a company needs to make a disclosure, the Listing Rules provide guidance on what constitutes a significant transaction.

A transaction is classified by assessing its size relative to that of the listed company proposing to make it. The size is measured against certain percentage tests of gross assets, capital or profits of the company or the consideration of the transaction. The transaction only needs to exceed the set percentages for any one of these four categories. In decreasing order of size the classes of transaction are:

Classification	Percentage test
Reverse takeover	100%
Class 1	25% or more
Class 2	5% or more
Class 3	Less than 5%

In a reverse takeover, the target company exceeds the size of the acquiring company in at least one of the criteria. The only exception to this is that it is still called a Class 1 transaction when the two entities are of similar size: so that no one test is exceeded by 125% and there is no change in voting control or board control.

5.4 Vote holder and issuer notification rules

The Disclosure Rules and Transparency Rules implement the requirements of the Transparency Directive that requires shareholders to disclose when they acquire a significant stake in a company. This information will then be published by a listed company so that there is transparency when a potential bidder starts to build up a stake in a target company.

The **initial threshold is 3%** and then transactions that go above or below a further full percentage point must also be disclosed. The holdings includes any financial instrument that would give control over a voting security. It therefore includes derivatives such as futures and options on a share. The disclosure must be made by the end of second business day after the transaction (known as T + 2).

The following example transactions by the same shareholder illustrate the notification requirements:

Transactions (all same shareholder)	Notification requirements
0% to 2.5% holding in shares	None (below 3% threshold)
Additional 0.6% via options on shares	Notify issuing company by T + 2 (total now 3.1%)
Acquire additional 0.5% shares	None (total 3.6% so same full percentage point of 3)
Acquire additional 2.5%	Notify issuing company by T + 2 (total now 6.1%)
Dispose of 3% of shares	Notify issuing company by T + 2 (total now 3.1%)
Dispose of 0.6% held via options	Notify issuing company by T + 2 (total now 2.5%)
Sell remaining 2.5% of shares	None (below 3% threshold)

There are exceptions of non-UK listed companies where notification is required at 5% steps up to 30% then 50% and 75% by T + 4.

Fund managers only have to disclose holdings at 5% and 10% and then at every single percentage point change above 10%.

5.5 Compliance with the Continuing Obligations

Failure to comply with the requirements of the Listing Rules, Prospectus Rules or Disclosure Rules and Transparency Rules may lead to

- Unlimited fines by the UKLA.
- Censure by the UKLA.
- Publication of the censure.
- Suspension or cancellation of a company's listing.

The last of these will mean that the company will be unable to use the facilities of the market.

In addition, any offending directors of the company may be censured and the UKLA may require their removal from the board as a condition for the company to retain its listing.

Companies should also be aware that in certain cases, failure to comply with the Listing Rules could also constitute an statutory offence under FSMA, particularly in relation to the market abuse regime.

6 THE ALTERNATIVE INVESTMENT MARKET (AIM)

6.1 Introduction

In June 1995, the London Stock Exchange introduced AIM, the Alternative Investment Market. This enables a company's shares to be traded through the Exchange in a lightly regulated regime. In contrast to the Main Market, which is regulated by the UKLA, AIM is regulated by the London Stock Exchange, which is responsible for writing and monitoring the AIM Rules. AIM is classified as an '**exchange regulated** market', whereas the Full List is classified as an 'EU regulated market'.

6.2 Requirements for AIM companies

There are **no minimum** market value, minimum public holding, required track record or advertising requirements.

Companies have to appoint a **nominated adviser (a NOMAD)** to guide and advise the directors of their responsibilities. The nominated adviser must be an authorised person under FSMA with recent relevant experience, and be on the Stock Exchange's register of nominated advisers, but need not be a member of the Stock Exchange. The AIM company must retain the NOMAD's services at all times.

If an AIM company ceases to have a nominated adviser the Exchange will suspend trading in its AIM securities. If within one month of that suspension the AIM company has failed to appoint a replacement nominated adviser its admission will be cancelled.

In addition, a company must at all times have a **nominated broker** (who must be an Exchange member) to support trading in the company's shares, and to assist in pricing and marketing in a flotation. If the company does not have a market maker registered for its shares, the nominated broker must use best endeavours to find matching business in the company's shares.

AIM companies have the following ongoing obligations.

- To publish price-sensitive information promptly.
- To disclose details of significant transactions.
- To seek shareholder approval for any transaction which qualifies as a reverse takeover.
- To adopt the Model Code on Directors' Share Dealings.

6.3 Duties of the nominated adviser

The main duties of the NOMAD are to confirm to the LSE that a company is appropriate for AIM, and ensure it is able to comply with the AIM Rules on an ongoing basis. This is broken down in the NOMAD rule book into the following rules:

- Assessing the appropriateness of an AIM company and informing AIM Regulation department when they consider it no longer appropriate

- Advising and guiding the AIM company for compliance with AIM Rules with at least two members of staff allocated to that company at least one of whom is a Qualified Executive

- Liaising with the Exchange in any requests for information and inform the Exchange as soon as practicable of any Rule breach

- Notifying the Exchange if ceasing to be a NOMAD. The reason for ceasing must be given

- Remaining independent and managing any conflicts of interest.

6.4 Comparison to requirements for an official listing

	Full List	AIM
Plc	Yes	Yes
Percentage in Public Hands	25%	None
Minimum Market Value	£700,000 for equity £200,000 for debt	None
Free Transferability	Yes	Yes
Documentation	Prospectus – Full PD	Prospectus – when issued to the public Admissions Document under AIM-PD – when issued to qualifying investors only
Rules	UKLA Listing Rules	LSE AIM Rules

BPP
LEARNING MEDIA

CHAPTER ROUNDUP

- Admission to the Full List is granted by the UK Listing Authority.

- A prospectus must comply with the requirements of the Prospectus Directive when issued onto an EU Regulated Market or to more than 100 persons.

- A junior market in the UK is the Alternative Investment Market (AIM).

- AIM is an exchange regulated market and therefore issuers must comply with a simpler version of the Prospectus Directive known as AIM-PD.

- The UKLA has six Listing Principles.

- The UKLA rules require a new security to have a minimum market value of £700,000 for shares and £200,000 for debt, a minimum free float of 25% and a maximum dilution of 20%.

- There are five main methods of issue for new companies. Offers for sale or subscriptions intermediaries offer and placing are known as marketing operations as they all raise new finance for the company. An introduction will only introduce existing shares onto the market.

- Once listed, an issuer must meet their continuing obligations to ensure a fair and orderly market.

- Major transactions of the issuer are given a classification with a class 1 transaction representing a 25% or more major change for the company.

- Holdings of 3% or more by one shareholder must be disclosed along with movements up or down through a full percentage point above 3%.

- An AIM company must have a nominated adviser to help them comply with the AIM rues.

TEST YOUR KNOWLEDGE

Check your knowledge of the chapter here, without referring back to the text.

1.   Who grants admission to the Official List?

2.   What is the number of people per EU state deemed to be the public for the Prospectus Directive?

3.   What is Principle 2 of the Listing Rules?

4.   What is the minimum free float for a UK Listed company?

5.   Which type of time method is not a marketing operation?

6.   What is the name given to investors who like to buy new shares for immediate sale on issue?

7.   What are the three components of a prospectus?

8.   As what is an outline prospectus prepared as part of initial marketing known?

9.   What is the size criterion for a class 2 transaction?

10. At what level and by when must a 3% or more shareholder disclose their holding in a Listed Company?

TEST YOUR KNOWLEDGE: ANSWERS

1.   The UK Listing Authority

     (See Section 1.1)

2.   100

     (See Section 2.1)

3.   A firm should take reasonable care to establish and maintain adequate procedures, systems and controls to ensure it complies with its obligations.

     (See Section 2.3)

4.   25%

     (See Section 2.4.1)

5.   Introduction

     (See Section 3.1)

6.   Stags

     (See Section 4.2.1)

7.   Registration document
     Securities note
     Summary document

     (See Section 4.3.1)

8.   A pathfinder prospectus

     (See Section 4.3.1)

9.   5% or more

     (See Section 5.3)

10. 3% or movements up and down through a percentage point above this level must be declared by T + 2

     (See Section 5.4)

7

Quantitative Methods

INTRODUCTION

The Unit 2 Technical Foundations requires you to have a sound knowledge of the mathematics behind risk assessment and the valuation models.

Risk is mainly assessed through the variability of returns in a portfolio either by the standard deviation or covariance of two portfolios. The valuation models are largely based on the discounted cash flow techniques.

You must ensure that you have memorised all the appropriate formulae as they are not given to you in the exam.

CHAPTER CONTENTS

Financial Mathematics

- **Understand** how to measure the risk and return of investments.

- **Be able to calculate** the expected return/arithmetic mean of investments.

- **Be able to calculate** the degree of variability of investments using the variance and standard deviation of returns.

- **Be able to calculate** the covariance of investments.

Discounted Cash Flows

- **Be able to calculate** the Present Value (PV) and Net Present Value (NPV) of future cash flows using the discounting formula.

- **Be able to calculate** the Internal rate of return (IRR) for a series of cash flows.

- **Be able to calculate** the market value of an annual coupon bond (3-year).

1 INTRODUCTION

1.1 Aim of measures of the average and of variability

In a certain world, we would always know what is going to happen, e.g. what dividend return a share is going to offer or how the stock market in general is going to perform. As a result we would be able to make perfect investment decisions.

In a more realistic world, we do not know such factors for certain. We may be able to make an estimate based on technical analysis of previous performance or fundamental analysis of relevant factors. However, we would have to accept that this forecast is likely to be incorrect and that the true position may vary away from this estimate.

In performing our technical analysis, we would review past returns and how these have varied, hoping that these may give us some guide to the future, though bearing in mind the dangers of making this link. It is in this context that estimating the average return and its variability measures may be of use.

In the context of, say, shares these measures will provide us with an indication of

- The expected future **returns** from the share (all other things being equal).

- The **risk** we are facing (the potential variability of the returns about this expected return value) in holding the shares.

1.2 Arithmetic mean

1.2.1 Calculation

The arithmetic mean is the simple average that we are probably all used to. It is calculated by adding up (arithmetically) the observed values and dividing by the number of observed values.

The calculation of the arithmetic mean can be expressed mathematically as

Formula to learn

$$\overline{x} = \frac{\sum x_i}{n}$$

where

$\overline{x}$ = the arithmetic mean

x_i = the observed values

$\sum$ represents the summation (i.e. the total) of those observed values

n = number of observed values

Alternatively, this could be shown (and will certainly be calculated) as

Formula to learn

$$\overline{x} = \frac{x_1 + x_2 + x_3 + ... + x_n}{n}$$

although the initial formula is the one we will be stating.

Example

$$\overline{x} = \frac{\sum x_i}{n} = \frac{1+2+3+3+4+5+5+5+6+7+8+9+20}{13} = \frac{78}{13} = 6$$

Since all observed values are considered, this measure can **be severely distorted by extreme values**.

Example

Suppose in our raw data example the last observed item had been 100 rather than 20. The mean would then be

$$\overline{x} = \frac{\sum x_i}{n} = \frac{1+2+3+3+4+5+5+5+6+7+8+9+100}{13} = \frac{158}{13} = 12.15$$

when clearly the majority of observed values are less than nine.

1.3 Standard deviation and variance

1.3.1 Definition

The standard deviation is a measure of variability that is related to the arithmetic mean. The idea behind the calculation is to establish how far each observed value falls from the mean, the standard deviation being a function of this divergence, and the variance being the square of the standard deviation.

The greater the divergence of the observed values from the mean, the greater the standard deviation (or risk).

1.3.2 Calculation

The standard deviation is calculated through the following steps.

- Calculate the arithmetic mean $\bar{x}$.

- Calculate the difference between each observed value and the arithmetic mean $(x - \bar{x})$, the sum of which must be zero, since some items lie above the mean and have positive values and some lie below the mean and have negative values.

- Square the differences to remove the negative signs from those lying below the mean, i.e. we are now considering just the absolute value (or square of the value) of the differences, ignoring whether they lie above or below the mean.

- Sum these squared differences.

- Calculate the average of these squared differences by dividing by the number of observed values.

- Take the square root of this average to cancel the effects of our earlier squaring up.

Since we square the differences up, then later take the square root, the units of the standard deviation will be the same as those for the mean, i.e. if the mean is the average number of miles travelled in several journeys, the standard deviation will also be in miles.

Raw data

Stating the above as a mathematical expression for the calculation of the standard deviation for raw data gives

Formula to learn

$$\text{Standard deviation} = \sigma = \sqrt{\frac{\sum(x - \bar{x})^2}{n}}$$

and the calculation of the variance is

Formula to learn

$$\text{Variance} = \sigma^2 = \frac{\sum(x - \bar{x})^2}{n}$$

i.e. **the variance is simply the square of the standard deviation**.

Example

We calculated earlier that the mean of this population was $\bar{x} = 6$. To calculate the standard deviation, it would be most convenient to tabulate the data as follows.

x	$(x - \bar{x})$	$(x - \bar{x})^2$
1	−5	25
2	−4	16
3	−3	9
3	−3	9
4	−2	4
5	−1	1
5	−1	1
5	−1	1
6	0	0
7	1	1
8	2	4
9	3	9
20	14	196
	0	276

$$\sum (x - \bar{x})^2$$

Giving

$$\text{Standard deviation} = \sigma = \sqrt{\frac{\sum (x - \bar{x})^2}{n}} = \sqrt{\frac{276}{13}} = \sqrt{21.23} = 4.61$$

and

$$\text{Variance} = \sigma^2 = 4.61^2 = 21.23$$

1.4 Covariance

In many business situations, we are trying to establish whether a relationship exists between two factors and what exactly that relationship is. For example, if we consider the profits that a company may generate, a company's profit is clearly a function of its sales revenues and its costs. The higher the sales, the higher the profits; the higher the costs, the lower the profits.

Many other relationships also exist in business and finance. For example, it is generally believed that a higher risk will result in a higher return from a security.

Where such relationships exist, it would be very useful to be able to quantify them. If we were able to do this, we would be placed in a much better position to make business and investment forecasts and decisions.

The final statistical measure that quantifies the extent to which two variables move together is the **covariance**. This gives a measure of how returns from two different investments vary in relation to one another. If the returns tend to move together they will have a positive covariance. If the returns move in opposite directions there will be a negative covariance.

Calculation

Covariance is calculated as follows.

Formula to learn

$$\text{cov}_{x,y} = \frac{\sum (x - \bar{x})(y - \bar{y})}{n}$$

Example

We now have two variables x and y with 13 observations in our population. To calculate the covariance, it would be most convenient to tabulate the data as follows.

x	$(x - \bar{x})$	y	$(y - \bar{y})$	$(x - \bar{x})(y - \bar{y})$
1	−5	1	−2	10
2	−4	1	−2	8
3	−3	1	−2	6
3	−3	3	0	0
4	−2	3	0	0
5	−1	3	0	0
5	−1	4	1	−1
5	−1	4	1	−1
6	0	4	1	0
7	1	4	1	1
8	2	4	1	2
9	3	4	1	3
20	14	4	1	14
$\bar{x} = 6$	0	$\bar{y} = 3$	0	42

$$\text{Covariance} = \text{cov}_{x,y} = \frac{42}{13} = 3.23$$

2 DISCOUNTED CASH FLOWS

2.1 Introduction to the time value of money and interest rates

Central to all our theories regarding the valuation of securities are discounted cash flows and the time value of money.

The exam will require you to calculate and apply the following.

- Terminal values or future values.
- Present value and net present value.
- Annuity discount factors.
- Perpetuity discount factors.
- Effective discount factors.

A starting point is the realisation and appreciation of the time value of money, which we will all be aware of as a result of the payment (or possibly the receipt) of bank interest.

Bank interest can take one of two forms

- Simple interest; or
- Compound interest

each of which are illustrated below.

2.2 Simple interest

If a bank account were to offer a **simple interest** rate, then the interest received each year would be based on the **original capital invested only**. Hence, in relation to the above example, we would have the following solution.

Example

£100 is deposited in an account paying interest at 10% p.a. (simple interest). How much interest will be earned during, and what will be the value of the deposit at the end of

- The first year?
- The nth year (say 5th)?

Solution

First Year

The interest earned in this year would be based on the capital originally invested (£100) and the simple rate of interest (10%). The interest could be calculated using the formula

Formula to learn

$$i_1 = D_0 \times r$$

where

i_1 = interest earned by the end of the first year (time = 1)

r = interest rate stated as a decimal, here 10% or 0.10

D_0 = original capital invested at the start of the first year (time = 0)

Giving

$$i_1 = £100 \times 0.10 = £10$$

At that date, the deposit will be worth £110.

n^{th} Year

With simple interest, the interest generated each subsequent year will be exactly the same, since it is only based on the original capital invested. Hence, we can apply the same formula to calculate this year's interest as

$$i_n = D_0' \times r$$

giving for the fifth year

$$i_5 = £100 \times 0.10 = £10$$

We can see that the value of our deposit is growing by £10 each year.

In conclusion, with simple interest, we earn the same amount of interest each year. At the end of n years, the total interest we will have earned will be

n × Annual interest

or

$$i_{tot} = n \times (D_0 \times r)$$

which, when added to our starting capital of D_0, gives the value of our deposit as

$$D_n = D_0 + n \times (D_0 \times r)$$

Applying this to the above example gives

$$D_5 = D_0 + n \times (D_0 \times r) = £100 + 5 \times (£100 \times 0.10) = £150$$

which is perhaps the result we expected. Five years' interest at 10% p.a. should add a total of 50% to the value of the deposit with flat interest.

2.3 Compound interest

Interest rates are described as **compound interest** if, in each year, interest is earned on the **total value of the deposit at the start of the year**, i.e. original capital plus any interest previously earned. With compound interest, we receive interest on our previous interest.

Example

£100 is deposited in an account paying interest at 10% per annum (compound interest). How much interest will be earned during, and what will be the value of the deposit at the end of

- The first year?
- The nth year (say 5th)?

Solution

First Year

The interest earned in this year would be based on the value of the deposit at the start of the year, i.e. the capital originally invested (£100) and the compound rate of interest (10%). The interest could again be calculated using the formula

$$i_1 = D_0 \times r$$

where

i_1 = interest earned by the end of the first year (time = 1)

r = interest rate stated as a decimal, here 10% or 0.10

D_0 = original capital invested at the outset (time = 0)

Giving

$$i_1 = £100 \times 0.10 = £10$$

At that date, the deposit will be worth £110, which we could have calculated directly using the formula

$$D_1 = D_0(1 + r) = £100 \times (1 + 0.10) = £100 \times 1.10 = £110$$

where D_1 = the value of the deposit at Time 1

We can see that, so far, this is identical to the simple interest example above. However, this is only true for the first year.

n^{th} Year

With compound interest, the interest generated each subsequent year will be based on the value of the deposit at the start of each year. We could state this in a formula as

$$i_n = D_{n-1} \times r$$

In order to calculate the interest for the fifth year, we would need to know the value of the deposit at the start of the fifth year/end of the fourth year. From our Year 1 illustration above, we noted that the value of the deposit at the end of the first year/start of the second was given by

$$D_1 = D_0(1 + r)$$

This amount would then grow by the end of the second year/start of the third year to

$$D_2 = D_1(1 + r) = D_0(1 + r)^2$$

In a similar way, we could calculate the value of the deposit at the end of each subsequent year as

$$D_3 = D_2(1 + r) = D_0(1 + r)^3 - \text{end of third/start of fourth}$$

$$D_4 = D_3(1 + r) = D_0(1 + r)^4 - \text{end of fourth/start of fifth}$$

$$D_5 = D_4(1 + r) = D_0(1 + r)^5 - \text{end of fifth/start of sixth}$$

which could be described generally as

$$D_n = D_0(1 + r)^n - \text{end of } n^{th}/\text{start of } n + 1^{th}$$

Hence, at the end of the fourth year/start of the fifth the value of the deposit would be

$$D_4 = D_0(1 + r)^n = £100 (1 + 0.10)^4 = £100 \times 1.1^4 = £146.41$$

and hence, the interest generated in the fifth year would be

$$i_5 = D_4 \times r = £146.41 \times 0.10 = £14.641$$

taking the value of the total deposit up to £161.051 (£146.41 + £14.641) by the end of the fifth year, which we can confirm with the formula

$$D_5 = D_0(1 + r)^5 = £100 (1 + 0.10)^5 = £100 \times 1.1^5 = £161.051$$

This is a larger sum than under simple interest, since we are getting interest on our previously earned interest.

2.4 Introduction to terminal values

A **terminal value** or **future value** is the value of a deposit at the end of a period of time having received interest over that period, i.e. D_n is the terminal value in the above examples.

A **present value** is the equivalent value of the same deposit before the effects of interest, i.e. D_0 is the present value in the above examples.

Calculating terminal or present values for investment opportunities provides a means of appraising them. Indeed, as we noted at the outset, the calculation of a present value provides a method for evaluating a security, i.e. determines its market value.

All calculations with regard to these ideas utilise the concept of **compound interest**.

2.4.1 Calculating terminal/future values

Terminal/Future value calculations consider

- Each cash flow generated by an investment
- The timing of the cash flow

and calculates how much cash could be generated to the end of the investment period if the earlier returns were banked each year to generate additional compound interest.

If the returns plus the interest that they can accumulate exceeds the total that could be generated had we simply banked the cash at the outset rather than buying the investment, then we accept the investment. The decision criteria could be stated as

> "An investment should be accepted if it produces a surplus in cash terms after accounting for interest"

Example

Two alternative investments to banking £100 are investments A and B, both of which will terminate in three years. Investment A will return £41.00 p.a. for the next three years. Ignoring the time value of money this gives a total return of £123 and a total profit of £23. Investment B will return £134.00 at the end of the third year, a profit of £34 ignoring any time value.

Which investment opportunity is superior and which, if either, should be accepted if the interest rate is 10%?

Solution 1

Since we can receive 10% p.a. on any cash generated, then the effects of selecting A or B would be as follows.

Investment A

Time	Balance b/f	Interest for Year	Receipt at Year End	Balance c/f
	£	£	£	£
1	–	–	41.00	41.00
2	41.00	4.10	41.00	86.10
3	86.10	8.61	41.00	135.71

Undertaking investment A will result in cash in the bank of £135.71 at the end of the three years – this is its terminal value.

Investment B

Investment B will result in a single receipt of £134.00 at the end of the third year, hence this is its terminal value.

Bank account

Time	Balance b/f £	Interest for Year £	Receipt at Year End £	Balance c/f £
1	100.00	10.00	–	110.00
2	110.00	11.00	–	121.00
3	121.00	12.10	–	133.10

Banking the £100 today will result in cash in the bank of £133.10 at the end of the three years.

Conclusion

Both investments produce a better end position than the simple investment in the bank. Investment A will result in £2.61 more cash (£135.71 – £133.10) and Investment B gives £0.90 more (£134.00 – £133.10). Comparing the two, Investment A now appears preferable to Investment B.

It would certainly seem that it is in the investor's interest to pay more attention to the cash flows expected from an investment and to the timing of these cash flows than to consider solely the level of profit.

Solution 2

An alternative way of dealing with the example would be by compounding the interest on each flow individually, using our earlier compound interest ideas.

Investment A

Time	Cash Flow £	Compound Factor	Terminal Value £
1	41.00	1.10_2	49.61
2	41.00	1.10_1	45.10
3	41.00	1	41.00
Terminal value at t_3			£135.71

Investment B

Time	Cash Flow £	Compound Factor	Terminal Value £
1	0.00	1.10_2	0.00
2	0.00	1.10_1	0.00
3	134.00	1	134.00
Terminal value at t_3			£134.00

Here, we have compounded each flow by adding on interest at 10% p.a. for the number of years remaining until the end of the investment lives. To achieve this, we have in each case multiplied the cash flow by the compound factor, which in general terms may be written as

Formula to learn

Compound factor with n years to run = $(1 + r)n$

where r is the rate of interest expressed as a decimal (here r = 0.10) and n is the number of years' compounding required.

Clearly, the calculations have produced the same result, but the method used here is somewhat neater. We have compounded the flows to produce what is known as the terminal value of each flow.

Again, this can be compared to the £133.10 terminal value from the bank account to show that the investments are both worthwhile.

2.4.2 Net terminal value

The net surplus or deficit from the investment (£2.61 for Investment A, £0.90 for Investment B as calculated above) is known as the Net Terminal Value (NTV), and since it is positive, indicating a surplus, the investments are worthwhile and should be accepted. Had it been negative, indicating a deficit, we would have rejected the investments.

Rather than calculating separately the terminal values of the investment and the bank account, we can combine them in one net terminal value calculation as follows.

Investment A

Time	Cash Flow £	Compound Factor	Terminal Value £
0	(100.00)	1.10_3	(133.10)
1	41.00	1.10_2	49.61
2	41.00	1.10_1	45.10
3	41.00	1	41.00
Net terminal value at t_3			£2.61

Here, we are considering the £100 invested initially as a cash outflow on which we will lose interest. In turn, we get the investment inflows that generate interest, but it is the net difference we are interested in.

Investment B

Time	Cash Flow £	Compound Factor	Terminal Value £
0	(100.00)	1.10_3	(133.10)
1	0.00	1.10_2	0.00
2	0.00	1.10_1	0.00
3	134.00	1	134.00
Net terminal value at t_3			£0.90

2.5 Conclusion

Net terminal values will be useful for evaluating individual investments or investments with the same end date. If, however, we are trying to evaluate investments with different end dates, then we cannot compare the terminal value of one directly to the terminal value of the other.

For example, how could we compare the terminal value of Investment A of £135.71 at the end of three years, to the terminal value of a third investment of £150 at the end of six years?

In order to do this comparison, we must compound the interest out to a common end date. Here, six years would be sensible. However, this method will get very cumbersome, especially if we have some investments that will continue forever and never terminate.

3 PRESENT VALUES AND NET PRESENT VALUES

3.1 Introduction to present values

One way of accounting for the interest is by compounding the flows and calculating the terminal values, as we have just seen. However, as we stated earlier, if we are to compare investments, we will have to calculate to a common date, say, the end of the longest investment time. An alternative approach is to use present values where we take the common date as the present.

Present value calculations consider for any investment

Each relevant cash flow; and

The timing of the cash flow

and calculates how much cash we would need to have invested now to generate these same amounts of cash at these same future dates.

If we can get the same amounts of cash at the same future dates by investing less up front now, then we should accept the investment.

Example

Two alternative investments to banking £100 are Investments A and B, both of which will terminate in three years.

Investment A will return £41.00 p.a. for the next three years; Investment B will return £134.00 at the end of the third year.

Which investment opportunity is superior and which, if either, should be accepted if the interest rate is 10%?

Solution

Investment A generates the following cash flows.

Time	Cash Flow £
1	41.00
2	41.00
3	41.00

Looking at each of these in turn, how much cash would we need to invest now at our 10% rate of return to have £41.00 in each year?

Year 1

If we invest x now, then in one year it will grow to $x \times 1.10 = 1.10x$. Since we know that this is £41.00, then we can calculate x as

$$1.10x = £41.00$$

or

$$x = \frac{1}{1.10} \times £41.00$$

$$= £37.27$$

Year 2

Similarly, x invested now will grow to $x \times 1.10^2 = 1.21x$ after two years, hence

$$1.21x = £41.00$$

or

$$x = \frac{1}{1.21} \times £41.00$$

$$= £33.89$$

Year 3

And x invested now will grow to $x \times 1.10^3 = 1.331x$ after three years, hence

$$1.331x = £41.00$$

or

$$x = \frac{1}{1.331} \times £41.00$$

$$= £30.80$$

Conclusion

Putting these all together, we have

Time	Cash Flow £	Discount Factor	Present Value £
1	41.00	$\frac{1}{1.10^1}$	37.27
2	41.00	$\frac{1}{1.10^2}$	33.89
3	41.00	$\frac{1}{1.10^3}$	30.80
Present value at t_0			£101.96

In total, the present value of these receipts is £101.96. This means that, given the 10% rate of return, we would be indifferent between £41.00 each year for three years and £101.96 now.

Rather than compounding up the cash values for interest generated to the end of the investment, we are **discounting down**, i.e. reducing future cash values to their equivalent value today.

This discounting is effectively the reverse of our compounding process and in a similar way, we could apply a general formula for any year.

Formula to learn

Discount factor at Time n = $\dfrac{1}{(1+r)^n}$

where r is the **discount rate**, i.e. rate of interest expressed as a decimal (here r = 0.10) and n is the number of years' discounting required.

Example

Calculating the present value for Investment B gives

Time	Cash Flow £	Discount Factor	Present Value £
3	134.00	$\dfrac{1}{1.10^3}$	100.68
Present value at t_0			£100.68

This means that we would be indifferent, given the 10% rate of return, between £134.00 in three years and £100.68 now.

3.1.1 Bank

What is the present value of our option to bank the cash for a comparison? Under this option, we left the cash in the bank until Year 3 when it had grown to £133.10. This is then the cash flow to discount, giving

Time	Cash Flow £	Discount Factor	Present Value £
3	133.10	$\dfrac{1}{1.10^3}$	100.00
Present value at t_0			£100.00

This one really proves the idea, as it shows that we would be indifferent between £133.10 in three years and £100.00 now, which stands to reason as to get £133.10 in three years, we will need to invest £100.00 in the bank now.

3.1.2 Net present value

The present value of Investment A is £1.96 higher than could be expected from the bank. Investment B has a present value that is £0.68 higher than that from the bank. These represent the **net present values** of these investments.

In a similar way to net terminal values, we could calculate a net present value in one go, rather than calculating separately the present value of the investment and the banking option, as follows.

Solution

Investment A

Time	Cash Flow £	Discount Factor	Present Value £
0	(100.00)	1	(100.00)
1	41.00	$\dfrac{1}{1.10^1}$	37.27
2	41.00	$\dfrac{1}{1.10^2}$	33.89
3	41.00	$\dfrac{1}{1.10^3}$	30.80
Net present value at t_0			£1.96

You will note in this that the cash flow at Time 0 (now) is not discounted. £100 now is worth £100 now. Discounting takes account of the time value of money.

Investment B

Similarly, for Investment B, we get

Time	Cash Flow £	Discount Factor	Present Value £
0	(100.00)	1	(100.00)
3	134.00	$\dfrac{1}{1.10^3}$	100.68
Net present value at t_0			£0.68

Conclusion

For an accept or reject decision, the criterion is as before – **a positive net present value (NPV) indicates a cash surplus after accounting for interest and therefore we should accept**. A negative NPV indicates a cash deficit and we should therefore reject.

If we were to choose between various investments, we would now simply select the investment with the highest NPV.

4 DISCOUNT FACTORS

4.1 Single cash flow discount factor

We established above that the general term for a discount factor to be applied to cash flows at Time n is

$$\text{Discount factor at Time n} = \frac{1}{(1+r)^n}$$

The above formula is suitable if we are only dealing with a few cash flows, or have a spreadsheet model to cope with a large number, but what if this is not the case? There are some other situations for which we can establish discount factor formulae to make manual calculations more straightforward, specifically in the situation of

- Level annuities; and
- Level perpetuities.

4.2 Annuity discount factor

An annuity describes the situation where we have equal annual cash flows for a set period, such as in investment A above. Here, we have £41.00 received at the end of each of the next three years and, so far, we have appraised each flow separately.

However, since for all the receipts we are multiplying the relevant discount factor by £41.00 each time, we can simplify the calculation by multiplying £41.00 by the sum of the discount factors, i.e.

$$£41.00 \times \left(\frac{1}{1.10^1} + \frac{1}{1.10^2} + \frac{1}{1.10^3} \right)$$

$$= £41.00 \times 2.48685$$

$$= £101.96 \text{ as before}$$

The discount factor of 2.48685 is termed the three-year annuity discount factor at 10%.

This annuity discount factor for cash flows arising from Time 1 to Time n can be calculated using the following formula.

$$\text{Annuity discount factor for Times 1 to n} = \frac{1}{r}\left(1 - \frac{1}{(1+r)^n}\right)$$

where r is the rate of interest p.a. expressed as a decimal which must be constant throughout the period.

4.2.1 Using the annuity discount factor formula

Wherever we pay or receive a level stream of payments over a period of time, e.g. a regular coupon from a bond assuming constant interest rates, we can use this formula to calculate their present value.

Example

Using this formula to calculate the three-year annuity discount factor at 10% gives

$$\text{Annuity discount factor for Times 1 to n} = \frac{1}{0.10}\left(1-\frac{1}{1.10^3}\right)$$

$$= \frac{1}{0.10}\left(1-\frac{1}{1.10^3}\right)$$

$$= \frac{1}{0.10}(1-0.751315)$$

$$= \frac{1}{0.10}(0.248685)$$

$$= 2.48685$$

Using this approach, we could calculate the net present value of Investment A above (which we earlier calculated as £1.96) as follows.

Time	Cash Flow £	Discount Factor	Present Value £
0	(100.00)	1	(100.00)
1-3	41.00	$\frac{1}{0.10}\left(1-\frac{1}{1.10^3}\right)$	101.96
Net present value at t_0			£1.96

This approach can lead to significant time savings as the annuity period gets longer.

4.3 Perpetuity discount factor

A perpetuity refers to an equal annual flow which will continue indefinitely.

NB: Any series of flows that continue beyond 50 years could be approximated to a perpetuity without much impact or loss of accuracy.

Clearly, it will be impossible for us to evaluate each individual cash flow going on forever. For this situation, we must have a short cut.

Example

We are going to receive £10,000 p.a. in perpetuity and the interest rate (which we will now start to refer to as a required rate of return or cost of capital) is 10% p.a. How would we value this series of flows?

To get a present value, we need to know how much cash invested now at 10% p.a. would provide £10,000 p.a. in perpetuity. We would be indifferent between these two things which, by definition, means that it is the present value.

Solution

If we are to receive exactly the same amount in perpetuity, then we must never add to or eat into our capital invested. We are looking for an income of exactly £10,000 p.a.

Since our interest rate is 10% p.a., we can achieve this level of income by investing £100,000, the relationship being £100,000 × 10% = £10,000.

Now, we know that £10,000 × Perpetuity discount factor = £100,000 (the present value), hence the perpetuity discount factor in this case is $\frac{1}{0.10}$.

NB: What we have found is the discount factor for a stream of cash flows starting in one year, i.e. at Time 1.

Discount factor

The general discount factor formula for a level perpetuity stream of cash flows starting at Time 1 is

Formula to learn	Perpetuity discount factor for Time 1 to infinity = $\dfrac{1}{r}$

where r is the rate of interest per annum expressed as a decimal.

4.4 Effective discount factor

Where a perpetuity is growing at a constant rate through time, starting at time 1, its present value can be calculated using the following formula.

Formula to learn	Perpetuity discount factor with constant growth = $\dfrac{1}{r-g}$

Effectively we are calculating the net effect of the conflicting increase for growth and decrease for time value. Therefore, this is also referred to as the effective discount factor.

For example, if there is cash flow at time 1 of £1,000, which will grow at a constant rate of 4%, i.e. a flow of £1,040 at time 2, £1,081.60 at time 3, etc., and the discount rate is 9%, the present value of the whole series can be calculated as follows.

$$PV = 1,000 \times \frac{1}{0.09 - 0.04} = £20,000$$

Note that the cash flow used must be the first one in the series, i.e. **the cash flow at time 1**.

4.5 Annuities and perpetuities not starting at Time 1

4.5.1 Introduction

As we noted in the calculation of the annuity or perpetuity discount factor, the first cash flow always arises at the end of the first time period (at Time 1). However, there will be situations when this will not be the case.

Example

An investment pays £41 at the end of Years 3, 4 and 5. Calculate the present value of the receipts assuming a 10% required rate of return.

Solution

Time	Cash Flow £	Discount Factor	Present Value £
3	41.00	$\dfrac{1}{1.10^3}$	30.8039
4	41.00	$\dfrac{1}{1.10^4}$	28.0036
5	41.00	$\dfrac{1}{1.10^5}$	25.4578
Present value at t_0			£84.2653

4.5.2 Alternative approaches

There are two alternative approaches that we could have adopted to calculate this, which could prove very useful in longer annuity or perpetuity situations.

Deducting unwanted years

We could view this cash stream as a normal five-year annuity (Time 1 to Time 5), but assume we must repay the Time 1 and Time 2 cash flows (hence not receive them).

Example

An investment pays £41 at the end of Years 3, 4 and 5. Calculate the present value of the receipts assuming a 10% required rate of return.

Solution

Time	Cash Flow £	Discount Factor	Present Value £
1-5	41.00	$\dfrac{1}{0.10}\left(1-\dfrac{1}{1.10^5}\right)$	155.4224
1-2	(41.00)	$\dfrac{1}{0.10}\left(1-\dfrac{1}{1.10^2}\right)$	(71.1571)
Present value at t_0			£84.2653

Discounting back

The alternative approach is to recognise that this is a three-year annuity, which starts to pay at Time 3 rather than Time 1, i.e. two years later than a standard annuity which starts at Time 1. If all of the cash flows are two years later than in a normal annuity or perpetuity, they must be discounted back a further two years. Hence

$$\text{Annuity Factor (3-5)} = \text{Annuity Factor (1-3)} \times \frac{1}{(1+r)^2}$$

Example

An investment pays £41 at the end of Years 3, 4 and 5. Calculate the present value of the receipts assuming a 10% required rate of return.

Solution

Time	Cash Flow £	Discount Factor	Present Value £
3-5	(41.00)	$\frac{1}{0.10}\left(1-\frac{1}{1.10^3}\right) \times \frac{1}{(1+r)^2}$	£84.2653

Conclusion

There are three alternative approaches for calculating present value when we do not start at Time 1.

- Evaluate each separate cash flow.
- Calculate by deducting the unwanted years.
- Calculate by discounting back.

All approaches will give the same answer, and you may choose whichever approach you prefer.

4.6 Relationship between present and terminal values

One final point to note is that there is a direct relationship between present and terminal values, either gross or net. If we take the present or net present value of any investment and compound it up for the appropriate number of years, we will get the corresponding terminal or net terminal value as we can see from our sample investments.

Example

Earlier, we calculated the terminal value, net terminal value, present value and net present value of two investments (A and B), based on A paying £41.00 each year for three years and B paying £134 at the end of the third year. Comparing the net present values and net terminal values we calculated earlier based on a required rate of return of 10%, we get

	Net Present Value £	Compound Factor	Net Terminal Value £
Investment A	1.96	1.10^3	2.61
Investment B	0.68	1.10^3	0.90

We can use this idea to determine the terminal value or net terminal value of anything for which we can calculate a present value or net present value (other than a perpetuity). That is, we can calculate the present value of the cash flows then compound them up to give the corresponding terminal value.

5   INTERNAL RATE OF RETURN

5.1 Definition

The **Internal Rate of Return (IRR)** is defined as follows.

IRR = The rate of interest that discounts the investment flows to a net present value of zero

7.5.2 Use of the IRR

The IRR may be used as a method for assessing the total return from an investment or a portfolio.

Example

An investment is bought for £100 and sold one year later for £110. Calculate the return realised.

Solution

Here, we are making a £10 gain on a £100 investment, corresponding to a 10% return.

Clearly, with this very simple investment it was very easy to assess the return without recourse to discounted cash flows. However, if we were to discount this investment's cash flows at different rates, we would find the following.

Time	Cash Flow £	Discount Factor (5%)	Present Value £	Discount Factor (10%)	Present Value £	Discount Factor (15%)	Present Value £
0	(100.00)	1	(100.00)	1	(100.00)	1	(100.00)
1	110.00	$\dfrac{1}{1.05^1}$	104.76	$\dfrac{1}{1.10^1}$	100.00	$\dfrac{1}{1.15^1}$	95.65
Net present values			£4.76		£0.00		(£4.35)

What we can see here is that there is an inverse relationship between NPVs and required rates of return – as rates rise NPVs fall. Appreciating this relationship is the key to understanding the examination approach to these questions.

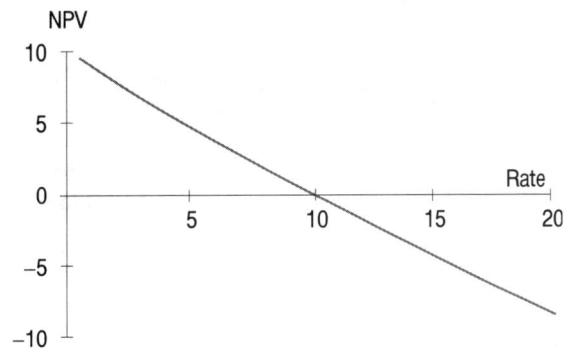

What we can also see in this example is that the IRR is 10% (the rate corresponding to a zero NPV), telling us that this investment is returning 10%. Clearly, we already knew the return from this very simple security was 10%, however the strength of this IRR approach is that it can be applied to investments that provide a much more complicated series of cash returns.

5.2 Assessment

An approximation to the IRR can be determined through a process called **interpolation**, although a trial and error approach is really the only way of finding the exact IRR. Through knowledge of the inverse relationship, however, the number of trials and errors can be minimised in a multiple choice exam, where four alternative rates are offered.

5.2.1 Steps for exam questions

Calculate the NPV of the various cash flows using the second highest rate, which will give rise to three possibilities.

- If the NPV is zero, then the correct rate has been selected first time.

- If the NPV is positive, then the selected rate is too low and the IRR is a higher rate. Since the second highest rate was originally selected, the correct answer must be the highest rate offered.

- If the NPV is negative, then the selected rate was too high and the IRR is one of the two lower rates offered in the question. One of these two lower rates will need to be tried to determine which it is.

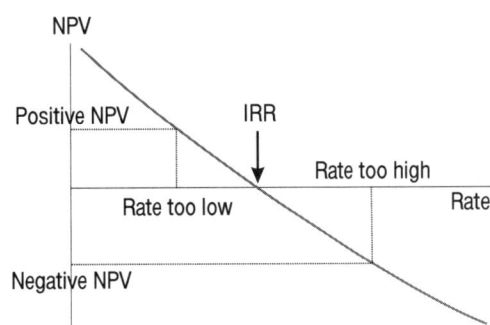

Example

An investment is bought for £88.33. It returns £6 each year for the next five years and is then sold for £100. Calculate the return realised on this investment.

    A   8.7%
    B   9.0%
    C   9.3%
    D   9.5%

Solution

Trying the second highest rate of 9.3%

Time	Cash Flow £	Discount Factor	Present Value £
0	(88.33)	1	(88.33)
1-5	6.00	$\dfrac{1}{0.093}\left(1-\dfrac{1}{1.093^5}\right)$	23.16
5	100.00	$\dfrac{1}{1.093^5}$	64.11
Net Present value			(£1.06)

Since this is negative, the rate we have selected is too high, so the correct answer must be either 8.7% or 9.0%.

Try 9.0%

Time	Cash Flow £	Discount Factor	Present Value £
0	(88.33)	1	(88.33)
1-5	6.00	$\dfrac{1}{0.090}\left(1-\dfrac{1}{1.090^5}\right)$	23.34
5	100.00	$\dfrac{1}{1.090^5}$	64.99
Net Present value			£0.00

The NPV is zero, hence the rate of return (the IRR) is 9.0%.

If you had tried a discount factor of 8.7%, this would have given a positive NPV of £1.70 and hence the rate would have been too low.

5.3 Summary of discount factors

Name	Formula	Use
Discount Factor	$\dfrac{1}{(1+r)^n}$	For single cash flows or different cash flows in each period.
Annuity Discount Factor	$\dfrac{1}{r}\left(1-\dfrac{1}{(1+r)^n}\right)$	For constant cash flows for a number of periods.
Perpetuity Discount Factor	$\dfrac{1}{r}$	For constant cash flows in perpetuity.
Effective Discount Factor	$\dfrac{1}{r-g}$	For growing perpetuities to give an effective rate.

6 CALCULATING THE MARKET VALUE OF A BOND

The exam syllabus requires you to be able to calculate the market value of a bond with annual coupons and a maturity of three years. We may use the DCF method to calculate the expected market value.

6.1 Present value of a three-year bond

Example

A bond pays an annual coupon of £9 and is to be redeemed at £100 in three years. The required return on the bond (prevailing interest rate) is 8%. What will be the market value?

Solution

The market value can be established by calculating the present value of the associated cash flows at the required rate of 8%. The cash flows from the bond will be £9.00 coupon at the end of each year, and £100 capital redemption at the end of the third year, i.e. £109 is received in total at that time.

The market value can, therefore, be calculated as

Time	Cash Flow £	Discount Factor	Present Value £
1	9.00	$\dfrac{1}{1.08}$	8.33
2	9.00	$\dfrac{1}{1.08^2}$	7.72
3	109.00	$\dfrac{1}{1.08^3}$	86.53
Market value			£102.58

6.2 Assumptions underlying Discounted Cash Flow (DCF)

Finally, it is worthwhile to consider the assumptions we have implicitly been making in all of the NPV and IRR calculations to date.

6.2.1 The basic assumptions

- The cash flows expected to accrue from any investment can be considered in isolation, and are independent of decisions relating to any other investment.

- The cash flows are known with certainty.

- No firm or individual has sufficient funds to affect the price of funds.

- Investors have a time preference for money and make rational decisions accordingly.

6.2.2 The assumptions as to reinvestment rates

The fundamental difference between NPV and IRR is the assumption made about reinvestment rates. Under NPV, we are implicitly assuming that any surplus funds generated can be reinvested to earn a return equal to the required rate of return.

However, the IRR calculation assumes that surplus funds will be reinvested to earn a return equal to the IRR, that the time value placed on money is this rate.

Conceptually, NPV is superior because, regardless of the actual investment that is generating the cash flows, we always assume the flows can be reinvested at the same rate. There is no real justification for saying that returns from one investment can be reinvested to earn a return in excess of the returns earned from any other investment, as assumed with the IRR.

CHAPTER ROUNDUP

- Make sure you have learnt all the formulae from this chapter as they are not given to you in the exam.

Mean $\qquad = \bar{x} = \dfrac{\sum x_i}{n}$

Standard deviation $\qquad = \sqrt{\dfrac{\sum (x - \bar{x})^2}{n}}$

Covariance $\qquad = \dfrac{\sum (x - \bar{x})(y - \bar{y})}{n}$

Single cash flow discount factor $\quad = \dfrac{1}{(1+r)^n}$

Annuity discount factor $\qquad = \dfrac{1}{r}\left(1 - \dfrac{1}{(1+r)^n}\right)$

Perpetuity discount factor $\qquad = \dfrac{1}{r}$

Perpetuity with growth $\qquad = \dfrac{1}{r-g}$

Check your knowledge of the chapter here, without referring back to the text.

1. What is the mean of the following numbers: 8.3, 7.2, 5.8, 6.9, 11.4 and 8.2?

2. What is the covariance of the following two populations?

X	Y
6	3
4	5
8	1

3. Calculate the present value of the following.

    A   A single cash flow of £1,000 in three years' time if interest rates are 12%

    B   An annuity of £5,000 starting in one year's time and continuing for ten years when interest rates are 8%

    C   A cash flow of £10,000 in one year that will last forever and grow at 2% per annum when the discount rate is 6%

4. What is the IRR?

TEST YOUR KNOWLEDGE: ANSWERS

1. $\bar{x} = \dfrac{(8.3 + 7.2 + 5.8 + 6.9 + 11.4 + 8.2)}{6} = 7.97$

    (See Section 1.2.1)

2. $\bar{x} = \left(\dfrac{6 + 4 + 8}{3}\right) = 6$

    $\bar{y} = \dfrac{(3 + 5 + 1)}{3} = 3$

$(x - \bar{x})$	$(y - \bar{y})$		$(x - \bar{x})(y - \bar{y})$
$(6 - 6)$	$(3 - 3)$	=	0
$(4 - 6)$	$(5 - 3)$	=	−4
$(8 - 6)$	$(1 - 3)$	=	$\underline{-4}$
			-8

$COVAR_{x,y} = \dfrac{-8}{3} = -2.67$

(See Section 1.4)

3. A $\dfrac{£1,000}{1.12^3} = £711.78$

    (See Section 4.1)

    B $£5,000 \times \dfrac{1}{0.08}\left(1 - \dfrac{1}{1.08^{10}}\right) = £33,550.41$

    (See Section 4.2)

    C $£10,000 \times \dfrac{1}{(0.06 - 0.02)} = £250,000$

    (See Section 4.4)

4. The Internal Rate of Return: the rate of return that discounts the investment flows to a net present value of zero.

    (See Section 5.1)

8

Accounting Analysis

INTRODUCTION

The Corporate Finance exam does not require you to be able to perform accounting operations or prepare accounts. You just need to be a competent reader and user of accounts. Therefore, we will examine the layout of the main components of the financial statements, the Balance Sheet, Profit and Loss Account and the Cash Flow Statement.

The formulae used for the analysis of accounts are fairly straightforward, but as with Chapter 7 you are required to memorise them for the exam.

CHAPTER CONTENTS

CHAPTER LEARNING OBJECTIVES

Basic Principles

- **Understand** the purpose of financial statements.

- **Understand** the Companies Acts' requirement for companies and groups to prepare accounts in accordance with applicable accounting standards.

- **Know** the purpose of

    – International Accounting Standards (IAS).
    – International Financing Reporting Standards (IFRS).
    – Statements of Standard Accounting Policies (SSAPs).
    – UK Financial Reporting Standards (FRSs).
    – US Generally Accepted Accounting Principles (GAAP).

- **Know** for what periods the IFRS apply to AIM companies' accounts.

- **Understand** the difference between group accounts and company accounts and why companies are required to prepare group accounts. (Candidates should understand the concept of goodwill and minority interests, but will not be required to calculate these.)

Company Balance Sheets

- **Know** the purpose of the balance sheet, its format and main contents (including on and off-balance sheet items).

- **Understand** the concept of depreciation and amortisation.

- **Understand** the difference between authorised and issued share capital, capital reserves and revenue reserves.

- **Know** how loans and indebtedness are included within a balance sheet.

Profit and Loss Account

- **Know** the purpose of the profit and loss account , its format and main contents.
- **Understand** the difference between capital and revenue expenditure.

Cash Flow Statement

- **Know** the purpose of the cash flow statement and its format as set out in IAS 7.

- **Understand** the difference between profit and cash and their impact on the long-term future of the business.

- **Understand** the purpose of free cash flow and the difference between enterprise cash flow and equity cash flow.

BPP
LEARNING MEDIA

Financial Statement Analysis

- **Understand** the following key ratios.

    - Profitability ratios (gross profit and operating profit margins).
    - Return on capital employed.

- **Be able to calculate** profitability ratios (gross profit and operating profit margins) and return on capital employed.

- **Understand** the following financial gearing ratios.

    - Investors' debt to equity ratio.
    - Net debt to equity ratio.
    - Interest cover.

- **Be able to calculate** changes in investors' debt to equity ratio, net debt to equity ratio and interest cover.

- **Understand** the following investors' ratios.

    - Earnings per share.

    - Diluted earnings per share.

    - Price/earnings ratio (both historic and prospective).

    - Enterprise value to EBIT.

    - Enterprise value to EBITDA.

    - Net dividend yield.

    - Net dividend cover.

- **Be able to calculate** changes in earnings per share, diluted earnings per share, price/earnings ratio (both historic and prospective), net dividend yield and net dividend cover.

1 PURPOSE OF FINANCIAL STATEMENTS

1.1 Introduction

A company is a business organisation, created in law, which is owned by its members or shareholders.

Generally, for listed companies and larger unlisted ones, the shareholders appoint directors to manage the company on their behalf, having little involvement in the day-to-day operations of the companies themselves.

The primary purpose of annual financial statements is to provide a medium enabling the directors to report to the shareholders on the performance of the company.

The financial statements are, however, frequently used by other interested parties, such as lenders, creditors, potential investors, tax authorities, the Government etc., to help them assess the returns they are receiving and the risks that they may face.

2 REGULATION OF ACCOUNTS

2.1 Introduction

As a result of the segregation of management and ownership, and the limitation of liability, strict reporting rules/regulations have been developed to ensure that the shareholders are kept fully informed to enable them to assess their risks and returns.

There are three sources of regulations in relation to a quoted company's accounts.

- Legal rules (the Companies Acts).
- UKLA's rules (the Listing Rules).
- Professional accounting rules (Financial Reporting Standards).

The first two are concerned with what should be disclosed in the accounts. The latter are principally concerned with tackling the accounting methods that should be used, although they frequently also give additional disclosure guidance.

2.2 Legal rules

2.2.1 Introduction

As with most UK legislation, the Companies Acts rules have developed gradually over the years. The Companies Act 1985 (CA 1985) consolidated the previous statutes regarding the form and content of a set of financial statements. The Companies Act 1989 (CA 1989) updated certain provisions of this Act, principally those regarding group accounts.

2.2.2 True and fair view

One of the requirements of the Companies Acts is that the accounts should give a **true and fair view** of the performance of the company for the period and its financial position at the end of that period. The requirement to show a true and fair view **overrides all other requirements** in the preparation of accounts.

2.2.3 Formats of disclosure

In line with EU practice, UK accounts are now prepared in accordance with strict formats. Both the balance sheet and the profit and loss account are obliged to be presented in prescribed formats.

2.3 UK Listing Authority

Companies whose shares are listed on the Stock Exchange must comply with certain additional disclosure requirements laid out in the UKLA's **Listing Rules**.

They must also produce a half-yearly or interim report for shareholders.

2.4 Professional accounting rules

The UK accounting profession, the Stock Exchange and the Government have jointly formed the **Financial Reporting Council** (FRC). This body is responsible for

- The development of Accounting Standards, through a subsidiary, the **Accounting Standards Board** (ASB).
- The monitoring and enforcement of the application of those standards via another subsidiary the **Financial Reporting Review Panel**.

Accounting Standards must be applied by all companies. They set out acceptable methods for the treatment and presentation of a wide range of aspects of company accounts. There are two forms of Accounting Standards in issue at present. Firstly, there are **Financial Reporting Standards (FRSs)** which are standards prepared by the Accounting Standards Board. Secondly there are **Statements of Standard Accounting Practice (SSAPs)**. These were prepared by a committee (now defunct) which was superseded by the Accounting Standards Board.

In addition, the ASB has a subsidiary – the **Urgent Issues Task Force (UITF)** – whose role is to assist the ASB in areas where no accounting standard or Companies Act rule exists but where unsatisfactory or conflicting interpretations have/are likely to be applied. The UITF issues **Abstracts** which, although they are not proper standards, must be applied by all companies if their accounts are to give a true and fair view.

2.5 International Financial Reporting Standards

Accounting principles have largely been developed on a national basis, often with significant differences from country to country. The accounts prepared in line with these standards are therefore said to be prepared under Generally Accepted Accounting Principles (GAAP) of that country, e.g. UK GAAP or US GAAP. The need for uniform accounting principles for international financial reporting has been recognised for many years.

A major step towards realising this objective was taken with the creation of the International Accounting Standards Board (IASB), now widely recognised as the authoritative global accounting standard-setting body.

The IASB publishes its standards in a series of pronouncements called International Financial Reporting Standards (IFRSs). Upon its inception, the IASB adopted the existing International Accounting Standards (IASs). The term 'International Financial Reporting Standards' includes IFRSs and IASs.

2.5.1 Adoption of International Financial Reporting Standards

The European Commission has recently adopted a regulation that all EU companies **listed on a regulated market** must prepare consolidated accounts in accordance with IFRSs, effective by 2005 at the latest. From 1 January 2005 UK-listed companies must prepare their accounts in line with IFRSs. **AIM companies** must implement the IFRS for all accounting periods commencing on or after **1 January 2007**.

3 REPORTING REQUIREMENTS

3.1 Responsibility for accounts preparation and audit

It is the **directors'** legal **responsibility** to prepare the accounts for the shareholders that must

- Give a true and fair view.
- Comply with the requirements of the Companies Acts.

The auditor is an independent third party appointed by the shareholders (to whom they report) to give an opinion as to whether the directors have correctly fulfilled these responsibilities. The auditor's report is also a legally required part of the annual report and accounts.

3.2 Format and contents of accounts

As a result of these regulations, the annual report and accounts of listed companies must contain the following elements.

Item	Regulation		
	Companies Act	UKLA	FRS
Director's report	✓		
Auditor's report	✓		
Financial statements			
Profit and loss account	✓		
Balance sheet	✓		
Statement of total recognised gains and losses			✓
Cash flow statement			✓
Notes to the accounts	✓		
Accounting policies	✓		
Figures for this year plus previous year's comparatives	✓		
Five-year summary		✓*	

Note that the Chairman's Statement and other similar documents are not required to be prepared, even though they are present in most annual reports.

Furthermore, the UKLA's five-year summary is a **recommendation** rather than an absolute requirement.

3.3 Fundamental accounting principles

3.3.1 Introduction

The Companies Act sets out **five fundamental accounting principles** that must be used when preparing accounts. The first **four** were known as the **fundamental accounting concepts** and were originally outlined in **SSAP 2** – *Disclosure of Accounting Policies*. Now just the first two are set out as bedrocks of accounting in FRS 18.

3.3.2 Going concern

This concept assumes that the enterprise will continue in operational existence for the foreseeable future. This means, in particular, that the profit and loss account and balance sheet assume no intention or necessity to liquidate or curtail significantly the scale of operations.

3.3.3 Accruals (or matching)

This concept assumes that the revenue and costs are

- Accrued, i.e. recognised as they are earned or incurred, not as money received or paid.
- Matched with one another so far as their relationship can be established or justifiably assumed.
- Dealt with in the profit and loss account of the **period to which they relate**.

Note where the accrual concept is inconsistent with the **prudence concept, the latter prevails**.

3.3.4 Consistency

This concept assumes that there is consistency of accounting treatment of like items within each accounting period and from one period to the next.

3.3.5 Prudence

This concept assumes

- **Revenue and profits are not anticipated**, but are recognised by inclusion in the profit and loss account only when realised in the form of cash or other realisable assets.

- **Provision is made for all known liabilities** arising as a result of actions taken.

3.3.6 No netting-off

In determining the aggregate amount of any item, the amount of each individual asset or liability that falls to be taken into account should be determined and disclosed separately, i.e. they should **not** be netted off against each other and hence omitted altogether. This principle was not part of the original SSAP but was included in the Companies Act. It is therefore not one of the accounting concepts.

3.3.7 Historic cost

Most items are recorded in the accounts at their original value at the time of purchase or creation, known as the historic cost. It is possible to revalue upwards to their current market value all assets except goodwill. Revaluation is most commonly used for properties.

4 BALANCE SHEET

4.1 Introduction

The balance sheet is a statement of the financial position of the business at a specific point in time, such as the year end.

It is the product of the accounting equation and as its name suggests, must always equate or balance.

It should always be borne in mind that it is only a picture of the company at the **specific point of time**. Each transaction impacts on the accounting equation, hence the balance sheet just after the year end may be significantly different from that at the year end if a company has undertaken significant transactions.

4.2 Accounting equation

4.2.1 Introduction

The accounting equation can be stated as

Formula to learn

> Net assets = Shareholders' funds

The format usually adopted by UK companies presents this equation vertically with net assets above shareholders' funds, rather than horizontally where they are alongside one another. In outline, a UK balance sheet appears as follows (note brackets are used to denote negatives).

Balance Sheet Outline

	£'000
Net Assets	
Assets	400
Liabilities	(150)
	250
Shareholders' Funds	
Share capital	100
Reserves	150
	250

As we can see the accounting equation holds – the balance sheet balances.

The four categories we have outlined are as follows.

1. Assets

These represent resources owned or controlled by the company and available for its use, such as stocks of goods for sale or production equipment. These can be sub-categorised under two headings.

Fixed assets

Assets acquired for continued use in the business to earn profit, not for resale. Examples of such items would include office and production buildings and equipment. Clearly, we intend to use these long term, not to simply sell them on at a profit.

Current assets

Assets acquired for conversion to cash during the ordinary course of business. Examples of such assets would include stocks of goods available for sale to customers, or customers' account balances which will be settled for cash. By convention, assets which are to be converted into cash within **12 months** are deemed to be **current**.

2. Liabilities

These represent amounts owed by the company to outside suppliers and lenders. These too are sub-categorised as

- Creditors: amounts falling due within one year.
- Creditors: amounts falling due after more than one year.

The purpose of the above classification is to provide a clear indication of the timescales for settlement.

3. Share capital

This is money invested in the company by shareholders, i.e. money subscribed for shares.

4. Reserves

These generally represent profits earned and retained by the company since it began trading, although there may be other types of reserves as we will see later.

This is only a broad outline and in reality the balance sheet will contain much more detail.

4.3 Balance sheet format

4.3.1 Format

The general format for a balance sheet is prescribed in the Companies Acts and can be illustrated by the following example.

XYZ plc – group balance sheet as at 31 August 2005

	Notes	2005 £'000	2004 £'000
Fixed assets	1		
Intangible	2	877	662
Tangible	3	19,798	19,854
Investments	4	37	39
		20,712	20,555
Current assets	5		
Stock		19,420	19,101
Debtors	7	27,882	35,980
Investments		1,487	2,116
Cash		3,923	4,804
		52,712	62,001
Creditors: amounts falling due within one year	6 & 7	(48,817)	(45,218)
Net current assets		3,895	16,783
Total assets less current liabilities	8	24,607	37,338
Creditors: amounts falling due after more than one year	9	(3,695)	(18,553)
Provisions for liabilities and charges	10	(1,484)	(2,193)
		19,428	16,592
Capital and reserves			
Called-up share capital	11	1,743	1,725
Share premium account reserve	12	2,237	2,182
Revaluation reserve	13	4,687	3,806
Other reserves	14	1,204	1,204
Profit and loss account reserve	15	8,557	6,875
Total shareholders' funds		18,428	15,792
Minority interests	16	1,000	800
		19,428	16,592

You will notice that the balance sheet is shown for both this year end (31 August 2005) and the previous year end (31 August 2004) for comparison. The notes referred to above would normally provide further detailed analysis, but here they are being used to provide additional explanations of the terminology.

The accounts are called group accounts as they consolidate the position of all subsidiary companies with the parent company's balance sheet to show the net assets of the whole group.

4.4 Terminology – net assets

1. Fixed assets

As already noted, fixed assets are assets acquired for continued use within the business and not for resale. As we can see, these should be sub-classified into

- Intangibles.
- Tangibles.
- Investments.

The Companies Act requires that all fixed assets that have limited useful economical lives must be depreciated. Depreciation is the method by which the cost of using the asset is matched against its related benefit.

The following examples illustrate the two main methods of depreciation used (straight line and reducing balance), but note that you will **not** be required to perform these calculations in the exam.

Example – straight line method

A company buys some production machinery at a cost of £60,000. It expects, from previous experience, that it will last five years, after which time it will be sold for £5,000. It will therefore cost the company £55,000 (£60,000 cost less £5,000 expected sale proceeds) to use the equipment over these five years.

Applying the matching concept, this £55,000 cost should be spread over the five years, i.e. an expense of £11,000 charged against the profit each year.

On the balance sheet, fixed assets are usually stated at net book value (NBV), i.e. cost less the accumulated depreciation provision. Thus, at the end of each of the next five years the fixed asset will be valued in the balance sheet as follows.

	Year 1	Year 2	Year 3	Year 4	Year 5
	£'000	£'000	£'000	£'000	£'000
Cost	60	60	60	60	60
Depreciation provision	(11)	(22)	(33)	(44)	(55)
Net book value	49	38	27	16	5

As we can see, the balance sheet net book value of the equipment falls by £11,000 each year (as the amount is charged as an expense – depreciation) until in Year 5, it has dropped to the estimated sales proceeds of £5,000.

Example – reducing balance method

It is also possible to calculate depreciation by a **reducing balance method**. This aims to accurately reflect the consumption of more of the value of an asset in its earlier years.

For example, if a company buys an asset for £10,000, it may charge depreciation at 33% of its net book value each year. This would give a depreciation profile as follows.

	Year 1	Year 2	Year 3
	£'000	£'000	£'000
Cost or NBV	10.0	6.7	4.5
Annual depreciation	3.3	2.2	1.5
Net Book Value	6.7	4.5	3.0

2. Intangible fixed assets

Intangibles are literally assets without physical form. They frequently represent intellectual property rights of the company, or abilities of its staff, that enable it to operate and generate profits in a way that competitors cannot. This is most commonly referred to as **goodwill**. It usually arises in accounts when paying more to acquire a subsidiary than its separable net assets. In essence, the whole subsidiary is worth more than the sum of its parts and this excess is purchased goodwill.

The types of intangible assets that most frequently appear on the balance sheet are as follows.

- Research and development expenditure.
- Patents, licences and trademarks.
- Publishing rights and titles.
- Goodwill.
- Brands.

Depreciation of intangible fixed assets is usually referred to as **amortisation**.

3. Tangible fixed assets

These are physical assets that are used within the business over a number of years with a view to deriving some benefit from this use, e.g. through their use in the manufacture of goods for resale.

Tangible fixed assets include items such as

- Freehold land and buildings (including buildings under construction).
- Leasehold land and buildings.
- Plant and machinery.
- Motor vehicles.
- Fixtures and fittings.

Note that, although buildings will be depreciated, freehold land is held in perpetuity and, therefore, is **not** depreciated.

4. Investments

These represent long-term ownership of shares in other companies and are usually reported in the balance sheet at historical cost. Additional reporting regulations apply to significant levels of shareholdings that have caused the investments to be classified as either a subsidiary (50%+) or an associated undertaking (20%+).

5. Current assets

Strictly speaking these are assets other than fixed assets, although perhaps the best description is that current assets are assets held for conversion into cash in the ordinary course of business. As we can see, current assets are sub-categorised into (in order of liquidity).

- **Stock** – goods held available for sale.

- **Debtors** – amounts owed to the company, perhaps as a result of selling goods on credit.

- **Investments** – shares held in the short term with the intention of reselling, e.g. short-term speculative investments.

- **Cash**.

- In valuing current assets the fundamental accounting concept of **prudence** is applied, in that they are valued at the lower of

- **Costs**.

- **Net realisable value (NRV),** i.e. estimated selling price less any cost incurred in order to sell.

Thus

- If the NRV exceeds cost the asset is valued at cost, i.e. no profit is anticipated.
- If the NRV is less than cost the asset is devalued down to NRV, i.e. a loss is recognised.

6. Creditors – amounts falling due within one year

Creditors due within one year should fully reflect all liabilities payable within 12 months of the year end.

They include bank overdrafts and both dividends and taxation payable within one year, as well as amounts owed to suppliers known as trade creditors.

7. Prepayments and accruals

Accruals and prepayments arise in the balance sheet when the amount charged as an expense in the profit and loss account for the year is not the same as the amount paid out of the cash balance.

Accruals

An accrual is an amount due in respect of goods and services used during the year but not yet invoiced. Since we owe the amount even though we have not yet been invoiced for it, we have to show it as part of our liabilities. Accruals are therefore shown as part of **creditors**.

Prepayments

Prepayments are amounts paid before the balance sheet date which relate to the period after that date. Since we have paid the money over but not yet received the benefit due from the expenditure, we still have an asset at the balance sheet date. Prepayments are therefore shown as part of **debtors**.

8. Total assets less current liabilities

This is the sum of the fixed asset NBV (£20,712,000) and the net current assets (£3,895,000).

9. Creditors – amounts falling due after more than one year

This will typically include such items as

- Long-term bank loans.
- Loan stock and debentures issued by the company.

Both of these must be repaid long term. It would also include any other known liabilities such as trade creditors that do not require settlement within the next 12-month period. This section of the balance sheet is, therefore, the main part, showing the total loans and indebtedness of the group.

10. Provisions for liabilities and charges

These represent amounts set aside by the company to meet foreseeable future costs arising as a result of past events. An example of such a provision is the costs associated with the demolition and site clearance of a factory closed down during the year.

The amounts are estimated because they are not yet known with certainty and will not be until the process is completed some time in the future. Their value is, therefore, less reliable than items in creditors such as bank loans where it is known with certainty what is owed and when it is due to be paid.

Another example is deferred tax reserve, which represents the cumulative difference between the tax payable on the accounting profits versus the taxable profits. Although called a reserve, it is not part of the capital and reserves in shareholders' funds.

4.5 Terminology – shareholders' funds

If the net assets tell us in accounting terms what the company is worth to its shareholders, the shareholders' funds explain how that value was put into the company. We therefore distinguish between the share capital injected and the increase in value reserved in the business. The reserves are separated into those that are not distributable (capital) or distributable (revenue), i.e. whether they can be paid out as a dividend. Generally, only the profit and loss account reserve is a revenue reserve.

11. Called-up share capital

This represents the total nominal value of the shares in issue at the year end, e.g. our company has in issue 100,000 shares, each with a £1 nominal value giving £100,000 share capital. Note that the company may be **authorised** to issue more share capital in the future, but the balance sheet will only record the amount of **issued** share capital. The total amount of authorised share capital will be contained in the company's Memorandum of Association.

Under the Companies Act, UK companies must ascribe a nominal or par value to each share. This represents

- The minimum value at which shares can be issued. The company is not allowed to issue fully paid shares at a price below nominal value.

- The limits of the liability of the shareholder. If the company becomes insolvent, shareholders' liability is limited to any unpaid element of this nominal value. Where the share is a fully paid share, the shareholder has no further liability.

12. Share premium account reserve

If a company trades profitably and retains those profits to finance expansion, then its value will grow. As a result it will be able to raise cash in later years by issuing more shares at a price in excess of their nominal value, i.e. at a premium.

Example

A company could raise £20,000 by issuing 5,000 new £1 ordinary shares at a price of £4 each. This results in a premium of £3 per share (full price of £4 less nominal value of £1).

Under the Companies Act, the company must record the issue of these shares by increasing the called-up share capital by only the **nominal value** of the shares issued, i.e. £5,000. The premium of £15,000 must be added to the share premium account. The impact on the accounting equation is

	£'000
Impact on net assets	
Cash up	+20
	+20
Impact on shareholders' funds	
Share capital up	+5
Share premium account up	+15
	+20

Having been created, the share premium account can only subsequently be reduced in **five** circumstances without the court's permission.

1. To issue **bonus shares**. Bonus shares are issued by a company when it feels that the share price has gone too high. A bonus issue, like a rights issue, is made to the existing shareholders and gives them a number of free shares proportionate to their existing holding.

   In terms of the balance sheet the effect is

Impact on net assets	None.
Impact on shareholders' funds	Share capital up.
	Share premium account down.

2. To write off **preliminary expenses** of forming a company.

3. To write off **expenses of issue** of shares or debentures.

4. To charge **the premium on repayment on debentures**.

5. To charge the **discount on issue of debentures**.

The share premium account can **never be reduced to pay dividends** to the shareholders, as it is one of the company's non-distributable or capital reserves.

13. Revaluation reserve

UK companies are permitted by the Companies Act to revalue all assets other than goodwill upwards, increasing net assets and shareholders' funds.

Where a company does revalue its fixed assets upwards, it would be imprudent to treat this increase in shareholders' funds as part of the company's realised profits for the year. It has not been generated by the operational performance of the company and it is certainly not represented by cash. It is, therefore, considered unrealised and non-distributable, i.e. the company cannot use the revaluation reserve to pay a dividend.

In this situation, the increase in the net book value of the assets is reflected within shareholders' funds in the revaluation reserve.

Impact on net assets	Fixed assets up
Impact on shareholders' funds	Revaluation reserve up.

Revaluation is not compulsory and assets may remain in the accounts at their original purchase price. This is known as **historic cost** accounting.

14. Other reserves

Any other reserves generally represent an apportionment or allocation of profits from the profit and loss account. This is frequently done for the following reasons.

- To indicate that a certain element of profit is being retained for a specific reason.
- To indicate that a portion of profits will never be paid out as a dividend.
- To account for the treatment of unusual terms such as goodwill written off.

15. Profit and loss account reserve

The profit and loss account balance on the balance sheet represents the **accumulated profits made by the company since it started to trade**, which have **not been paid out as dividends** or transferred to other reserves. As such it is a distributable or revenue reserve under the Companies Act rules, i.e. it can be used to cover the payment of dividends to shareholders.

The separate **profit and loss account statement details the impact of this year's trading activities on this accumulated figure**. Any profits retained this year, which are detailed in the separate profit and loss account statement, will be added to the accumulated retained profits (or reserves) brought forward, giving the accumulated position at the end of the year. This could be viewed like a bank statement, where the statement only shows the movements for the month, but these are added to the opening cash balance to arrive at the closing one.

It is all too easy to become confused by two items having the same name of profit and loss account, so make sure that you can distinguish them in your mind, i.e.

- The balance sheet figure represents the accumulated position since the company started trading.
- The profit and loss account statement (covered next) details the movements for the year.

16. Minority interests

Minority interests arise when a company has a partly owned subsidiary company. For example, XYZ plc (holding or parent company) may own 80% of ABC Ltd (subsidiary). The balance of the shares in ABC Ltd are owned by other shareholders, referred to as the minority interest.

When XYZ plc prepares its consolidated accounts, it will include all the assets and liabilities of ABC Ltd on the top half of its balance sheet as being part of the group's assets and liabilities. The reason that it does this is that it controls all of ABC Ltd's assets, since it has a majority of voting rights.

However, it only owns 80% of ABC Ltd's net assets, with the other 20% being owned by the minority interest. XYZ plc recognises this fact by analysing out total shareholder financing into group shareholders' funds and minority interest. The minority interest shows how much of the net assets belong to the minority shareholders in ABC Ltd.

5 PROFIT AND LOSS ACCOUNT

5.1 Introduction

The profit and loss account statement provides a detailed analysis of how the company has generated its profit or loss for the accounting period. As already noted, it reconciles the change in the balance sheet profit and loss figure from one year to the next.

5.2 Profit and loss account format

The Companies Act describes the format of the profit and loss account. As for the balance sheet, the notes normally refer to further detailed analysis, but in our example they refer to additional explanations of the terminology.

All companies in the UK must comply with the requirements of **FRS 3** when preparing their profit and loss account. In broad terms, the key difference is that the profit and loss account must give a breakdown on a line-by-line basis of

- Generated from continuing activities.
- Generated from activities acquired during the year.
- Generated from activities which have been disposed of during the year.

XYZ plc – group profit and loss account for the year ended 31 August 2006

	Notes	2006 £'000	2005 £'000
Turnover	1	135,761	141,013
Cost of sales	2	(85,604)	(91,011)
Gross profit	3	50,157	50,002
Distribution costs	4	(22,961)	(21,636)
Administrative expenses	4	(19,620)	(16,752)
Other operating income		100	200
Operating profit	4	7,676	11,814
Exceptional items	5	(270)	(1,296)
		7,406	10,518
Income from fixed asset investments		100	100
Interest receivable and similar income		30	161
Interest payable and similar charges	6	(3,176)	(3,521)
Profit on ordinary activities before taxation		4,360	7,258
Tax on profit on ordinary activities	7	(1,104)	(2,000)
Profit on ordinary activities after taxation		3,256	5,258
Minority interests	8	(60)	(20)
Extraordinary items	9	–	–
Profit/(loss) for the financial year		3,196	5,238
Dividends paid and proposed	10	(2,064)	(6,527)
Retained profit/(loss) for the financial year		1,132	(1,289)
Earnings per ordinary share		5.08p	9.06p

5.3 Terminology

In accordance with the accruals or matching concept, income and expenses are recognised in the profit and loss account when earned regardless of when paid. Any difference between the recognition of these items and the corresponding cash flow will be reflected in a balance sheet debtor or creditor.

1. Turnover

The turnover or sales figure represents the total value of goods or services provided to customers during the accounting period whether they have been paid for or not, in accordance with the accruals concept. Thus, turnover will include both cash and credit sales.

2. Cost of sales

The cost of sales represents the total cost to the business of buying or making the actual items sold.

3. Gross profit

Gross profit is the difference between the value of the sales and the value of the cost of goods sold. One measure frequently used in determining the performance of the business is to consider its gross profit margin which can be calculated as

Formula to learn

$$\text{Gross profit margin} = \frac{\text{Gross profit}}{\text{Turnover}} \times 100\%$$

Clearly, the higher the margin for a particular level of operations, the higher the profit. However, this does not mean that low margins result in low profits. A number of businesses generate very healthy profits through selling very large numbers of items (achieving correspondingly large turnover) at low margins.

4. Various operating costs and operating profit

These costs include all other expenses incurred in generating the turnover for the period by way of administrative involvement and delivery/distribution. The operating profit is often referred to as **Earnings Before Interest payable and Tax (EBIT)**. It is a measure of how well management have used the factors directly under their control. Similarly to the gross profit, we can calculate an operating profit margin.

Formula to learn

$$\text{Operating profit margin} = \frac{\text{Operating profit}}{\text{Turnover}} \times 100\%$$

5. Exceptional items

Exceptional items are unusually large items of income or expense arising during the year. They are separately classified as exceptional items to highlight their one-off nature. An exceptional item

- Is material.

- Derives from events or transactions that fall within the ordinary activities of the business.

- Needs to be separately disclosed by virtue of their size or incidence if the financial statements are to give a true and fair view.

Removing such items from the normal ongoing costs and separately highlighting them in this way should enable us to see trends in the performance of the company which may otherwise be obscured.

6. Interest payable

In common with most other business expenses, any interest payable goes to reduce the company's profit before tax and hence taxable profit by the gross amount payable. For example, if a company has in issue £100,000 of 10% loan stock, then the interest charge in its accounts each year will be £10,000.

7. Tax on profit on ordinary activities

UK companies pay corporation tax, normally at 30%, on **all** their taxable profits. The element of the total tax charge shown here is the tax on the ordinary activities of the business, excluding any extraordinary items.

8. Minority interests

Minority interests arise in a similar way as in the balance sheet. Where XYZ plc owns 80% of ABC Ltd, it will include all of ABC Ltd's profit after tax in its own consolidated accounts on the basis that it controls all of ABC Ltd's operations. However, it does not own all of that profit, with 20% belonging to the minority interests. The 20% of ABC Ltd's profit after tax that belongs to the minority interests is deducted from the profit after tax, leaving the amount of profit attributable to the shareholders in XYZ plc.

9. Extraordinary items

An extraordinary item is a large one-off item, similar to an exceptional item, that requires separate disclosure in order to ensure that the truth in the accounts (the trends, ratios, etc.) is not distorted. An extraordinary item

- Is material.

- Possesses a **high degree of abnormality** which arises from events or transactions that fall **outside** the ordinary activities of the business.

- Is not expected to recur.

Note that this definition is exceedingly restrictive and it is highly unusual that a profit and loss account will have an extraordinary item shown. For that reason our illustrative accounts have shown the positioning of the item in the accounts but given a nil amount. In such a case, a company would dispense with the line altogether.

Tax is payable on extraordinary items. The figure that would be shown on the face of the profit and loss account would be a net of tax figure.

10. Dividends

These represent the cash dividends paid out or proposed to be paid out to shareholders net of lower rate income tax (10%).

Most of the time companies pay out dividends which are less than their profits after tax, i.e. the dividend is being paid from this year's profits and is said to be covered. It is **not essential for a dividend to be covered**, however. It may be financed from previously retained profits which, as we have seen, are accumulated in the balance sheet profit and loss account balance. XYZ plc's dividend for 2004 is uncovered in our example.

In most cases, UK companies pay dividends in two stages.

- **Interim dividend paid** – this is paid out during the year based on the half year's performance.

- **Final dividend proposed** – this is paid to shareholders following the approval of the year-end accounts at the annual general meeting.

5.4 Capital and revenue expenditure

5.4.1 Capital expenditure

Capital expenditure is expenditure on acquiring or enhancing fixed assets or their operating capacity. As such the benefits will be derived from this expenditure over the remaining life of the asset. Hence this expenditure is added to the value of fixed assets (is capitalised) on the balance sheet and will subsequently be depreciated through the profit and loss account.

5.4.2 Revenue expenditure

Revenue expenditure is expenditure incurred in

- Acquiring assets to be sold for conversion into cash, e.g. stock.
- Manufacturing, selling, distributing goods, e.g. wages.
- Day-to-day administrative expenses, e.g. electricity, telephone.
- Maintenance of fixed assets, e.g. repairs.

Revenue expenditure is charged directly against profits for the period to which it relates.

6 CASH FLOW STATEMENTS

6.1 Introduction

6.1.1 Background

The balance sheet and profit and loss account are prepared on an accruals basis. They give no indication of the effects of the operations of the business on its cash flows. It should always be noted that profits do not correspond exactly to cash. A company may be very profitable but almost bankrupt (unable to pay its liabilities as they fall due).

Since cash is such an important figure in determining the continuing existence of a company, we need a statement showing how the company's financial resources have been acquired and have been used in order to highlight the liquidity position and trends of the company.

FRS 1 *Cash Flow Statements* lays down the current rules to be followed in the preparation of the cash flow statement for UK companies. However, the exam only requires you to know the format of the cash flow statement under International Accounting Standard 7 (IAS 7).

6.2 Cash flow format (IAS 7)

International Accounting Standard 7 requires the cash flow of the company or group to be analysed under the following three headings.

- **Operating Activities** – The main revenue-producing activities of the company comprising cash received from customers for sales made and cash paid to suppliers and employees for costs. It also includes the tax and interest payments.

- **Investing Activities** – The acquisition and disposal of long-term assets.

- **Financing Activities** – Cash flows that alter the company's equity capital and borrowing structure.

The illustration below shows how a cash flow statement will appear in the accounts of XYZ plc under IAS 7 after its implementation in 2005.

XYZ plc – group cash flow statement for the year ended 31 December 2005

	2006 £'000	2005 £'000
Operating activities		
Cash receipts from customers	X	X
Cash paid to suppliers and employees	(X)	(X)
Income taxes paid	(X)	(X)
Interest paid	(X)	(X)
Net cash from operating activities	X	X
Investing activities		
Interest received	X	X
Dividends received	X	X
Proceeds on disposal of fixed assets	X	X
Purchases of fixed assets (CAPEX)	(X)	(X)
Net cash used in investing activities	(X)	(X)
Financing activities		
Dividends paid	(X)	(X)
Repayments of borrowings	(X)	(X)
Proceeds on issue of bonds or equities	X	X
New bank loans raised	X	X
Increase (decrease) in bank overdrafts	X	(X)
Net cash from financing activities	X	X
Net increase/(decrease) in cash and cash equivalents	X	(X)

6.3 Profit v cash

Trade certainly causes cash to flow, for example when customers pay or suppliers are paid, therefore trade does impact on cash flows. However, not all profit and loss items result in an immediate cash flow or even any cash flow at all, for example

- **Depreciation:** the cash flow arises when the original fixed asset is purchased from the supplier, the profit and loss account depreciation charge is **not** a cash flow.

- **Sales on credit/purchases on credit:** cash flows in relation to these items arise when the amounts are actually received/paid which is after they have been credited/charged within the profit and loss account.

- **Accrued expenses/prepaid expenses:** cash flows arise when these expenses are settled which, again, differs from when they are recognised in the profit and loss account.

These differences between accounting entries and movements of the actual cash must be reconciled in the notes to the accounts to show the net cash flow of operations.

6.3.1 Net cash inflow from/absorbed by operating activities

The net cash arising from operations, i.e. the cash generated corresponding to the operating profit in the profit and loss account. This figure will be supported by a note that reconciles from the operating profit figure. What factors do we need to take into account to undertake this reconciliation?

The answer turns out to be three types of transaction.

- Income or expenses that are not the direct result of any cash flow, e.g. depreciation or profits and losses on disposal of fixed assets.

- Provisions and expenditure incurred in respect of previously provided costs.

- Movements in working capital.

We will illustrate these points by building up a simple example. Please note that the exam does not require you to be able to calculate a cash flow statement and so this example is just to aid your understanding of non-cash items.

Illustration

Cash only business

If we had a cash only business (i.e. hold no other assets) that generated cash sales of £5,000 and cash purchases (cost of sales) of £4,000 then its profit and cash from operations would both be £1,000. For this type of business, cash does correspond to profit.

Depreciation and profits on disposal

If this business owns a fixed asset bought some time ago that it is depreciating at £200 per annum then the operating profit would now be reduced to £800, though the cash from operations is still £1,000, i.e. the reconciliation is

Reconciliation from Operating Profit to Net Cash from Operations

	£
Operating profit	800
Add: depreciation	200
Net cash generated by operations	1,000

That is we need to add back any expenses deducted in arriving at the operating profit that do not cause cash to flow. Similarly, we would need to deduct any income that has not caused a direct cash inflow, such as profits on disposal.

Provisions

A provision can impact on the cash flow statement in two ways.

- When it is set up.
- When the provided expenditure is paid.

Setting up a provision

The impact on this reconciliation of setting up a provision is identical to that for depreciation, in that it is an expense that does not result from a cash flow. Hence, in a year when provisions are set up we will need to add these in to this reconciliation. For example, if our company above made a restructuring provision of £100, then the operating profit would be reduced down to £700 and the reconciliation would become

Reconciliation from Operating Profit to Net Cash from Operations

	£
Operating profit	700
Add: depreciation	200
restructuring provision set up	100
Net cash generated by operations	1,000

Paying for previously provided costs

When we make a payment against previously provided expenses, this does not impact on this year's operating profit (it impacted when the provision was set up), but it clearly does reduce cash.

If our company had paid £50 this year against previously provided costs, then our net cash from operations would be reduced to £950 without there being any impact on this year's operating profit, and our reconciliation would become

Reconciliation from Operating Profit to Net Cash from Operations

	£
Operating profit	700
Add: depreciation	200
restructuring provision set up	100
Less: previously provided cost paid	(50)
Net cash generated by operations	950

Thus, we need to deduct such items from this reconciliation.

Working capital items

Finally, if our sales had been on credit, then we would not have received this £5,000 cash and hence, our cash absorbed by operations would be down £5,000 to (£4,050). The reconciliation would then be

Reconciliation from Operating Profit to Net Cash from Operations

	£
Operating profit	700
Add: depreciation	200
restructuring provision set up	100
Less: previously provided cost paid	(50)
	950
Less: increase in debtors	(5,000)
Net cash absorbed by operations	(4,050)

Thus, the increase in debtors must be deducted.

Thinking about this logically for a second, if we increase non-cash working capital, it must be at the expense of cash, all other things being equal, e.g. buying stock for cash increases stock but reduces cash. Hence, this same rule applies for all non-cash working capital items (stock and creditors).

An increase in stock or debtors causes a deduction, an increase in creditors an addition to this reconciliation.

6.4 Free cash flow

6.4.1 The purpose of free cash flow

The purpose of the calculation of free cash flow is to identify the surplus cash flow that a company is generating. This free cash flow can then be used to evaluate a company. At a simplistic level, the current level of free cash flow can be compared to the value of the company, giving a multiple for comparison with other companies. At a more complex level, free cash flow can be forecast into the future and the present value of the free cash flow calculated, giving a valuation of the business.

6.4.2 The definition of free cash flow

The definition of free cash flow varies quite substantially between companies and analysts, largely because of what they are trying to achieve with their definition. As a result, it is not possible to be exhaustive when defining free cash flow and the various ways in which it may be calculated. We will, therefore, focus on two major categories of definitions – free cash flow to equity and free cash flow to the enterprise.

6.4.3 Enterprise cash flow and equity cash flow

Enterprise cash flow represents the total cash flow generated by a business or enterprise that is available to service all providers of capital, including equity investors, preference share investors, debt investors and minority interests.

Equity cash flow represents the cash flow generated by a business that is available to service the providers of equity finance.

Although it may seem more appropriate to focus on equity cash flow at first sight, since we are trying to assess the business from the point of view of its equity investors, enterprise cash flow has an important part to play in the analysis process. The reason for this is that it ignores the level of gearing and other related financial factors when analysing a business.

In addition, enterprise cash flow is a useful benchmark for comparisons across companies. Since many companies in different countries will have different gearing levels, even though they are in the same industry, it will not be easy to compare their businesses based on equity cash flows. A more appropriate comparison would be to look at multiples based on enterprise cash flow. For example, cash flow multiples based on turnover, research and development costs, number of locations, etc. can be calculated and compared across the international sector.

6.4.4 Free cash flow for equity

If we wish to establish the free cash flow for equity, the analyst would aim to identify the surplus cash flow available after all other non-discretionary costs have been met. This could therefore be defined as follows.

	£
Net cash from operating activities (after tax and interest)	X
Less: capital expenditure	(x)
Less: preference dividends	(x)
Free cash flow for equity	**X**

Note that this is not the only possible definition of free cash flow for equity – however, it does aim to highlight the key issues to consider when calculating such a cash flow figure.

6.4.5 Free cash flow for the enterprise

The free cash flow to the enterprise is often referred to as 'net operating cash flow' and it can be calculated in the following way.

	£
Net cash from operating activities	X
Less: tax payments	(x)
Less: capital expenditure	(x)
Free cash flow for the enterprise	**X**

The free cash flow is the total amount of cash the company generates after funding purchases of fixed assets and any required increases in working capital, assuming that there is no debt. As such, it represents the maximum amount that a company could pay out to all its investors, assuming that the company is ungeared and has no commitment to pay interest to debt investors.

7 ANALYSIS OF ACCOUNTS

7.1 Introduction

The financial statements, incorporating the profit and loss account statement, the balance sheet, the cash flow statement and all the associated notes, contain a vast amount of information. The role of ratios is to distil this information into a more usable form for analysis purposes.

The financial statements are primarily prepared for company shareholders, however, they may have several other users, such as lenders, creditors, the Government, tax authorities etc. Each of these groups will use the account to provide an indication of the

- Returns they are receiving.
- Risks they are facing.

Ratios are most effective for analysing the performance of companies in the **same or similar industry** sector. A number of fairly standard ratios have been developed to assist with this process, and these can be grouped under three headings.

7.1.1 Profitability ratios

Ratios that assess the trading or operating performance of the company, i.e. levels of trading profits generated, and the productivity of trading assets. We have already met two measures in this area: gross profit margin and operating profit margin.

7.1.2 Financial gearing ratios

Ratios that assess the risks to the providers of finance, by analysing the company's exposure to debt.

7.1.3 Investors' ratios

Ratios that assess the returns to the providers of finance, who may be either shareholders or lenders.

Throughout our review of ratios, we will draw examples from the balance sheet and profit and loss account data for Illustration plc, which can be found at the end of this chapter.

7.2 Profitability ratios

7.2.1 Return on capital employed

This is a measure of the level of profitability generated by the management of a company.

Basic calculation

The return on capital employed is calculated as

Formula to learn

$$\text{ROCE} = \frac{\text{Profit before interest payable and tax}}{\text{Capital employed}} \times 100\%$$

Profit

This profit figure can be viewed as **operating profit**, i.e. the profits that management have generated from the resources they have available. It is specifically **before** interest payable since this will clearly be dependent on the financing of the business – the larger the loan, the larger the interest payable.

In the examination, you may be given the profit before tax figure and the interest payable and be asked to calculate operating profit, as follows.

	£
Profit before tax	3,673
Add back: interest payable	2,811
Operating profit	6,484

Capital employed

Capital employed could be viewed from the financing side as

Formula to learn

> Capital employed = Shareholders' funds + Loans

£37,486 = £33,041 + £4,445

or from the trading side as

Formula to learn

> Capital employed = Total assets − Current liabilities

£37,486 = (£23,499 + £57,653) − £43,666

Example – Illustration plc

$$\text{ROCE} = \frac{£6,484}{£37,486} \times 100\%$$

$$\text{ROCE} = 17.3\%$$

7.3 Financial gearing ratios

These ratios deal with the financing side of the balance sheet and consider the relationships between

- Interest-bearing borrowed capital on which the return (i.e. coupon or dividends) must be paid.
- Shareholders' capital on which the return (i.e. dividend distribution) is optional.

It is generally accepted that high levels of gearing imply high financial risks for the company.

7.3.1 Debt to equity ratio

Basic calculation

This is a relationship that shareholders would consider as a measure of the risk to their dividends.

Formula to learn

> $$\text{Debt to equity} = \frac{\text{Interest bearing loans}}{\text{Equity shareholders' funds}} \times 100\%$$

Considerations

We consider only interest-bearing debt since this is what is causing the risk to profit before tax, hence ultimately the profits after tax and amounts available for payment as dividends to our shareholders.

Example – Illustration plc

$$\text{Debt to equity} = \frac{£2,372 + £2,073}{£33,041} \times 100\%$$

$$\text{Debt to equity} = \frac{£4,445}{£33,041} \times 100\%$$

$$\text{Debt to equity} = 13.5\%$$

Equity shareholders' funds are given by the equity share capital and all of the reserves.

7.3.2 Net debt to equity ratio

This is an alternative to the above, and takes account of the cash that a business may also hold that could be used to repay debt.

Formula to learn

$$\text{Net debt to equity} = \frac{\text{Debt (as above)} - \text{Cash and current asset investments}}{\text{Equity shareholders' funds}} \times 100\%$$

Considerations

We should consider the ability of the company to use the cash it has available to repay debt.

Example – Illustration plc

$$\text{Net debt to equity} = \frac{£4,445 \,(\text{as above}) - £1,000 - £926}{£33,041} \times 100\%$$

$$\text{Net debt to equity} = \frac{£2,519}{£33,041} \times 100\%$$

$$\text{Net debt to equity} = 7.6\%$$

7.3.3 Interest cover

Basic calculation

This ratio considers gearing from the viewpoint of the profit and loss account statement and measuring the capacity of the firm to meet its interest obligations.

Formula to learn

$$\text{Interest cover} = \frac{\text{Profit before interest payable and tax}}{\text{Interest payable}}$$

Considerations

The interest cover provides a measure of the ability of the company to pay the fixed interest on borrowings from profits for the year. Clearly, the higher the level of interest cover, the less risk there is to either shareholders or lenders. However, there is no optimal level.

Example – Illustration plc

$$\text{Interest cover} = \frac{£6,484 \text{ (see ROCE above)}}{£2,811}$$

Interest cover = 2.31×

7.4 Investors' ratios

Earnings per share

Earnings per share (EPS) is the one ratio for which there are some rules regarding the calculation. These are laid out in FRS 14, which defines the EPS as

Formula to learn

$$\text{EPS} = \frac{\text{Earnings attributable to ordinary shareholders}}{\text{Number of ordinary shares}}$$

Earnings are defined as consolidated profit **after**

- Tax.
- Minority interests.
- Extraordinary items.
- **Preference** dividends.

Earnings therefore represent the remaining profits available to the ordinary shareholders.

Example – Illustration plc

$$\text{EPS} = \frac{£2,301}{18,762 \text{ shares}}$$

EPS = 12.3p

Fully diluted earnings per share

The objective of the fully diluted earnings per share figure is to warn shareholders of the company's possible future deterioration in the earnings per share figure, as a result of an obligation to issue new shares. There are a number of reasons why earnings could be diluted in the future.

- Convertible loan stock in issue.
- Convertible preference shares in issue.
- Options issued by and exercisable on the company.
- Warrants in issue.

Each of these circumstances may result in more shares being issued in future years. These would be taken into account when calculating the fully diluted earnings per share.

Fully diluted earnings per share is calculated on the basis that conversion of the debentures/preference shares or the exercise of warrants/options has already occurred. The impact of the notional conversion/exercise on earnings per share is calculated, and the result is fully diluted earnings per share.

7.4.1 Price/earnings (P/E) ratio

The Price/Earnings ratio is calculated as follows.

Formula to learn

$$\text{Price/Earnings} = \frac{\text{Current market price per share}}{\text{Earnings per share}}$$

Considerations

The P/E ratio expresses the number of years' earnings represented by the current market price.

Example – Illustration plc

If we take our current share price as £2.20 and our EPS figure as 12.3p, the P/E ratio is

$$\text{Price/Earnings} = \frac{220p}{12.3p}$$

$$= 17.9 \text{ years}$$

Analysis points

The significance of a P/E ratio can only be judged in relation to the ratios of other companies in the same type of business. If the median P/E ratio for an industry sector was 8, a ratio of 12 for a particular company would suggest that the shares of that company were in great demand, possibly because a rapid growth of earnings was expected. Note that **growth** (and therefore a **high P/E**) can be generated by retaining a large proportion of earnings and paying **low dividends** and reinvesting the earnings to grow the business. A **low ratio**, say 4 for example, would indicate a company, not greatly favoured by investors, which probably has **poor growth prospects**.

Alternatively, a high P/E ratio might indicate that a company is overpriced (overvalued) and a low P/E ratio might indicate that a company is underpriced (undervalued).

Historic versus prospective price/earnings ratios

If the earnings figures used are the published figures for the last year, this gives the historic price/earnings ratio. Alternatively, an analyst may look at the earnings which have been forecast by equity research analysts and calculate a prospective or future predicted price/earnings ratio.

7.4.2 Net dividend yield

The net dividend yield of an ordinary share is calculated as follows.

Formula to learn

$$\text{Net dividend yield} = \frac{\text{Net dividend per share}}{\text{Current market price per share}} \times 100\%$$

Example – Illustration plc

$$\text{Net dividend yield} = \frac{6.42p}{220p} \times 100\%$$

$$\text{Net dividend yield} = 2.92\%$$

Analysis points

A high net dividend yield suggests that the company is paying reasonable levels of income. However, a high yield may be due, in part, to a relatively low share price, indicating that the company has low growth prospects. Investors who believe that the company has good growth prospects would buy the share, driving the price up and reducing the yield.

Therefore, it is also true that companies with high P/E ratios tend to have low dividend yields, and vice versa.

7.4.3 Dividend cover

Dividend cover is used to assess the likelihood of the existing dividend being maintained. The dividend cover is calculated as follows.

Formula to learn

$$\text{Dividend cover} = \frac{\text{Earnings per share}}{\text{Net dividend per share}}$$

Example – Illustration plc

$$\text{Dividend cover} = \frac{12.3p}{6.42p}$$

$$\text{Dividend cover} = 1.92\times$$

Analysis points

An unusually high dividend cover implies that the company is retaining the majority of its earnings, presumably with the intention of reinvesting to generate growth.

A company **may** choose to pay a **larger dividend than that year's earnings** (in which case dividend cover will be <1). Where this occurs, the company is drawing on past reserves and is said to be paying an **uncovered dividend**.

7.5 Enterprise value to EBITDA

7.5.1 Definition

EV to EBITDA is calculated as follows.

Formula to learn

$$\text{EV to EBITDA} = \frac{\text{Enterprise value}}{\text{EBITDA}}$$

7.5.2 Enterprise value

Enterprise value is the total value of all the ordinary shareholders' equity, preference shares and net debt.

Formula to learn

Enterprise value = Market value of ordinary shares + Market value of preference shares + Market value of debt – Cash and investments

7.5.3 EBITDA (earnings before interest, tax, depreciation and amortisation)

Earnings	X
Add: corporation taxes	X
Add: net interest expense	X
Add: depreciation and amortisation	X
EBITDA	X

7.5.4 Key issues regarding EV/EBITDA

This ratio looks at the amount of debt **and** equity that a company has and then looks at the returns available to debt **and** equity holders. Contrast this with the P/E ratio, which looks at earnings (returns available to equity holders only) and the amount of equity a company has. This means that EV/EBITDA can be used to compare companies with different amounts of debt.

It is not affected by differences in depreciation and amortisation methods. It is, therefore, frequently used in capital intensive industries with high depreciation charges, e.g. utility companies.

Illustration plc

Balance sheet as at 31 December

	£	£
Fixed assets		
Intangible		3,926
Tangible		18,731
Investments		842
		23,499
Current assets		
Stock	19,420	
Debtors	36,307	
Investments	926	
Cash	1,000	
	57,653	
Current liabilities		
Trade creditors	35,781	
Tax	1,625	
Others	6,260	
	43,666	
Net Current Assets		13,987
Total assets less current liabilities		37,486
Long-term liabilities		
Secured loans	2,073	
Unsecured loans	2,372	
		(4,445)
Net Assets		33,041

	£
Share Capital	
£1 (NV) ordinary shares	18,762
Reserves	
Share premium account reserve	2,455
Revaluation reserve	2,681
Profit and loss account reserve	9,143
Shareholders' Funds	33,041

Profit and loss account statement

	£
Turnover	135,761
Cost of sales	(83,604)
Gross profit	52,157
Distribution costs	(22,961)
Administration costs	(22,712)
Operating profit	6,484
Interest paid	(2,811)
Profit before tax	3,673
Tax	(1,372)
Profit after tax	2,301
Dividends	(1,204)
Retained profit	1,097
Earnings per share	12.30p
Dividend per share	6.42p

CHAPTER ROUNDUP

- There are three sources of regulation relating to the accounts of a quoted company. They are Companies Acts, the UKLA Listing Rules and the Professional Accounting Standards.

- There are three financial reports that are crucial to the accounting process at a company. These are the Balance Sheet, Income Statement (Profit and Loss Account) and the Cash Flow Statement.

- The balance sheet shows the accounting value of a company at one particular date split into:
    - Fixed assets
    - Current assets
    - Current liabilities
    - Long-term liabilities

  The net of these items is described as net assets.

  This is represented by shareholder funds made up of:
    - Share capital
    - Share premium reserve
    - Revaluation reserve
    - Other reserves
    - Profit and loss account reserve

- Capital employed = Fixed assets + current assets – current liabilities (how funds are being used in a company).

  Capital employed = shareholders funds + long term liabilities (where the funds came from: equity plus debt).

- The profit and loss account analyses how the company has generated the profit or loss for the period. It is split into gross profit, operating profit, profit before tax, profit after tax and retained profit to show the effect of each set of deductions from the turnover of a company.

- The cash flow statement will analyse the cash movements through the year under three headings (operating, investing and financing cash flows).

- The profitability ratio Return on Capital Employed (ROCE) shows PBIT return on capital employed.

- Two important measures to be familiar with are Earnings per Share (EPS) and Dividend per Share (DPS). These lead on to the calculation of the "P/E Ratio" and "Dividend Cover".

- Financial gearing ratios show the ratio of debt to equity finance. Interest cover analyses whether PBIT is enough to pay the current interest payable.

- Investors' ratios look at the dividend or earnings per share compared to the share price. The sustainability of dividend returns may be assessed by dividend cover. The EV/EBITDA ratio will assess the return to both equity and debt.

EQUATION ROUNDUP

Net assets $= $ Shareholders' funds

Gross profit margin $= \dfrac{\text{Gross profit}}{\text{Turnover}} \times 100\%$

ROCE $= \dfrac{\text{Profit before interest payable and tax}}{\text{Capital employed}} \times 100\%$

Capital employed $= $ Shareholders' funds + Loans

Capital employed $= $ Total assets - Current liabilities

Debt of equity $= \dfrac{\text{Interest bearing loans}}{\text{Equity shareholders' funds}} \times 100\%$

Net debt of equity $= \dfrac{\text{Debt (as above)} - \text{Cash and current asset investments}}{\text{Equity shareholders' funds}} \times 100\%$

Interest cover $= \dfrac{\text{Profit before interest payable and tax}}{\text{Interest payable}}$

EPS $= \dfrac{\text{Earnings attributable to ordinary shareholders}}{\text{Number of ordinary shares}}$

Price/Earnings $= \dfrac{\text{Current market price per share}}{\text{Earnings per share}}$

Net dividend yield $= \dfrac{\text{Net dividend per share}}{\text{Current market price per share}} \times 100\%$

Dividend cover $= \dfrac{\text{Earnings per share}}{\text{Net dividend per share}}$

EV to EBITDA $= \dfrac{\text{Enterprise value}}{\text{EBITDA}}$

Enterprise value $= $ Market value of ordinary shares + Market value of preference shares + Market value of debt − Cash and investments

TEST YOUR KNOWLEDGE

Check your knowledge of the chapter here, without referring back to the text.

1. What are three sources of regulations in relation to listed companies' accounts?

2. List three possible current liabilities.

3. What is the accounting term for goods and services used during the year but not yet paid for?

4. What are the three major headings for cash flow under IAS 7?

5. What is meant by 'capital employed'?

6. What is the equation for return on capital employed?

7. What is the significant difference between the debt to equity ratio and the net debt to equity ratio?

TEST YOUR KNOWLEDGE: ANSWERS

1. (i) Legal Rules (Companies Act).
    (ii) The UK Listing Authority (UKLA) Listing Rules.
    (iii) Professional accounting rules (International Accounting Standards).

    See Section 2.1

2. Current liabilities include, bank overdrafts, corporation tax payable, trade accounts payable, accruals and loans repayable within one year.

    See Section 4.4.(note 6)

3. This is referred to as accrued expenses and appears in current liabilities.

    See Section 4.4.(note 7)

4. (i)   Operating cash flow
    (ii)   Investing cash flow
    (iii) Financing cash flow

    See Section 6.2

5. Capital employed refers to shareholders' funds plus long-term liabilities. It can also be shown as total assets minus current liabilities.

    See Section 7.2.1

6. ROCE = PBIT/Capital employed × 100%

    See Section 7.2.1

7. The debt to equity ratio calculates interest bearing loans divided by equity shareholder funds, where net debt to equity adjusts the debt by using only 'interest bearing loans – cash and current asset investments.' This is because the cash and current assets could be used to repay debt.

    See Section 7.3.2

9

Capital Structure

INTRODUCTION

When a company wishes to raise finance there are two main types of securities it can issue: equities and debt. This chapter looks at the main characteristics of both securities and their secondary issue methods (such as a rights issue).

The cost of capital will vary according to its type. It is important to realise the tax advantages of issuing debt, but at the same time be aware of their priority on interest and debt repayments.

CHAPTER CONTENTS

CHAPTER LEARNING OBJECTIVES

Equity Capital

- **Know** the typical characteristics of ordinary shares including voting rights, rights to dividends and rights to participate in a surplus on winding-up.

- **Know** the typical characteristics of preference shares including redeemable, cumulative and convertible preference shares.

- **Know** the tax treatment of dividends for the issuer of shares.

- **Understand** the meaning of the term 'listed' in relation to a company's shares.

- **Know** the *main* types of investor in listed and unlisted shares and their typical reasons for investing, including: pension funds, insurance companies, mutual funds, venture capital investors (including VCTs in the UK), directors/employees and private individuals.

- **Understand** the roles of the professional advisers in an IPO.

  - Reporting accountants.
  - Sponsor.
  - Book runner/global co-ordinator.
  - Underwriting syndicate.
  - Lawyers.
  - PR consultants.

- **Understand** why a company may choose to raise additional capital via a rights issue or through a placing/open offer (pre-emptive and non pre-emptive).

- **Understand** the basic mechanics of a rights issue and placing/open offer including the options available to a shareholder and the role of the underwriters.

- **Be able to calculate** the theoretical ex-rights price.

- **Understand** pricing of secondary issues as required by UK Listing Rules, AIM Rules, Association of British Insurers and National Association of Pension Funds.

- **Understand** the effect of clawback by qualifying shareholders under a placing or an open offer.

- **Understand** how the bookbuilding and pricing process works.

Debt Capital

- **Know** the typical characteristics of the main types of debt instrument (including loans, bonds, convertibles, mandatory convertibles, exchangeables and zero coupon bonds).

- **Know** the principal characteristics of the following alternative forms of debt financing: invoice factoring, finance leasing and sale and repurchase agreements.

- **Know** the difference between fixed rate and floating rate interest.

- **Understand** that debt can be secured, and that security can be given through either a fixed or floating charge.

- **Understand** the difference between senior and subordinated debt.

- **Understand** the difference between par and premium redemption.

- **Understand** the tax treatment of interest for the issuer of debt.

- **Understand** that debt can be listed or unlisted.

Cost of Capital

- **Understand** the meaning of the weighted average cost of capital.

- **Know** that the cost of equity is equal to the expected rate of total return on shares.

- **Know** that the expected rate of total return on shares can be estimated using the Capital Asset Pricing Model (CAPM).

- **Understand** what beta means in relation to equities.

- **Be able to apply** beta to share price movements.

1 EQUITY CAPITAL

1.1 The nature of a share

The shareholders of a company are the **owners** of the company. Historically, businesses were so small that one individual could finance the whole enterprise. As businesses became larger, it was difficult for one individual to provide sufficient finance for the operation. Companies allow a large number of individuals to pool their capital into one organisation, therefore facilitating the formation of larger companies.

Each owner (shareholder) contributes capital and, in return, receives shares (i.e. share of ownership). The more an individual contributes, the greater the allotment of shares. As the owners, the shareholders take the greatest risks. If the company performs badly, they will lose their money. However, they normally have only a **limited liability**; limited to the amount that they agreed to contribute.

On the other hand, if the company prospers, then the shareholders will reap the rewards. Debt, such as a corporate bond, will only ever receive its interest, or coupon payments and the capital repayment upon maturity, whereas shares do not normally have a fixed return, and participate fully in the remaining profits of the business.

1.2 Equity shares

Ordinary shares are often referred to as **equity shares**. Here, the term equity means that they have an equal right to share in the profits of the company. For example, if a company has 10,000 ordinary shares, each share is entitled to $\dfrac{1}{10,000}$ of the profits made during any period. These profits may be distributed by way of a dividend, or can be retained within the operation in order to increase the potential for future profit.

1.3 The normal characteristics

The rights of ordinary shares are detailed in the company's constitutional documents and in particular, the **Articles of Association**.

1. It is normal for ordinary shares to carry the **right to vote**. This means that the holder of any ordinary shares may attend, speak and vote at any meetings held by the company. Whilst the day-to-day control and management of the company is dealt with by the directors and managers,

the shareholders must retain the right to decide upon the most important issues that affect the business.

2. The shareholders also have an equal right to share in any **dividends** that are distributed by the company. However, a dividend distribution is not guaranteed. If profits for the year are low, the company will be unlikely to pay a dividend. The dividend of a UK company is received net of 10% withholding tax. This is referred to as 'franked investment income'.

3. Additionally, on a **winding-up** of the company, the ordinary shareholders are entitled to participate in any surplus funds available after all the creditors have been paid and preference shareholders have been redeemed.

1.4 Special types of ordinary shares

1.4.1 Founder shares

A business may find itself requiring additional equity finance but the original, or founding shareholders, may not wish to relinquish control of the company. One solution is to issue a new class of shares to the original shareholders (**founder shares**), with **enhanced voting rights** (say, 100 votes per share) to ensure the original shareholders will retain control of the company whilst still raising additional equity finance.

1.4.2 'A' class ordinary shares

An alternative to holding shares with enhanced voting rights, in order to maintain control, would be to issue new shares with **no voting rights**. These are commonly referred to as 'A' class ordinary shares.

1.4.3 Deferred shares

Deferred shares are shares with **some form of deferred rights** – either dividend or voting rights deferred for a period of time.

2 PREFERENCE SHARES

As mentioned above, ordinary shares carry the full risks and rewards of ownership. Another type of share which a company can issue is a **preference share**. These take on debt-like characteristics and offer only limited risks and returns.

2.1 The normal characteristics

A preference share is preferred in two basic ways.

1. The preference share **dividend must be paid out before any ordinary dividend can be paid**. It is conventional for preference shares to be **cumulative** and if the dividend is not paid in any one year, the arrears and the current year's preference dividend must be paid before any ordinary dividend can be paid in the future. The assumption is that preference shares are cumulative unless stated otherwise.

2. The second form of preferencing is on the order of payout on a winding-up. Preference shares **will be redeemed prior to ordinary shares**. On liquidation of the company, the preference shareholders will only ever receive the **nominal value** of the shares. This is not the case for ordinary or equity shares. Equity shares would receive anything that remains after all other investors have been paid (i.e. it could be more than nominal value).

In order to receive these benefits, preference shareholders must relinquish a number of rights normally attached to shares.

Firstly, the dividend on preference shares is **normally a fixed dividend**, expressed as a percentage of the nominal value. For example, 7% £1 preference shares: these shares would pay a dividend each year of 7p per share. The quoted rate on a preference share is **net** of income tax at 10%.

Secondly, it is conventional for preference shares to carry **no voting rights**. However, most company constitutions contain a clause which states that if the dividend on a cumulative preference share has not been paid for **five years**, preference shareholders will receive the right to attend and vote at general meetings of the company. It should be remembered that, as with all dividends, the payment is at the discretion of the directors and no shareholder may sue for a dividend.

2.1.1 Preference shares as investments

As we can see, preference shares offer the rewards one would normally see attached to a debt instrument – a fixed return with no voting rights. However, they carry greater risk since they are nearer the bottom of the liquidation priority table in the event of a winding-up.

There are, however, a number of special features that can be added to preference shares to enhance their attractiveness and make them interesting potential investments for individuals.

2.2 Special types of preference shares

Some preference shares can be specified as **participating shares**. A participating share has a right, when profits reach certain levels, to take a share of those profits as opposed to simply receiving a fixed return. This participation right **may** also apply to the proceeds on a winding-up (liquidation).

Preference shares may also be issued **with conversion rights**. These rights will allow the preference shares to be converted into a specified number of ordinary shares at a specified point in the future. As such, the preference share in this instance is more like a convertible debt instrument than a share.

Finally, preference shares may be given **specified redemption dates**. For the most part, ordinary shares are not redeemable but preference shares frequently carry a redemption date, making them seem once again more like debt than shares.

One key difference between preference shares and debt lies in the **tax treatment of the dividends**. Preference dividends, as well as ordinary dividends, are paid out of the company's after-tax profits and are therefore not allowable deductions for corporation tax. The dividends are subject to income tax, and are paid to the investor net of 10% withholding tax. Interest on debt, by contrast, is paid out of the company's pre-tax profits and is therefore an allowable deduction which reduces the company's profits for corporation tax purposes.

3　SECONDARY ISSUES OF SHARES

Once a company has done its Initial Public Offer of securities, it may use one of the following methods of secondary issuance of new securities. These include

- Rights issues.
- Open offers.
- Vendor placings.
- Placings.

Various advisors and professionals will assist the company in raising this additional finance. The sponsor will co-ordinate the activities of the other advisers, who may include

- **Reporting accountants**. The sponsor appoints independent reporting accountants to carry out detailed due diligence into the past record, current status and future prospects of the issuer. The accountants provide a **long form report** to the sponsor, giving full details of their findings. They will usually also provide a **working capital statement**, to support the sponsor's report to UKLA on the company's working capital position. Where necessary, the reporting accountants will also report on any profit forecasts or pro-forma accounts to be published by the issuer.

- **Lawyers**. The sponsor will also appoint lawyers to carry out legal due diligence on the company, to ensure that there is no legal or regulatory obstacle to its issue of securities. Additionally, lawyers to the issue will ensure that the process is carried out in accordance with the regulations.

- **PR consultants**. PR consultants are appointed at an early stage to ensure that the issue has wide publicity, that it is marketed as effectively as possible, and to enhance the attractiveness of the prospectus and of any advertising.

- **Book runner/global coordinator**. Where shares are being placed with institutions, the price is generally determined using the book building process (see below). The sponsor co-ordinates this process.

- **Underwriting syndicate**. Where the issue is underwritten the sponsor arranges and co-ordinates the process. The underwriter guarantees to buy any unsold shares under the issue.

3.1 Bookbuilding

Bookbuilding is an approach frequently used in the placing of larger issues. The issuing house sets a price range for the securities, based on the current market price of existing securities, its own in-house valuation and the reaction of potential investors to presentations by management. It then approaches potential institutional investors to solicit interest at this price range. The level of interest of investors, i.e. the number who wish to be on the issuing house's 'book', determines whether the final price is set at the higher or lower end of the price range.

3.2 Rights issues

A rights issue is an offer to existing shareholders to subscribe for new shares in the company in proportion to their existing holding of shares. It will usually be implemented by means of a renounceable letter or other negotiable document. This means that ownership of the document which evidences entitlement to the new shares can be transferred to a third party.

3.2.1 Pre-emption rights

Section 89 of the Companies Act 1985 states that where a company issues equity shares **for cash**, then it is obliged to offer them first to existing shareholders on a pro rata basis to their existing holding in the company. The shareholders must be given at least 21 days to decide whether to purchase the shares. If they do not, then the shares can be sold to outsiders, but the price must not be better than that offered to existing shareholders.

The objective of this law is to protect the equitable interests of existing shareholders and prevent shares in the company being issued by the directors to new shareholders, possibly at cheap prices, thus diluting the existing shareholders' interests.

3.2.2 Exemption for private companies

A private company is able to exclude the requirement for these pre-emption rights in its Articles of Association if it so desires. This exclusion is not allowed for public companies.

3.2.3 Disapplication of pre-emption rights by listed companies

Under S95 of the Companies Act, shareholders in listed companies may pass a special resolution disapplying pre-emption rights for a maximum period of **five years**. This maximum period is also confirmed in the Listing Rules.

However, listed companies will normally be allowed to disapply pre-emption rights only for issues of new shares amounting to a maximum of **5%** of the issued share capital in any **one year**, or 7½% on a **rolling three-year** basis, so long as they obtain shareholder approval. In addition, the Listing Rules do not normally permit non-pre-emptive issues at a discount of more than **10%** to the middle market price of the shares. Any discount greater than 10% requires shareholder approval.

3.2.4 Mechanics of a rights issue

Rights issues are made at a discount to the current market price to encourage shareholders to buy the shares and to ensure that the issue is a success. The greater the discount, the more incentive the shareholders have to take up the rights issue. There is no maximum share price discount for a rights issue. A deeply discounted rights issue does not therefore require underwriters to guarantee to buy any unsold shares under the rights issue.

For example, a 1 for 3 rights issue is made at a price of £4.00, when the current market price is £5.00 (the **cum rights price**).

A rights letter will be dispatched to each shareholder, telling them of their right to subscribe for a certain number of shares. For example, shareholders who currently own 3,000 shares will receive a letter telling them of their right to subscribe for 1,000 new shares at a price of £4.00 each, total £4,000. This letter may be referred to as a Provisional Allotment Letter, or PAL. An example letter is shown later in this section.

The rights letter will be dispatched to all shareholders who are on the register of shareholders on a particular date set by the company, referred to as the **on-register** day.

Once the rights letter has been dispatched to the owner of the shares on the 'on-register' day, the owner has four courses of action from which to choose.

1. To take up the shares and hold them.
2. To take up the shares and sell them.
3. To sell the rights 'nil paid'.
4. To do nothing.

If the shareholder does nothing before the rights expire, the company will then sell these nil-paid rights in the market place. Any surplus over the subscription price of £4.00 will then be dispatched to the shareholder. It should be noted that this fourth option is subject to the charges of the company, and may result in a very small payment, if any, to the shareholder.

The shareholder must be allowed **at least 21 calendar days** after the dispatch of the rights letter to consider which option to take. If, by the end of these 21 days, the shareholder has not taken up these rights, they will be deemed to have lapsed (point 4 above). If the shareholder wishes to take up the rights, he must return the rights letter to the company's registrars, together with a cheque for the appropriate amount.

The registrar then stamps the rights letter to indicate that the amount due has been paid and returns it to the original owner. From this point on, the receipted rights letter acts as a **temporary document of title**, and provides evidence of ownership of the underlying shares. The shareholder can then do one of two things: hold the shares, in which case a real share certificate (the **definitive document of title**) will be dispatched some time after the rights issue; or sell the shares.

If the shareholder elects to sell the shares using his temporary document of title, transfer of the shares is slightly different from that using registered share certificates. On the reverse of the rights letter are two forms: form X and form Y. **Form X** states that the owner transfers the rights to shares to the new shareholders named in **form Y**. Normally, the original owner signs form X and gives it with a blank form Y to the purchaser of the shares, which creates, in effect, a bearer document. The new owner **must register** his or her rights to these shares by a specified date – **the Registration of Renunciation** – which is generally four or so weeks prior to the dispatch of share certificates.

Rights Letter Timings

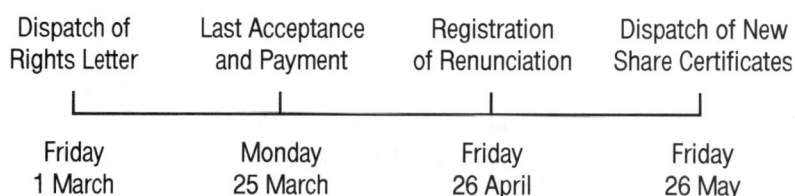

Dispatch of Rights Letter	Last Acceptance and Payment	Registration of Renunciation	Dispatch of New Share Certificates
Friday 1 March	Monday 25 March	Friday 26 April	Friday 26 May

In the example above, the rights letter is dispatched on Friday, 1 March. The recipient must accept the rights letter by sending payment by Monday 25 March. Failure to do so results in the lapse of the rights. In this event, the company would normally enter the market the following day and sell the shares at the then market price, any balance (in excess of the subscription price) being returned to the original shareholder.

Once the shareholder has received the receipted rights letter from the registrar, it can be converted into bearer form and can be used to trade, with form Y still blank, until Friday 26 April, when the registration of renunciation takes place. By that time, anyone who has purchased the receipted rights letter in renounceable form must have completed form Y and sent it to the registrar. This ensures that the share certificates are sent to the new holder on Friday 26 May.

Failure to register the transfer before the registration of renunciation date means that any subsequent transfer must be accompanied by a stock transfer form.

The third option open to the holder is **selling the rights nil paid**. The rights letter gives a shareholder the right to buy a share at a discounted price. Consequently, the holder can simply sell on his rights to this discount without having accepted it himself.

In order to sell the rights nil paid, the holder once again signs form X on the reverse of the rights letter, but this time, prior to applying to buy the new shares or paying for them. It is then the responsibility of the purchaser of the rights letter to accept the rights (i.e. by applying to buy new shares at the discounted price) by the **Last Acceptance and Payment** date which, in this example, is Monday 25 March.

To do this, form Y must also be completed – the registration of renunciation – and sent to the registrar, who stamps it and returns the receipted rights letter in the purchaser's own name. If the purchaser fails to take up the rights he has purchased, the company enters the market and sells the shares on behalf of the original shareholder, who receives any value resulting from the sale.

An example provisional allotment letter for a rights issue is shown on the following page.

PROVISIONAL ALLOTMENT LETTER

	ACCOUNT No.	ALLOTMENT No.
00708745	T4200116	15341916

BRITISH TELECOMMUNICATIONS PUBLIC LIMITED COMPANY

(Incorporated and registered in England No. 1800000)

RIGHTS ISSUE OF UP TO 1,975,580,052 NEW BT SHARES OF 25 PENCE EACH AT 300 PENCE PER SHARE
payable in full on acceptance not later than 9.30 a.m. on 15 June 2001

60171
MR ANDREW ROBERT DOUGHTY

15341916

Box 1 Registered holding of BT Shares at close of business on 9 May 2001	Box 2 Number of new BT Shares provisionally allotted to you	Box 3 Amount payable in full on acceptance at 300 pence per new BT Share not later than 9.30 a.m. on 15 June 2001
120	***36***	***£108.00***

All enquiries in connection with this letter should be made to:
Lloyds TSB Registrars
Antholin House
71 Queen Street
London EC4N 1SL
Telephone: 0808 100 4141 (UK only)
+44 20 7864 9074 (International calls)

Latest time and date for:	2001
Depositing Nil Paid Rights into CREST	3.00 p.m. on 11 June
Splitting nil paid	3.00 p.m. on 12 June
Acceptance and payment in full	9.30 a.m. on 15 June
Depositing fully paid rights into CREST	3.00 p.m. on 27 June
Splitting Fully Paid	3.00 p.m. on 27 June
Registration of renunciation	3.00 p.m. on 29 June
CREST accounts to be credited	2 July
Expected despatch of share certificates	by 16 July

TO ACCEPT IN FULL, PLEASE RETURN THE WHOLE OF THIS LETTER WITH A CHEQUE FOR THE AMOUNT SHOWN IN BOX 3 ABOVE (MADE PAYABLE TO "LLOYDS TSB BANK PLC — BT RIGHTS ISSUE" AND CROSSED "A/C PAYEE ONLY") TO LLOYDS TSB REGISTRARS AT THE ABOVE ADDRESS BY 9.30 A.M. ON 15 JUNE 2001. IF YOU WISH TO HAVE THE NEW BT SHARES REGISTERED IN YOUR NAME, YOU DO NOT NEED TO COMPLETE ANY OF THE DETAILS IN THE REST OF THIS LETTER.

Application has been made to the UK Listing Authority for the new BT Shares to be admitted to the Official List and application has been made to the London Stock Exchange for the new BT Shares to be admitted to trading on its market for listed securities. It is expected that Admission will become effective on 20 May 2001 and that dealings in rights to the new BT Shares will commence, nil paid, at 8.00 a.m. on 21 May 2001. If Admission has not become effective by such time (or such later time and/or date as Cazenove & Co. Ltd and Merrill Lynch International may agree with the Company, not being later than 3.00 p.m. on 29 May 2001) this document shall cease to be of any value and the provisional allotment will lapse and any payments received will be returned without interest. Copies of the UK Prospectus have been delivered to the Registrar of Companies in England and Wales for registration in accordance with section 149 of the Act and may be obtained from or inspected at the offices of Linklaters & Alliance, One Silk Street, London EC2Y 8HQ and the registered office of the Company. Copies of the US Prospectus may also be obtained from or inspected at Morgan Guaranty Trust Company of New York, JP Morgan Service Centre, P.O. Box 842006, Boston MA 02284-2006 ("Morgan Guaranty") or Georgeson Shareholder Communications Inc., 17 State Street, New York, New York or the registered office of the Company. Save where the context otherwise requires, words and expressions defined in the Prospectus shall have the same meaning in this PAL.

If you are a holder of BT Shares in the United States and you take up or transfer the rights represented by this Provisional Allotment Letter, you will be deemed to represent that you have received and read a copy of the US Prospectus. If you have not received a copy of the US Prospectus, you should contact, Georgeson Shareholder Communications Inc., 17 State Street, New York, New York 1000Y on +1 888 382 8303 to obtain a copy.

The attention of Qualifying Shareholders who have registered addresses outside the United Kingdom or who are citizens or residents of countries other than the United Kingdom or who are holding BT Shares for the benefit of such persons is drawn to note 7 on page 2 of this document, relating to Overseas Shareholders, and to the section headed "Overseas Shareholders" in paragraph 7 of Part 3 of the UK Prospectus or the paragraph entitled "Non-UK Holders of Shares" on page 32 of the US Prospectus.

If you wish to accept your rights and then wish the fully paid Provisional Allotment Letter to be returned to you, please tick this box. You need to have the fully paid Provisional Allotment Letter returned to you only if you want to deal in your Fully Paid Rights. Otherwise, the next document you receive will be a share certificate for your new BT Shares.

Box 4

Name and address of lodging agent. (If this box is not completed by the agent lodging this form for payment, this Provisional Allotment Letter will be returned, if requested, to the person(s) named above)	Received the amount payable on acceptance	Account No.	Allotment No.
		T4200116	15341916
		36	
		£108.00	
	For Lloyds TSB Registrars	02787537	

36

ACCOUNT No.

T4200116

ALLOTMENT No.

15341916

FORM X   **FORM OF RENUNCIATION**

To be completed if the original allottee(s) desire(s):

(i) to renounce all the Nil Paid Rights or Fully Paid Rights comprised herein (the original allottee may do so up to 3.00 p.m. on 29 June 2001); or

(ii) to obtain split Provisional Allotment Letters (the original allottee may do so up to 3.00 p.m. on 12 June 2001 (if nil paid) and up to 3.00 p.m. on 27 June 2001 (if fully paid)); or

(iii) (where the original allottee is a CREST member or CREST personal member) to convert the Nil Paid Rights or Fully Paid Rights represented by this letter into uncertificated form (that is, to deposit them in CREST).

To the Directors of British Telecommunications public limited company

I/We hereby renounce my/our right to the new BT Shares comprised in this Provisional Allotment Letter for the purposes of splitting or in favour of the person (s) named in the Registration Application Form (Form Y) or CREST Deposit Form below.

Notes for completion of this form

All joint allottees must sign. Any forms completed under a power of attorney must be accompanied by a certified copy of the power of attorney. A company must execute under its common seal which should be affixed in accordance with its articles of association or other regulations. Alternatively, a company to which section 36A of the Companies Act 1985 applies may execute this letter by a director and the company secretary or by two directors of the company signing the letter and bearing the name of the company above their signatures. Each of the officers signing the letter should state the office which he or she holds under his or her signature. Before signing, please read paragraph 7 on page 2 relating to Overseas Shareholders. If all the new BT Shares are to be registered in the name of the person(s) on page 1 of the document this Form X should not be completed. In the case of split letters, this Form X will be endorsed "Original Duly Renounced".

Dated ....

Signature(s) of
person (s)
named on
page 1 of this
document
{
....
....
....
....

FORM Y   **REGISTRATION APPLICATION FORM**

In the event of renunciation, this Form Y must be completed by or on behalf of the person(s) in whose name(s) the new BT Shares are to be registered unless such person(s) is/are (a) CREST member(s) and wish(es) to hold the new BT Shares in CREST, in which case the CREST Deposit Form below must be completed. THIS FORM Y SHOULD NOT BE COMPLETED IN THE NAME(S) OF THE ORIGINAL ALLOTTEE(S).

(1) Forename (s).. Surname...
(in full)   Mr., Mrs., Miss or title
(2) Forename (s).. Surname...
(in full)   Mr., Mrs., Miss or title
(3) Forename (s).. Surname...
(in full)   Mr., Mrs, Miss or title
(4) Forename (s).. Surname...
(in full)   Mr., Mrs., Miss or title
FULL POSTAL ADDRESS OF FIRST-NAMED APPLICANT OR FULL REGISTRATION DETAILS IF CORPORATE BODY

....

.... Postcode...................................

Stamp and/or name and address of agent (if any) lodging this Provisional Allotment Letter for a Share Certificate

For use between 18 June 2001 and 3.00 p.m. on 29 June 2001 (see paragraph 4 on page 2 of this document, relating to Share Certificates).

Name:...

Address:..

....
Note: to be completed only if share certificates are to be sent to an address other than shown on page 1 or, if Form Y on this page 4 is completed, other than to the address inserted in Form Y.

CONSOLIDATION LISTING FORM	
Allotment number of letter	No. of new BT Shares
Total number of allotment letters	Total number of new BT Shares
Allotment number of Principal Letter	

CREST DEPOSIT FORM

Before completing this form, please refer to paragraph 4 on page 3 of this letter and to the notes below. This form should only be completed by either: (i) the original allottee(s) (where the original allottee is a CREST member) if he/she wishes to convert the Nil Paid Rights or Fully Paid Rights (as appropriate) represented by this letter into uncertificated form (that is, to deposit them in CREST); or (ii) a person or persons to whom this letter has been renounced and who (being a CREST member) wish(es) to hold the Nil Paid Rights or Fully Paid Rights (as appropriate) represented by this letter in uncertificated form. Form X above must therefore also have been completed. Do not complete Form Y if you are completing the CREST Deposit Form.

Counter Location Stamp (a).	SDRN (b). Bar Code or Reference.

Full name(s) of the person(s) who wishes to convert Nil Paid Rights or Fully Paid Rights (as appropriate) into uncertificated form or to whom the Nil Paid Rights or Fully Paid Rights have been renounced. Such person(s) must be a CREST member (c).

Participant ID (d).	Member account ID (d).	Stamp of depositing CREST participant (e).

To the Directors of the Company

I/we (being the person(s) lodging this form) request you to enter on the relevant register of securities that the Nil Paid Rights or Fully Paid Rights (as appropriate) represented by this Provisional Allotment Letter are held in uncertificated form by the CREST member specified above to whom such rights have been renounced or as a result of conversion of Nil Paid Rights or Fully Paid Rights (as appropriate) from certificated form into uncertificated form.

Notes for completion of this form

(a) The Counter Location Stamp identifies the CCSS Counter where this letter has been processed and is applied by the Counter.
(b) The Stock Deposit Reference Number (SDRN) should be written or bar-coded in this space.
(c) No address is required, as the CREST member will be identifiable by its participant ID.
(d) Insert the participant ID of the CREST member to whom this letter has been renounced and the member account ID under which the Nil Paid Rights or Fully Paid Rights will be held in CREST.
(e) This should contain the Broker ID of the depositing CREST participant.
The depositing CREST participant by delivering this letter to CRESTCo authorises CRESTCo to deliver this letter to the Company and agrees to be deemed for all purposes to be the person(s) actually so delivering this letter. CRESTCo is delivering this letter at the direction and on behalf of the depositing CREST participant whose stamp appears herein and does not in any manner or to any extent warrant or represent the validity, genuineness or correctness of the instructions contained herein or the genuineness of the signature(s) of the transferor(s).

0325084

3.3 Theoretical Ex-Rights Price (TERP)

It is possible to calculate a theoretical change in the company's share price as a result of a rights issue, much in the same way as for a bonus issue. The theoretical ex-rights price may also be referred to as the TERP.

Example

A 1 for 3 rights issue @ £4.00, when market price (or cum-rights price) is £5.00.

Existing holding	3 shares	@ £5.00	£15.00
		=	
Shares issued as a result of the		@ £4.00	
rights issue	1 share	=	£4.00
	4 shares	@ ? =	£19.00

As a result of the rights issue, the shareholder has four indistinguishable (fungible) shares, with a total value of £19.00.

Therefore, each share now has a value of

$$\frac{£19.00}{4} = £4.75$$

As a result of the rights issue, the share price will, theoretically, fall from its current market level of £5.00 to £4.75. This new price of £4.75 is referred to as the theoretical ex-rights price. This reflects the dilution aspect of issuing one new share at £4.00 when the existing market price of shares is £5.00.

3.3.1 Nil paid values

If the new share price is £4.75, then the maximum price that anybody would be prepared to pay for the rights letter, which gives the right to buy the shares at £4.00, would be **75p**. Anything more than that and buyers may as well go into the market and buy the shares after the rights issue.

It must be stressed that we are dealing here with a purely **theoretical** situation. In reality, prices might reflect a number of other factors, and rise and fall by different amounts.

3.3.2 Maximum subscription at nil cost

A final point to consider is that the investor may have insufficient funds available to take up the rights, although he may be very keen to buy as many shares as possible. One solution to this is to split the rights letter into two components. One portion is sold at the nil paid value to raise finance. This money is then used to purchase the shares for as many of the remaining rights as possible. There is a simple formula for working out the number of shares that can be purchased in this fashion.

Example

If the investor owns 3,000 shares, he will receive the right to purchase an additional 1,000 shares (following the example of a 1 for 3 rights issue).

In order to take up as many rights to shares as possible, it will be necessary to sell the following number of rights.

$$\text{Number of rights available} \times \frac{\text{Subscription price}}{\text{Theoretical ex-rights price}}$$

$$1,000 \times \frac{\pounds4}{\pounds4.75} = 842.1\ (843)\ \text{(always round-up)}$$

Proof

	Rights		
Sell	843	@ £0.75 =	£632.25
Buy/Take up	157	@ £4.00 =	£628.00
	1,000		£4.25

It will be impossible to better this situation. If the investor sold one less right, there would be insufficient funds to take up this extra right.

3.4 Open offers

3.4.1 What is an open offer?

An open offer is pre-emptive offer to existing shareholders which is not allotted on renounceable documents. This means that the shareholder cannot sell on the right to subscribe for the open offer shares, unlike in a rights issue. An open offer will still be made pro rata to existing shareholdings in the company.

3.4.2 Requirements for open offers

The Listing Rules provide that in order to ensure that shareholders have adequate time to claim shares being offered by means of an open offer, there must be at least 15 business days between posting of the application forms to shareholders and when the offer closes.

An open offer will not be permitted where the offer price is at a discount of more than 10% to the middle market price of the shares when the offer is announced, unless the company is in severe financial difficulties or there are other exceptional circumstances and the company obtains shareholder approval.

3.4.3 Use of open offers

An open offer is often used in conjunction with a secondary placing, when it may be described as a 'placing with clawback'. Here, the offer shares are first placed conditionally with institutional investors, and then offered on a pre-emptive basis to the company's existing shareholders. To the extent that shareholders take up their entitlement to new shares, these shares are 'clawed back' from the institutional places. This structure has the effect of an underwriting of the open offer.

3.5 Placing

A company may select to market shares solely to external institutional investors, rather than issue shares to its existing shareholders. Provided it has complied with the requirements to disapply pre-emption rights, this is permissible and may be a quick and inexpensive way of raising additional capital for the company.

As with an open offer, a placing will not be permitted where the offer price is at a discount of more than 10% to the middle market price of the shares when the offer is announced, unless the company is in severe financial difficulties or there are other exceptional circumstances and the company obtains shareholder approval.

4 INVESTORS IN COMPANIES

A company may be incorporated as a private company (limited, or ltd) or as a public company (public limited company or plc). Only a plc may offer shares to the public, although it is not obliged to do so.

4.1 Who invests in equity?

Over its life, the company's shareholder base may change considerably.

- When first incorporated, it is usual for the managers and founders to be the first and only shareholders, perhaps supported by friends and family.

- As the business grows, it may seek additional finance. This may come from venture capital/private equity firms, which usually operate collective investment schemes for investment over a three-to-five year timescale in private companies. It might also offer shares to employees as rewards or inducements for their commitment to the business.

- Many companies will, at some stage, seek to raise equity capital by offering shares to the investment community at large. This will include major institutional investors such as insurance companies, pension funds, mutual funds and banks, as well as retail investors.

Once shares are offered to the public, the total capital of the company will be divided among a wide number of investors, each potentially taking on a small minority shareholding. To compensate them for the relatively low level of control that these investors will have, the company will typically offer some or all of the following incentives.

4.1.1 Liquidity

The company may arrange for its shares to be traded on a stock exchange. This will provide a secondary market on which investors can realise their shares into the most liquid of all assets – cash.

4.1.2 Returns

Some investors are primarily 'income' investors and will seek a steady rise in the dividend income achieved from their investment. Others invest for capital growth, seeking an increase in the market value of the company over the life of the investment.

4.2 Rationale for equity investment

The rationale for equity investment varies according to the investor, as follows.

4.2.1 Pension funds and insurance companies

These investors are investing the money received by them in the form of pension contributions and insurance premiums, in the hope of making sufficient returns to meet their long-term obligations. Accordingly, they are usually seeking a relatively low level of risk, with long-term capital growth. To minimise risk, their investments comprise a balanced portfolio of bonds, deposits and liquid, listed equities.

4.2.2 Venture capital investors

These investors are seeking a substantial return on a portfolio of investments in private companies over a three to five-year timespan. On average, their required compound average annual return is in the region of 30%, most of which will be achieved from the capital gain on an eventual sale or flotation of the investment. They have relatively little requirement for dividend income but, because of the lack of liquidity in their investment, will seek voting control and significant board influence.

4.2.3 Venture capital trusts

In the UK, it is possible for retail investors to buy shares in a Venture Capital Trust (VCT). This is a company whose shares are traded on the London Stock Exchange, and which invests in the shares of unlisted companies. A VCT operates in the same way as a venture capital investor, investing in private companies for a three to five-year timespan to achieve significant capital gain on an eventual sale or flotation of the investment. However, the VCT shareholders have the ability to buy and sell shares in the VCT, providing them with liquidity in their investment. VCTs have tax advantages which make them attractive to investors.

4.2.4 Retail investors

Retail investors are typically long-term investors rather than short-term traders. As such, their rationale tends to be focused towards either dividend income or long-term capital gain. It is unusual for a retail investor to own shares in an unlisted company that he is not connected with as founder, manager or employee.

5 DEBT CAPITAL

5.1 Bank debt

Most companies will, at some point, borrow money from a bank to supplement the equity capital they have raised. The advantages to the company's directors of borrowing money from a bank are

- The shareholders, who may include directors, do not have to give up part of their ownership of the company.

- The interest paid on bank loans is tax-deductible, so that the cost of the bank loan becomes relatively low.

There are a number of products available from a bank.

5.1.1 Term loans

Term loan facilities are suitable for cash flow lending situations in which the loan proceeds are used for long-term needs, such as to finance equipment acquisitions, permanent working investment, stock repurchases, and the refunding of existing maturities of short-term debt as they become due. Some features of term loans are as follows.

- The loan may be **amortised** (i.e. repaid in instalments over the term of the loan) or **bullet** repayment (i.e. repaid in one single instalment at the end of the term).

- The interest rate may be **fixed or floating**. The floating rate is expressed as a fixed spread over a variable interest rate such as the London Interbank Offered Rate (LIBOR).

- It may be a **senior** loan or **subordinated**. Senior debt is debt provided by a bank which is designated the senior lender, and which therefore has priority in receiving interest and capital repayments and ranks ahead of other lenders on a winding-up. It is generally secured (see below). Subordinated debt is debt where the rights and returns are subordinated to those of the senior lender. It is therefore typically more expensive for the company than senior debt.

5.1.2 Commercial mortgage

A commercial mortgage is a flexible method of purchasing or improving a freehold or leasehold property. It may be owner occupied or for investment, commercial or industrial purposes. In essence, it is a long-term loan from the bank, secured on the property concerned. The main features are that it is provided over a long term, the interest base can be either floating or fixed, and the amount granted is based on the open market valuation of the property.

5.1.3 Syndicated loans

A syndicated loan is a loan provided by two or more banks to one or more borrowers. The loan is syndicated – spread among the banking community – usually because it is for a larger amount that one bank is prepared to lend on its own. The terms and conditions on which the loan is to be made by the banks to the borrower are set out in a loan agreement, to which all lenders and the borrower are a party. Consequently, all lenders are bound by the same terms, which are enforced on their behalf by the **lead arranger**.

5.1.4 Overdraft

Some borrowers will borrow on a **demand basis**. This means that the bank itself can demand immediate repayment at any time. The usual mechanism for this is the **overdraft** – where a company's account is allowed to go into debit up to a certain limit. This is highly flexible for the borrower since it can alter the balance of its borrowings at will. However, it imposes a high degree of risk on the borrower, since the bank can demand repayment immediately (although banks will often quote a non-binding 'review date'), and the borrower would have to seek emergency refinancing from another source. The interest rate for UK overdrafts is normally variable, calculated by reference to a margin above the base rate.

5.1.5 Revolving credits

A revolving credit is a formal legal agreement in which the bank agrees to lend up to a certain amount for a specific purpose over a specified period of time, usually two to five years. The borrower has complete flexibility in borrowing all or a portion of the total amount as necessary and repaying any amount at any time during the life of the commitment. In other words, revolving credit arrangements do not have set repayment schedules. The interest basis is normally variable, calculated by reference to a margin above LIBOR, payable on the amounts drawn down. Additionally, the borrower must pay a commitment fee on amounts not drawn down.

5.2 Other forms of financing

5.2.1 Leasing

Leasing is a tax-effective source of finance for fixed asset acquisition. A lease is an agreement in which the owner of an item (e.g. a business asset) or a piece of real estate allows someone else to use it for a specified time, in return for a rental. The owner of the leased asset is the lessor and the user of the asset is the lessee.

5.2.2 Factoring

Factoring means selling trade debts for immediate cash to a 'factor' who charges commission. Most factors offer three basic services, although clients are under no obligation to take them all.

The services provided by a factor are as follows.

- An accounting, credit checking and debt collection service.
- Credit insurance against bad debts, for 'approved' debts.

- The provision of immediate cash against invoices, up to 75-85% of the face value of the invoices and, because of the credit insurance, a guarantee of payment of the remainder within an agreed period of time.

Invoice discounting is similar to factoring, except that only the financing service is used; copies of invoices sent to customers are discounted with a financial institution. The trading company still collects the debts as agents for the financial institution and remits the cash on receipt. Factoring generally refers to purchasing a client's entire turnover (excluding cash sales), whereas invoice discounting refers to purchasing individual debts on a 'one-off' basis.

5.2.3 Sale and leaseback

A company may have a significant amount of its net worth represented by tangible fixed assets used in its commercial activities, such as factories or a head office. It may choose to sell one or more of its properties to a property company or bank, and then lease it from the new owners. This will have the effect of raising an immediate cash sum, although the cost of leasing the property back will dilute earnings in future years.

A company might choose to enter into a sale and leaseback agreement when

- It is seeking to raise cash to repay debt. It will seek to ensure that the leasing costs are lower than the interest on the debt repaid.

- It wishes to raise cash for an expansion of the business, or to improve a long-term liquidity position.

5.3 Bonds

In the same way that companies may seek to raise equity by selling shares to market investors, they may seek to raise debt by borrowing in the markets. In this case, rather than entering into a negotiated loan agreement with a specific bank or syndicate of banks, they will borrow money through a bank or stock exchange from a wide range of investors. Each investor advances a small proportion of the loan, and in exchange receives a bond. The bonds themselves are rather like an IOU ("I owe you"); they provide evidence of the loan, and details of the interest and repayment.

The main features of bonds include the following.

- **Term**. Bonds may be issued for any term from a year to 99 years or even in perpetuity.

- **Credit rating**. A corporate issuer will usually seek a credit rating for the bond from a ratings agency such as Standard & Poors or Moody's.

- **Certificates**. Bonds are commonly in bearer form, i.e. the issuer does not maintain a register of owners, and possession of the bond certificate is the only evidence of ownership.

- **Redemption**. Bonds are normally redeemed at par (nominal value). They may however be redeemed at a **premium to the par value**, particularly when the bond offers a low coupon or none at all (a **zero-coupon bond**).

- **Security**. Bonds may be secured or unsecured (see below).

- **Listing**. Bonds are freely transferable; they may be admitted to listing on a stock exchange in the same way as equities, or may be traded over-the-counter by agreement with a bank.

There are additionally some special features of bonds to consider.

5.4 Coupon

The interest on a bond is referred to as a coupon. Most corporate bonds are issued with a fixed coupon rate, paid either annually or semi-annually. The coupon to be received is based upon the nominal value of the corporate bond held, and the fixed coupon rate. There are, however, two major exceptions to this rule, namely floating rate notes (FRNs) and zero-coupon bonds.

5.4.1 Floating Rate Notes (FRNs)

With FRNs, the coupon is not fixed at the outset, but floats in line with market rates and is re-fixed on a regular basis. Every few months, the market rate of interest is assessed, often using a measure such as **LIBOR, and adding to it a margin**. LIBOR represents the rate the largest banks are prepared to lend to each other (the interbank deposit rate is called LIBID) and, therefore, provides a benchmark for market interest rates. The margin added reflects the additional risk the investor is taking in lending to a company.

With a fixed rate bond, a change in interest rates will cause the price of the bond to change (so that the yield reflects the market rate of interest). With a FRN, however, the coupon will change in line with market interest rates. This will result in the value of the bond remaining **constant at around the par value**.

5.4.2 Zero-coupon bonds

These are bonds that carry no coupon rate but are issued at a discount to their face value. The discount reflects the interest that is liable over the life of the bond. The tax treatment of zero-coupon bonds is that the company receives corporation tax relief on a notional interest charge each year, while the investor suffers **income tax** (not capital gains tax) **on the gain** made, but only in the year the bond is **redeemed**.

The same effect is achieved if the bond is redeemed at a premium to its nominal value. For example, if a bond of £100 nominal value has a redemption premium of 15% at redemption the issuer will pay back £115.

5.5 Convertible bonds

In addition to security, the issuers of a bond may attach various rights to the issue in order to encourage investors to buy in.

A **conversion right** gives the bondholder the right, at a specified date or dates in the future, to convert their bond into shares of the company. The rate of conversion will be fixed at the time of issue and represents an option to purchase the shares at a given price. Depending on the movement in the underlying share price this conversion right or option may be very valuable indeed. The trade-off in this sort of issue is that the coupon will often be much lower than the market would otherwise expect on a bond from that particular company.

The attraction of convertible bonds is that they offer a two-way bet. If the share price rises, then the conversion right itself has value. If the share price falls, then, at worst, the bondholder is left with a lower coupon bond (compared with a conventional corporate bond).

5.5.1 Mandatory convertibles

However, sometimes the bondholder will be required to convert the nominal value into ordinary shares of the company at a set redemption date. These are known as mandatory convertibles.

For example, equity contract notes will be redeemed for the equivalent of the bond's nominal value in current market value of shares of the company.

5.5.2 Exchangeables

Exchangeable bonds are ones that are convertible into the ordinary shares of a subsidiary or associate company of the issuer.

5.6 Eurobonds

In essence, a **Eurobond is a debt instrument issued by a borrower (typically a government or a large company) normally, or predominantly, outside of the country in whose currency it is denominated**. For example, a US dollar Eurobond could be issued anywhere in the world except for the US. As such, a better name for it might be an 'international bond'. Eurobonds frequently carry no security, other than the name and credit rating of the issuer.

Another important feature of bonds issued in this market is that, for the most part, they are issued in **bearer form**, with no formal register of ownership held by the company. These bearer documents are immobilised at central depositories, such as Euroclear and Clearstream, which provide clearing and stocklending facilities.

It should be noted that for a number of pragmatic reasons, the clearing houses in the Euromarkets do maintain a form of register of ownership. However, this register is not normally open either to government or tax authorities. Combined with the feature of being bearer documents, a vital aspect of the Eurobond is that, unlike most government bonds, it does not attract withholding tax. **Eurobonds pay coupons gross** and usually **annually**.

Most Eurobonds are issued in **bullet form**, redeemed at one specified date in the future. However, a number of issues have alternative redemption patterns. Some bonds are redeemed over a number of years, with a proportion of the issue being redeemed each year. Whilst Eurobonds are not issued in registered form, each will have an identifying number. A **drawing** of numbers is made every year from the pool of bonds in issue. The numbers drawn are published and the bonds are called in and redeemed. This redemption process is known as a drawing on a Eurobond.

5.7 Security

Companies have the ability to issue debt which is secured against the company's assets. There are two types of legal charge that a company can issue over its assets.

5.7.1 Fixed charges

A fixed charge security is security given over a specific asset of the business. Where a particular asset has a fixed charge security over it, the company cannot dispose of the asset without the permission of the fixed charge holders. If the company defaults on the loan, the holder of the fixed charge has the right to appoint a receiver to remove the asset in question, dispose of it and use the proceeds to repay the debt to the bondholder. Any surplus on disposal must be returned to the company.

Bonds secured under a fixed charge are often referred to as **debentures or debenture stock**. The term stock means a loan which can be broken down into small units. With a straight debenture, an investor can buy all of it or none of it. With a debenture stock, as with a gilt-edged stock, the investor can buy as much, or as little, as desired.

5.7.2 Floating charges

A floating charge security is secured against the assets in general (including current assets) rather than against specific assets. A floating charge has no effect until the company defaults on a loan. At this stage, the holder of a floating charge may appoint an administrator or receiver to take over the running of the company. He will then manage the company and any money generated will be used to repay the chargeholder's debt.

Unlike a fixed charge, where the company loses the right to dispose of an asset covered by a fixed charge, the company has full rights over the assets of the business until there is an event of default. At that stage, and at that stage only, does the charge crystallise.

Both fixed and floating charges must be **recorded with the Registrar of Companies**.

Fixed charges are a more effective way than floating charges of ensuring repayment in the event of default. This is demonstrated by looking at the order of payout on the liquidation of a company. The process of liquidation is one in which the company is wound up by a liquidator. The company is turned into its liquid asset – cash. Assets are sold, money is collected and then used to pay the creditors of the company in a legally specified order.

5.8 Priority on liquidation of a company

The liquidator's task is to convert the company into cash as quickly and efficiently as possible. The order of payout, determined by the Insolvency Act 1986 and amended by the Enterprise Act 2002, is as follows.

Priority on liquidation
1. The liquidator's costs
2. Fixed charge security holders
3. Preferential creditors (employees' wage arrears)
4. Floating charge security holders
5. Unsecured creditors
6. Subordinated creditors
7. Preference shareholders
8. Ordinary shareholders

The liquidator will pay each category in full before moving on to the next. Since most liquidations are a result of insolvency, the likelihood is that there will be insufficient funds left to meet all debts. The order of liquidation is an attempt to reward those who have some form of security first, before moving on to the unsecured creditors. Only those of the liquidator's costs which relate to the realisation of floating charge assets take priority.

When the liquidator runs out of money, the category being dealt with at that stage will receive, on a pro rata basis, the proportion of their debt that can be covered by available funds. For example, the unsecured creditors in a liquidation may receive only 14p in the pound.

The important point to note is that shareholders receive their money last. As owners of the company, they must take the risks as well as reap the rewards. However, if the company is wound up and there is a surplus on liquidation, this surplus would be paid to the ordinary shareholders.

It should be noted from the order of priority on liquidation that **subordinated** debt can be issued. A subordinated loan is one which on liquidation ranks below the unsecured creditors for payout. As such, subordinated creditors take on board a higher degree of risk and will obviously require a higher degree of return to compensate. It is possible that subordinated debt is secured by a second charge over the company's assets; if this is the case, it would rank above the unsecured creditors.

Finally, it is possible that the debt itself has been guaranteed by another company. Often within groups of companies, one of the subsidiaries may borrow money from the market place. Its loan may have been guaranteed by the **parent or holding company** and is then referred to as **guarantee stock**. The value of this guarantee obviously depends upon the credit rating of the holding company and it would be classified as an **unsecured creditor**.

6 THE COST OF CAPITAL

When considering their capital structure, a major consideration for companies is the relative cost of the different forms of capital. The cost of capital may be expressed in two ways.

- It is equivalent to both the **cost of funds** that a company raises and uses, and the **return that investors expect** to be paid for putting funds into the company.

- It is therefore the **minimum return that a company must make** on its own investments to earn the cash flows out of which investors can be paid their return.

The cost of capital of a business can be measured by studying the returns required by investors in that business. This cost of capital can then be used to calculate a discount rate for discounted cash flow (DCF) analysis and a 'required' rate of return for investment appraisal.

The two basic sources of finance for a company are

- Debt.
- Equity.

Each form of capital has a separate cost.

7 THE COST OF DEBT

The cost of debt is relatively straightforward to calculate. It equates to the interest on the debt, net of tax relief.

The formula used for calculating the cost of debt is

Formula to learn

$$Kd = i \times (1 - t)$$

where

i = the interest rate

t = the tax rate

Example

Geared Co. Ltd has debt paying interest of 6.5% pa. The corporation tax rate is now 30%. What is Geared's cost of debt?

Solution

$$Kd = 6.5\% \times (1 - 30\%)$$

i.e. $= 6.5\% \times 70\% = 4.55\%$

The company's cost of debt is the interest it must pay to its lenders, less the tax relief it will receive.

8 THE COST OF EQUITY

The cost of equity capital is the expected long-term average annual returns to shareholders, expressed as a percentage of the share price.

In the UK, equity is usually more expensive than debt capital. Shareholders expect a higher long-term average return to compensate them for the greater risk factor in their investment. Equity is, by its nature, a more risky investment than debt. The annual income of the company is affected by a wide range of factors, and can fluctuate from one year to the next. If actual profits turn out to be much lower than expected, returns from dividend income may be lower and the share price could fall, giving disappointing returns in some years.

Unlike providers of debt capital who have a **right** to regular fixed interest payments (and the repayment of the debt principal), equity shareholders rely for their dividend income on the discretion and judgement of the company's directors. To compensate for this uncertainty, **equity shareholders require a higher return** on their investment than debt providers. The other side of the coin is therefore that the **cost** of equity is higher than the cost of debt.

An estimate can be made of the cost of equity for each company quoted on a stock market. The main method used for estimating this is the **Capital Asset Pricing Model (CAPM)**.

8.1 Capital Asset Pricing Model

The Capital Asset Pricing model (CAPM) is a mathematical model for estimating a company's cost of equity, based on the expected average returns from individual shares (or a portfolio of shares). The model, in broad outline, is based on a comparison of

- The yield available on **risk-free investments** (long-term domestic government bonds), R_f.

- The **average market yield**, i.e. the comparable average returns generated historically from the stock market as a whole. Over time, this is higher than the risk-free investment yield, R_m.

- Subtracting R_f from R_m shows us the difference between the return generated from a portfolio of risk-free investments, and the return generated by a portfolio of equity investments which mirrors the risk of the equity market as a whole; i.e. the **premium return generated by investing in equity, R_p**.

- The **additional return** required to reflect the risk of investing in the shares of a particular company, relative to the risk of investing in the equity market as a whole. This could be higher or lower than the average market yield, depending on whether the shares are high risk or low risk: the measure is referred to as β **(beta)**.

Another way of expressing this is to say that CAPM

- Measures the return any investor would require for a 'risk-free' investment.

- Adds to this the additional return he would require solely to justify investing in equity (as opposed to, say, government bonds).

- Then increases or reduces this to reflect the additional return required (or not required) if the specific equity invested in is riskier (or less risky) than the 'average' equity investment.

8.1.1 The CAPM formula

The CAPM formula for the expected return on an individual share is as follows.

Formula to learn

$$K_e = r_f + \beta(r_m - r_f)$$

where

K_e = cost of equity

r_m = the return expected from the market portfolio

r_f = the return offered by a risk-free security

β = the risk of the investment opportunity relative to that of the market portfolio (systematic risk only)

The calculation of cost of equity is shown as follows.

$$K_e = r_f + \beta(r_m - r_f)$$

Example

Equity Co. Ltd has a beta of 1.2. The risk-free rate is 4.5% and the market return historically has been 10.8%. What is its cost of equity, using CAPM?

Solution

$$
\begin{aligned}
K_e &= 4.5\% + 1.2 \times (10.8\% - 4.5\%) \\
&= 4.5\% + 7.56\% = 12.06\%
\end{aligned}
$$

This represents the minimum return that the company must generate for its equity investors in order to satisfy their investment requirements.

Note that the Certificate in Corporate Finance syllabus only requires you to "know the total return on shares can be estimated using CAPM". You should not be required to calculate the cost of equity in the exam.

8.2 Systematic and unsystematic risk

The risk in investing in the shares of an individual company depends on two groups of factors.

- Those that affect all firms in the economy, to a greater or lesser extent, and not just the individual company. These factors give rise to **'market risk' or 'systematic risk'**, and the risk is measured as R_m. The extent to which an individual's company's risks are in line with the market as a whole is measured by β (beta).

- Those that are specific or special to the company, e.g. the quality of its management. These factors give rise to **'specific' or 'unsystematic' risk**.

CAPM takes into account both the systematic risk for shares in individual companies, and the return that an investor with an efficient portfolio of investments should expect to receive from his shares overall. This expected yield should determine the share's cost of capital and its market price.

8.3 Beta

Each listed share has its own beta factor (β), established from a comparative analysis over time of market returns and returns on the share. The beta factor is a measure of how much the individual share moves in relation to the market as a whole, i.e. volatility relative to the market. It is taken as a proxy for how much risk is attached to an investment in this particular share, as opposed to the risk implicit in investing in equities in general.

When a share's beta factor is between **0 and 1**, its **systematic risk is lower** than for the stock market as a whole. When average market returns rise or fall, returns from the share should rise or fall by a lesser amount, i.e. they are more stable. Low beta factors are associated with **'defensive'** stocks. When a share's beta factor is **greater than 1**, its **systematic risk is greater** than for the stock market as a whole. When average market returns rise or fall, returns from the share should rise or fall by a larger amount. High beta factors are associated with **'cyclical'** stocks.

The sign of the beta (+/−) indicates whether, on average, the investment's returns move with (+) the market, rising and falling when it does, or in the opposite direction (−) to the market. T

8.3.1 Summary

Beta > 1

On average, the investment's returns will move in the same direction as the market's returns but to a greater extent.

Beta = 1

On average, the investment's returns will move in the same direction as the market's returns and to the same extent.

0 < Beta< 1

On average, the investment's returns will move in the same direction as the market's returns but to a lesser extent.

Beta = 0

The investment's returns are uncorrelated with those of the market. This would be the case if the investment were risk free but, more generally, this situation will arise when all of the investment's risk is unsystematic.

Beta < 0

On average, the investment's returns will move in the opposite direction to the market, to a lesser extent if Beta> −1, to the same extent if Beta = −1 and to a greater extent if Beta < −1.

Example

Company A has a Beta of 2 and Company B has a Beta of 0.5. Which share price will fall the furthest in a bear market.

Solution

Company A's share price will fall the furthest as it is a cyclical stock. So when there is a fall in prices in a bear market, Company A's share price will fall by twice the amount of the market as a whole. Meanwhile, Company B's share price will only fall by half the amount of the whole market.

CHAPTER ROUNDUP

- Equity are the owners of a company giving an equal share in profits and voting rights.

- Preference shares rank above equity in receipt of a usually fixed dividend and capital repayment in the case of liquidation of the company.

- A rights issue is when a UK company raises new finance by giving existing shareholders the first right to buy new shares in the company.

- On receipt of a rights letter the holder has four choices:

    - Take up the shares and hold

    - Take up the shares and then sell the allotment letter

    - Sell the rights 'nil paid' for their intrinsic value

    - Do nothing and receive any value in the rights when they are sold on to other shareholders after the last acceptance and payment date

- The theoretical ex-rights price is calculated by adding the original value of the holding to the subscription price and then dividing the result by the total number of shares held after the rights issue.

- Open offers are a form of rights issue but the original holder may not renounce or sell on their rights.

- Bonds may be issued with different levels of security and different rewards in the form of their coupons or conversion rights.

- A fixed coupon bond price will move inversely to interest rates to reflect the attractiveness (or not) of the fixed coupon as market yields move.

- A floating rate note will refix its coupon to LIBOR on a frequent basis and so its price will remain around par.

- Eurobonds are international bearer bonds.

- Adding security to a bond through fixed or floating charges will reduce the credit risk and therefore pay a lower yield.

- The cost of debt is given by $Kd = i \times (1 - t)$.

- The cost of equity under CAPM is given by $K_e = r_f + \beta(r_m - r_f)$

- Beta shows how much an individual share moves in relation to the market as a whole.

TEST YOUR KNOWLEDGE

Check your knowledge of the chapter here, without referring back to the text.

1.   Name three special types of preference shares.

2.   How long is the minimum period between sending out the provisional allotment letters and the last acceptance and payment date?

3.   What is a venture capitalist?

4.   What is the difference between an overdraft and a revolving credit?

5.   What is a mandatory convertible bond?

6.   Rank the following on priority in liquidation: Eurobond, debenture, subordinated loan, preference share.

7.   What is the major advantage of debt finance?

8.   What would be the beta of a share that fell by 10% when the market increased by 8%?

TEST YOUR KNOWLEDGE: ANSWERS

1.   Participating, convertible and redeemable.

   (See Section 2.2)

2.   21 calendar days

   (See Section 3.2.4)

3.   A venture capitalist is an investor who seeks a substantial return having taken the risk of investing in young, start-up companies. Most of their return will be the capital gain on the floatation or sale of the business after a few years.

   (See Section 4.2.2)

4.   Both are relatively short-term borrowing from banks. The main difference is that overdrafts can be called in for repayment on demand by the bank, whereas a revolving credit is a committed facility of usually two to five years when the bank promises not to call any money drawn down.

   (See Sections 5.1.4 and 5.1.5)

5.   The issuing company can require the bondholder to take ordinary shares in the company instead of cash at the redemption date.

   (See Section 5.5.1)

6.   Debenture, Eurobond, subordinated loan, preference share.

   (See Section 5.8)

7.   Debt interest payments are tax deductible.

   (See Section 7)

8. $\beta = -1.25$

   (See Section 8.3)

10

Introduction to Business Valuations

First of all, this chapter examines the different parts of a company that can be valued (enterprise or equity) and the different reasons for a valuation (stock market, transaction and break-up).

There are four methods of valuation. For each one you need to know the method used, purpose and limitation.

CHAPTER CONTENTS

BPP
LEARNING MEDIA

Chapter Learning Objectives

Equity Value and Enterprise Value

- **Understand** the distinction between Equity Value and Enterprise Value.
- **Understand** the use of Enterprise Value.

Stock Market, Transaction and Break up Values

- **Understand** the distinction between stock market, transaction and break up values of a business.

- **Know how** to calculate the stock market value of a quoted company.

- **Understand** how to compare the stock market values of companies in similar sectors by use of multiples such as P/E ratio, EBIT and EBITDA multiples.

Asset-based Valuations

- **Understand** the use of asset-based models.
- **Know** the limitations of asset-based valuations.

Dividend-based Valuations

- **Understand** the use of dividend-based valuations.
- **Be able to calculate** a valuation of a business using the dividend valuation model.
- **Understand** the limitations of the dividend-based valuation.

Earnings-based Valuations

- **Understand** the use of an earnings-based valuation.
- **Be able to calculate** the equity value of a business using P/E ratio.
- **Be able to calculate** the enterprise value of a business using EBIT and EBITDA multiples.

Cash-based Valuations

- **Understand** the use of cash-based valuation.
- **Know how to calculate** free cash flow.
- **Understand** the key stages that need to be followed in a cash flow-based valuation.

    - Historical analysis.
    - Forecasting.
    - Calculating a terminal value.
    - Identifying an appropriate discount rate, Weighted Average Cost of Capital (WACC).

- **Be able to calculate** a terminal value assuming no growth and growth.
- **Be able to calculate** a simple cash flow-based valuation.

1 INTRODUCTION TO BUSINESS VALUATIONS

1.1 Listed and unlisted companies and valuation purpose

In terms of valuation, companies can be split into two main categories – listed and unlisted. For the former, there is already a market value available as a starting point. For the latter, there is no market value readily available and more work needs to be done to establish what the company is worth.

It is also worth noting that there can be different measures of value even for the same asset or liability, according to the perspective of the individual assessing the value and the purpose of the valuation.

- Is it a board of directors seeking to value an asset for the purposes of balance sheet presentation?

- Is it a banker wanting to identify value in the circumstances of taking a charge over an asset as security for a loan?

- Is it a minority shareholder wishing to establish the value of his shareholding in order to sell it?

- Is it an acquirer wishing to rationalise the return on investment that he can obtain after changes are implemented?

- Is it a board of directors seeking a corporate restructuring to reduce the company's vulnerability to a hostile takeover bid?

- Is it the marketing agent wanting to pitch the price of shares in a flotation?

The **value of a business is therefore subjective** – it will always depend on the perspective of the valuer, and on the purposes for which the valuation is carried out.

2 EQUITY VALUE AND ENTERPRISE VALUE

2.1 The distinction between equity value and enterprise value

Enterprise value represents the total value of a business or enterprise to all providers of capital, including equity investors, preference share investors, debt investors and minority interests. It can be calculated by adding the company's market capitalisation and the market value of its gross debt, and deducting any cash balances. Short-term liquid financial investments that can readily converted to cash are also deducted. Any additional sources of capital should also be added, i.e. the market value of preference shares and minority interest.

EV = Market capitalisation + Gross debt – Cash + Preference Shares + Minority Interest

Equity value represents the value of the business to the providers of equity finance. It is calculated after deducting the values of debt, preference shares and minority interests from enterprise value.

2.1.1 The use of enterprise value

Although it may seem more appropriate to focus on equity values at first sight, since we are trying to identify the value of the business to its equity investors, enterprise value has an important part to play in the valuation process. The reason for this is that it **ignores the level of gearing** and other related financial factors when calculating the value of any business. As such, it can be an easy and consistent way to value equity – first through calculating the enterprise value and then deducting the value of other sources of finance.

Enterprise value	X
Less: Value of net debt	X
Equity value	X

In addition, enterprise value is a useful benchmark for comparisons across companies. Since many companies in different countries will have different gearing levels, even though they are in the same industry, it will not be easy to compare their businesses based on equity values. A more appropriate comparison would be to look at multiples based on enterprise values. For example, multiples based on turnover, research and development costs, number of locations, etc., can be calculated and compared across the international sector.

2.2 Stock Market, Transaction and Break-up Values

2.2.1 Stock market value

This is the value of a quoted company on the London Stock Exchange. It is calculated as the share price multiplied by the number of shares in issue. It is of relevance to investors with **small stakes in the listed company** in question.

Formula to learn

> Full market capitalisation = Total number of shares × Market price per share

However, when considering the stock market value for index purposes, it is common practice to only include shares that are available for trading on that exchange, known as the '**free float**'. This would therefore exclude holdings by significant shareholders which are not expected to trade in the market.

> The Free Float is defined as the total shares outstanding less shares held by owners of more than 5%, less shares held by executives and other insider holdings (e.g. founders and other strategic investors).

The stock market value of the company can be compared to other companies in the same sector by using multiples, such as the P/E ratio or the EBIT multiple. Where the comparison is being done on a basis of equity value, an earnings figure relevant to equity should be used (i.e. after tax and minority interests such as P/E ratio). Where the comparison is being made on the basis of enterprise value, an earnings figure should be based upon profits available to all providers of finance (i.e. before interest and tax such as EBIT).

Finding a company on either a high or low multiple relative to its sector does not, of course, tell you whether or not the company is a good buy. An expensive company may be justifiably on a high multiple due to expectations of growth arising from its competitive advantages in the market place in question. A cheap company may be on a low multiple because it has no distinguishing characteristics and can offer no competitive threat. Alternatively, it may be that the stock market has failed to value the company in question correctly. One of the objectives of analysis is to identify which is likely to be the correct answer.

2.2.2 Transaction value

Transaction value assumes a **change of control**. It reflects the cost of buying the entire company or a controlling stake in it. Transaction value should usually be higher than stock market value, since the acquirer of the company will need to pay a control premium, to reflect the value of a controlling stake. In addition, it is likely that the acquirer is expecting to reap synergistic benefits, in which the sellers of the business will want to participate.

When applying a control premium to the value of a company, the premium should be applied to the equity value rather than the enterprise value. The reason for this is that it is equity that controls the business rather than debt. As a result, there is no reason to pay a control premium for the debt element of the business.

The transaction value of a company will often be calculated on a fundamental cash basis, since the acquirer will need to obtain a detailed knowledge of the company prior to purchasing it and integrating it in the group. In addition, he will need to identify from where synergies are going to arise. When a company is listed on the stock market, its stock market value may move towards its transaction value if the market anticipates that a bid is likely.

2.2.3 Break-up value

This describes the value that might be achieved by disaggregating the different parts of the group and valuing them separately on a break-up basis. It links in to the unbundling approach referred to above. The break-up valuation might involve selling some divisions as going concerns, floating some divisions as separate listed companies, but closing others and disposing of surplus assets. Depending on the approach to be adopted, a stock market value or transaction value might be appropriate for valuing the separate divisions.

Where it is intended to float a division separately, it should be remembered that the owner will receive less than the stock market value of the division, since the flotation will need to be priced at a discount. This will reduce the overall break-up value. Other factors that will also reduce overall value include the other costs associated with a break up, such as redundancy, reorganisation and tax. Break up may actually destroy some value, if it removes economies of scale or links between the value chains of the divisions concerned.

2.3 Approaches to valuation

The main techniques for valuing companies are as follows.

- Asset based.
- Dividends based.
- Earnings based.
- Cash based, including discounted cash flows.

We will look at each in turn, focussing on their key applications, advantages and disadvantages.

In practice, a valuer will use a combination of valuation methods. This will depend on the information available at the time, any standard practices in a given industry or country and their own investment criteria.

In the exam you will be expected to identify which valuation technique is most appropriate to a particular industry or situation and the key drawbacks of each approach.

3 ASSET-BASED VALUATIONS

3.1 Introduction

A business can be seen as a collection of individual assets and the value of the business could be calculated as what it would cost to buy the assets separately or what the assets would realise if sold off separately.

This means that an asset-based valuation is **not relevant for a minority investor** who owns shares in a company that is a going concern. Since the company is not going to be wound up, the asset value will never be realised.

If an investor owns 75% of the shares in the company, however, he or she can force a liquidation of the company and realise the asset value. In this case, or if the company is definitely in the process of being wound up, then the asset value will be relevant.

Asset-based valuation is also useful to an extent for shareholders who own more than 50% of the shares. Although they cannot force a liquidation of the company, they can arrange for the disposal of surplus or under-used assets and receive a share of the cash on disposal by means of dividend.

3.2 Net Realisable Value of Assets

3.2.1 The minimum selling price for a vendor

The net realisable value of the assets is of relevance to existing shareholders, since it represents the minimum sum for which they should be prepared to sell the company. There is no point in accepting £1m for a business when the assets could have been sold off separately for £3m.

3.2.2 Liquidation value

In addition, it establishes whether a business has a higher value as a going concern or on liquidation. If a company's cash flows from its operations have a lower present value than the liquidation value, then the company should be wound up and the proceeds reinvested in a more profitable area.

3.2.3 Establishing realisable values

In calculating realisable values, care needs to be taken in assessing the values of fixed assets and stocks. If the break up of the company is occurring over a rapid timescale or as a result of a forced sale, then values will be lower than if the business were run down in an orderly fashion over a period of time. In addition, any costs of disposal will need to be taken into account. These may include, for example, redundancy costs and taxation on asset disposals.

3.2.4 The maximum purchase price for an acquirer

The cost of buying the assets separately and forming the business from scratch will give a potential purchaser an indication of how much to pay for a business. The problem with this is that if the business has substantial goodwill built up over a number of years, then the cost of acquiring a similar business will not just be the cost of buying identical tangible assets. This means that the asset-based valuation method may significantly undervalue a business.

3.3 Uses of assets-based valuations

For shareholders with a controlling interest the net asset basis for valuation is used for the following purposes.

- To establish the **break-up or liquidation value**.
- To establish the minimum selling price for a vendor.

The net asset basis for valuations is also most suitable in the following circumstances.

- For **asset-based companies** such as property companies, banks and investment trusts, where asset-based valuations are the traditional approach.

- As a measure of **security** in a share value. The calculation provides an assessment of the asset backing of the company.

- For companies with **low or no profits or cash flows**. Net assets may be positive where profits are negative meaning that price/net asset ratios may be used instead of price/earnings ratios in these circumstances.

3.4 Problems with asset-based valuations

Asset based valuations **are not** suitable for

- Minority investors who have no influence on whether the assets may be disposed of

- Service Companies with few tangible assets and a focus on intangible assets that are not recorded on the balance sheet (e.g. internally generated goodwill, customer and employee loyalty).

The major problems with asset-based valuations are

- Net assets ignore many of the intangible assets of a company, such as human capital.

- Different companies in the same industry may use different business models. This could give different balance sheet structures. For example, a company that assembles parts rather than manufacturing and that operates tight stock control will have lower fixed assets and stocks than a company that manufactures the same equipment. As a result, it will have lower net assets.

- Net assets are affected by accounting choices of the management, particularly when doing international comparisons.

- Net assets are usually based on the historic cost of the assets. These could be out of date due to inflation and technological changes.

- The valuation of a business is ultimately related to earnings power going forward, whereas net assets are based on the assets' original cost. The two might be significantly different where the earnings power of the assets has changed significantly since the assets were bought.

4 DIVIDEND-BASED VALUATIONS

4.1 Introduction

Whereas an asset-based valuation relies on the assumption that the assets can or will be realised, the dividend-based approach assumes that a company is a going concern and values the company based on its dividend flows.

This methodology is suitable for the valuation of **small shareholdings in unquoted companies**, or for pricing small shareholdings in quoted companies. A minority investor has little influence over a company's affairs and just receives a regular dividend. Hence, to be persuaded to sell their shares, they must be paid a price that compensates them for the future dividends that they will be giving up. This takes into account the required yield on such an investment.

Moreover, small shareholdings in unquoted companies are not marketable, so that any capital element in the value of their shares is heavily discounted to reflect the risk that they cannot be sold.

4.2 The dividend valuation model

4.2.1 The present value of the future dividend stream

The dividend valuation model (DVM) states that a company's value is the present value of all the future cash flows to investors discounted at the investors' required rate of return for that company. It assumes that the only cash flows investors receive are dividends paid by the company.

4.2.2 What about capital gains?

This assumption may appear to be invalid for stock exchange investors, who sell their shares and earn a capital gain. However, the sale proceeds received by the investor will be determined by reference to the expected future dividend stream from the shares. As such, they merely represent the present value of the future dividends at the date of sale. The validity of the model is, therefore, not affected.

4.2.3 Constant annual dividends

If a company pays a constant dividend to perpetuity, then a simplified formula for valuing the company's shares is given by

Formula to learn

$$MV = \frac{D}{k_e}$$

where

MV = share price (ex-dividend)

D = constant annual dividend

k_e = required rate of return

4.2.4 Dividend stream with constant growth

The above formula may be adequate for preference shares where no growth is possible, but is unlikely to be sufficient for equity shares where dividend growth is probably expected. The formula can be developed to incorporate constant dividend growth as follows.

Formula to learn

$$MV = \frac{D_0 (1+g)}{k_e - g} = \frac{D_1}{k_e - g}$$

where

D_0 = the current dividend

D_1 = the prospective dividend in one year's time

g = the expected annual growth rate in dividends

Both formulae give an ex-dividend share price because the way the formulae are derived assumes that the first inflow occurs in one year's time. In addition, the growth formula also assumes that the growth rate is less than the required rate of return.

4.3 Estimating D_1, k_e and g

4.3.1 The prospective dividend, D_1

In order to be able to value a company, the three variables, D_1, k_e and g, will have to be identified. The prospective dividend is likely to be relatively easy to establish, typically from the company's own forecasts.

4.3.2 Expected growth, g

The expected growth rate for the company in question can be estimated by using expected growth rates for similar quoted companies as an indication or by more specific analysis of the company to establish its expected earnings and dividend stream. This may involve specific forecasting of profits and cash flows. Alternatively, it may be based on a more general analysis of a company's profitability and cash flows.

Depending on the level of sophistication used to identify dividend growth, the final valuation will be more or less rough and ready.

4.3.3 The required rate of return, k_e

There are three alternative approaches to calculating k_e:

- **The Capital Asset Pricing Model**. This was discussed in Chapter 9 – Capital Structure and derives the required return on equity/cost of equity as the sum of the risk-free rate plus a risk premium adjusted for the company's systematic risk as measured by the ß.

Formula to learn

$$k_e = r_f + \beta(r_m - r_f)$$

where

k_e = the required return from the share

r_f = the risk-free rate of return

r_m = the return required from the market overall

ß = the company's level of systematic risk relative to the overall market's risk

- **Bond yield** plus premium.

  This is used when analysts have no confidence in CAPM and involves looking at the company's cost of debt and adding a **judgemental** risk premium to it.

- **Dividend yield** approach. Here we apply the DVM to a comparable quoted company (with a known share price) and solve for k_e.

  DVM: $MV = \dfrac{D_1}{k_e - g}$

  Or rearranging for k_e

  $k_e = \dfrac{D_1}{MV} + g$

  The required rate of return/cost of equity equals the prospective dividend yield (D_1/MV) plus expected dividend growth.

  This third approach is most commonly associated with the DVM.

4.4 Uses of dividend based valuation

Dividend based valuations are appropriate for the valuation of **minority shareholdings** on both quoted and unquoted companies.

In addition, they are useful for companies with **predictable dividends and growth rates** and where a **suitable estimate of k_e** can be generated from comparable listed companies.

4.5 Link to price to earnings ratios

The DVM may be adapted to provide a formula for the P/E ratio of our unquoted company simply by dividing both sides of the equation by Earnings per Share (EPS).

$MV = \dfrac{D_1}{k_e - g}$

dividing by EPS

$$P/E = \frac{D_1/E}{k_e - g}$$

where D_1/E = the dividend payout ratio

The price/earnings ratio is equal to the dividend payout ratio divided by the cost of equity less **expected** dividend growth.

Since we have derived the P/E ratio from the DVM, we can also infer that a key assumption underlying the DVM is that the price/earnings ratio or "valuation multiple" is not expected to change.

4.6 Problems with dividend-based valuations

The DVM assumes dividends can be estimated as a steadily growing perpetuity. It is therefore not appropriate for

- Companies experiencing rapid growth. (Clearly the rate of growth (g) must be lower than k_e).
- Companies where the growth rate in dividends is expected to change.
- Companies where the price/earnings ratio or dividend payout ratio is expected to change.

In addition, where k_e is to be estimated from the prospective dividend yield and estimated dividend growth of a comparable quoted company, problems arise if the quoted company differs from the unquoted company that is being valued.

- The gearing company of the companies must be similar to avoid distortions.
- The business risk of the companies must be similar.
- The expected growth rate in dividends must be similar.
- The liquidity of the two stocks must be similar.

5 RELATIVE VALUATION MEASURES

5.1 Introduction

It is possible to value companies by reference to other comparable quoted companies. This will be satisfactory when there are many comparable companies and the market is not at an extreme of valuation.

The method of comparable analysis involves taking a price multiple for a comparable quoted company and applying it to the unquoted company that is being valued.

Alternative approaches involve using the average multiple for a group of comparable companies, the multiple for the industry or sector or, for private company M&A, a transactions multiple – the price at which private comparable companies were sold to trade or private equity buyers.

The price multiples that are in common use are described below.

5.2 Price-to-Earnings ratio

5.2.1 The calculation

The most popular price multiple is based on earnings levels and is called the price-to-earnings (P/E) ratio.

It is calculated as

Formula to learn

$$\text{P/E ratio} = \frac{\text{Price per share}}{\text{Earnings per share}}$$

The P/E ratio for a similar quoted company can be inserted into the formula along with the earnings per share of the company being valued. The required valuation will be the missing figure. The key assumption underlying the P/E valuation approach is that earnings yields are similar for comparable quoted and unquoted companies.

This may be appropriate where earnings are a good indicator of value, i.e. not distorted by dubious accountancy practices, and of high quality, i.e. a good indicator of underlying or trend earnings and not distorted by one-off exceptional items.

It also requires that the comparables being used are similar, not only in terms of their business mix, but also in their capital structure and choice of accounting policies.

5.3 Uses of P/E ratios

Reasons why the P/E multiple is commonly **used** are as follows.

- It is based on earnings, which is recognised as the key driver of value (**earnings power**).
- It is widely recognised and frequently used.

5.4 Problems with using P/E ratios

As with the dividend based approach, the problems relate to comparability of the quoted companies with the company being valued. These can be

- Differences in accounting policies.
- Different growth levels.
- Different levels of gearing.
- Different levels of liquidity.
- Different levels of business risk.

Moreover, the P/E approach cannot be used for loss-making companies (asset based or cash flow based valuations will be more appropriate). The earnings per share figure is extremely susceptible to differences in accounting policies. It is affected by different stock valuation, provisioning, depreciation and deferred taxation policies. The P/E ratio is therefore very subjective and difficult to compare between companies, sectors and countries.

Ideally, the P/E ratio could be adjusted to reflect these differences. For example, it is usually the case that unlisted companies are valued at, say, a 30% discount to an equivalent listed company to reflect the lack of liquidity in the shares. However, the assumptions that need to be made and the theoretical nature of such adjustments means that, if additional sophistication is required, it may be better to use a cash-based approach to valuation from the very start.

P/E ratios may also be based on 'pro-forma' earnings that have been adjusted to take account of the transaction under consideration. An example might be a flotation where the finance being raised is, for the most part, being used to reduce the indebtedness of the company. This is a common situation where the floating company was originally a management buy-out. The earnings are restated to allow for a much lower interest charge.

5.5 EBIT multiples

<table>
<tr><td>**Formula to learn**</td><td>$$\text{EBIT multiple} = \frac{\text{Enterprise value}}{\text{EBIT}}$$</td></tr>
</table>

Instead of using P/E ratios, which rely on a post-tax figure for earnings, it is possible to do a similar calculation based upon earnings before interest and tax (EBIT). Published EBIT multiples are not so widely available as P/E ratios.

The idea of the EBIT multiple is that it removes distortions caused by the company's gearing structure or tax position, which may change if the company is acquired and merged into a larger group.

Since the EBIT multiple is being based on an earnings figure before interest is paid, it is effectively valuing the whole of the firm rather than just the part of the firm that belongs to equity investors. The earnings before interest need to be used to pay off providers of debt as well as equity finance. In order to find the value of the firm's equity, the value of the debt financing will need to be deducted from the total value calculated.

As with the P/E ratio, the EBIT multiple has problems of comparability across companies. Even though it is based on a pre-interest figure some accounting distortions remain, such as differences in depreciation or stock valuation.

5.6 EBITDA multiples

<table>
<tr><td>**Formula to learn**</td><td>$$\text{EBITDA multiple} = \frac{\text{Enterprise value}}{\text{EBITDA}}$$</td></tr>
</table>

It is possible to base earnings multiples on various other definitions of earnings. For example, a multiple based on earnings before interest, tax, depreciation and amortisation (EBITDA). The benefit of EBITDA multiples is that they strip out the accounting items of depreciation and amortisation, which may vary substantially between companies. It could be viewed that such adjustments are actually aiming to move towards a normalised cash-based figure for the company in question.

6 CASH-BASED VALUATIONS

6.1 Introduction

Discounted cash flow-based valuations are theoretically superior to other valuation methods, since they are based on the fundamental determinant of corporate value, i.e. cash. We have already seen an example of cash-based valuations in the dividend valuation model based on cash dividends.

6.2 The use of cash-based valuations

6.2.1 An investor acquiring control of the company

The dividend valuation method can be used to value a company on the basis of its cash dividends. As such, it is particularly appropriate to minority investors who only get the dividends determined by the directors. The cash valuation used here focuses on the cash that the business generates before investors have received their returns. It is of use to a controlling shareholder who can decide whether to reinvest this 'free cash flow' of the business or to pay it out as a dividend.

There are two main ways in which the cash flow can be used for analysis and valuation purposes

- Compared to the market value of the company giving a multiple for comparison with other companies
- Forecasting into the future, with or without growth, and calculating the present value giving a valuation of the business

6.3 Free cash flow

6.3.1 What is free cash flow?

In order to produce a cash flow-based valuation of a company, it is first necessary to estimate the cash flows it can generate for its investors on an ongoing basis. This is often referred to as 'free cash flow'.

> The **free cash flow** is the total amount of cash the company generates after tax and after funding purchases of fixed assets and any required increases in working capital, assuming that there is no debt. As such, it represents the maximum amount that a company could pay out to its investors, assuming that the company is ungeared and has no commitment to pay interest to debt investors.

6.3.2 Calculation of free cash flow

Historical analysis

The starting point for the historical analysis of free cash flow is the net cash flow from operating activities in the cash flow statement of the company's accounts. Under IFRS (IAS7) this figure is after tax and after the payment of interest. To arrive at free cash flow the following adjustments are made.

	£
Free cash flow	
Cash flow from operating activities	X
Add: After-tax interest expense	X
Less: Capital expenditure	(X)
Less: Increase in working capital[1]	(X)
Free cash flow	X

[1] A decreased in working capital is added.

6.3.3 Forecasting free cash flow

When forecasting free cash flow it is more common to use a "top down" approach, i.e. starting from forecasts of operating profit (EBIT).

A possible layout for a free cash flow forecast is set out below.

	£
Operating profit	X
Less: Tax paid	(X)
After tax profit	X
Add: Depreciation	X
+/− Other non-cash items	X
Cash flow from operations[1]	X
Less: Capital expenditure	(X)
Less: Increase in working capital	(X)
Free cash flow	X

[1] After tax but **before** interest

Capital expenditure is the total amount of cash spent on purchasing new fixed assets less the proceeds from fixed assets. In the historical analysis total capital expenditure should be included. However, when forecasting capital expenditures some analysts prefer to forecast only replacement capital expenditures on the basis that any additional investment represents an application of free cash flow.

6.3.4 Working capital

An increase in working capital represents an increased investment in the asset base of the business, and means that a certain amount of profits has not yet been realised in cash. Working capital should only include stocks, debtors and prepayments as currents assets and creditors and accruals as current liabilities.

Financial items such as cash, short-term financial investments and financial interest-bearing short-term debt, though part of the accounting definition of working capital set out in Chapter 8, are excluded in the free cash flow calculation.

6.4 Stages in a cash flow valuation

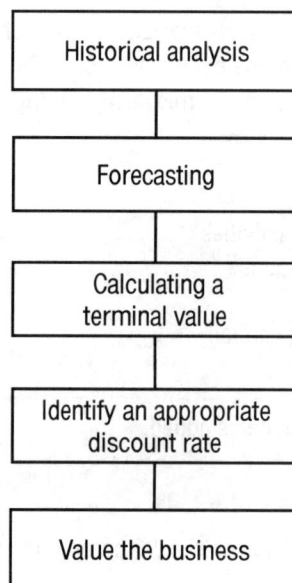

The following key stages need to be followed in a cash flow-based valuation of a business.

Stages in a Cash Flow Valuation

```
┌─────────────────────────┐
│   Historical analysis   │
└─────────────────────────┘
            │
┌─────────────────────────┐
│       Forecasting       │
└─────────────────────────┘
            │
┌─────────────────────────┐
│     Calculating a       │
│     terminal value      │
└─────────────────────────┘
            │
┌─────────────────────────┐
│ Identify an appropriate │
│      discount rate      │
└─────────────────────────┘
            │
┌─────────────────────────┐
│   Value the business    │
└─────────────────────────┘
```

6.5 Historical analysis of cash flows

6.5.1 Purpose of historical analysis

We have seen above how a company's free cash flow is derived from two main factors.

- Its ability to generate profits from its asset base.
- The level of reinvestment in the business.

In order to be able to forecast cash flows for the future by analysing these factors, it is important to analyse the past. By understanding how the company has generated cash in the past, we can examine the existing and forecast economic and industrial environment, to establish how it can continue to generate cash in the future.

6.6 Forecasting cash flows

6.6.1 The explicit forecasting period

The valuation of the company in question will be based on two main elements, namely the explicit forecasting period and the terminal value. The explicit forecasting period is the period for which detailed cash flow forecasts are completed. The terminal value is a more simplistic forecast for the remainder of the company's life, based on simplifying assumptions for growth and rates of return.

Since the terminal value is based on simplifying assumptions and, hence, may be a less rigorous valuation technique, it is desirable to make it of less significance in the context of the overall valuation. This is achieved by extending the length of the explicit forecasting period, with its more detailed analysis of the company and its cash flows. The problem with extending the explicit period is that any cash flow forecast for years further into the future is inherently less reliable than one for a closer period of time. It may, therefore, be that the additional accuracy obtained from a longer explicit forecast is spurious and a simpler approach is just as good. As always, valuation techniques are not absolute measures and a large element of judgement is required.

A theoretically sound approach is to make the explicit forecasting period the length of time for which the company is able to maintain a level of return on new investment in excess of the required returns to shareholders. The reason for this is considered below in relation to calculating the terminal value. In practice, analysts will usually establish a forecasting period of between five and ten years, depending on whether the company is in a stable or a growing industry.

6.6.2 Identifying key variables

In developing the forecast, the analyst will need to identify the key factors affecting cash flow over the forecast period. These will include

- The economic and industry scenario.
- The level of investment made by the company.
- The return on investment.

Having identified the key characteristics of the industry, it is usually the case that demand will be the key limiting factor for the company. Having identified the anticipated level of demand, the level of investment needed to sustain that demand and the level of operating costs can be derived by making assumptions for operating profit margins and asset turnover.

6.6.3 Sensitivity analysis

As with any investment appraisal decision, sensitivity analysis is required to establish the likely impact of a change in a key variable on the company's value. Key variables to consider will include estimated volumes and prices, for example.

6.7 Terminal value

6.7.1 The purpose of the terminal value calculation

When valuing a company, its total value is usually broken down into two components, as mentioned above.

Formula to learn

> Total value of the company's operations = Present value of operating cash flows in the explicit forecast period + Present value of the Terminal value

The terminal value calculation is designed to estimate the present value of the cash flows outside of the explicit forecast period. It can be incorporated into the cash flow forecast as the value of the business at the end of the explicit forecast period. The present value of the cash flows in the explicit forecast period and the terminal value can then be discounted back using an appropriate cost of capital to give the value of the company today.

6.8 Calculation of terminal value

The terminal value can be calculated using a number of different approaches, however the most common is to assume that cash flows outside the explicit forecasting period approximate a steadily growing perpetuity and calculate the terminal value using the perpetuity with growth formula:

$$\text{Terminal value at } t_x = \frac{FCF_X(1+g)}{WACC - g}$$

Where   g   =   steady state growth rate

       FCF_X =   the forecast free cash flow at period x (the final cash flow of our explicit forecasting period)

       WACC   =   the weighted average cost of capital

Note that the final forecast explicit period cash flow needs to be increased by the steady state growth rate since the perpetuity formula gives use the present value at time t when the first cash flow occurs one year later.

This formula is similar to that used in the dividend valuation model except that

- The relevant cash flow is free cash flow (i.e. returns available to both debt and equity investors).

- The relevant discount rate is the weighted average cost of capital (WACC) as opposed to the cost of equity.

6.8.1 Should growth be incorporated?

An alternative approach is to assume no further growth outside of the explicit forecasting period in which case terminal value can be estimated using the perpetuity with no growth formula.

$$\text{Terminal value at } t_x = \frac{AFCF_X}{WACC}$$

where $AFCF_x$ = Adjusted free cash flow at time x

Note that as no further growth is assumed the relevant cash flow $AFCF_x$ should be higher than used in the perpetuity with growth formula since capital expenditures may be reduced to replacement level, whereas they need to be higher to generate a growing asset base.

In practice, because we operate in an inflationary environment, where the money value of revenues is likely to increase overtime, it is common to incorporate a modest growth assumption.

6.8.2 Price-to-earnings ratios

An alternative approach is to assume that the company is going to be sold at the end of the explicit forecasting period. The analyst will need to identify the expected net operating profits after tax for the last year of the forecast period and apply an appropriate P/E ratio to these profits.

If this approach gives a significantly different valuation to the cash-based approach, the reasons for this will need to be analysed carefully. For example, it may be that the cash-based approach is using a different discount rate than that used by the market to value companies in the sector in general. If this is the case, then the discount rate being used for the cash-based valuation will need to be studied very carefully to ensure that it is appropriate.

6.9 Discounting

6.9.1 The present value of the free cash flows

Having established the cash flows the company is capable of generating and distributing to investors and a terminal value, these need to be discounted to a present value. The cost of capital used will reflect the risk of the business.

6.9.2 The weighted average cost of capital (WACC)

There are a number of different ways in which to identify the appropriate discount rate to calculate the present values. The usual method, however, is the Weighted Average Cost of Capital (WACC). This takes account of the relative costs of debt versus equity finance and is calculated using the specific gearing ratio (level of debt to equity) of each company.

Since a company will be financed by a combination of debt and equity, the WACC provides a single discount rate that reflects all the sources of finance in their correct proportions.

6.9.3 Calculating the weighted average cost of capital

The WACC is calculated using the formula below.

$$WACC = k_e \times \frac{E}{E+D} + k_d \times \frac{D}{E+D}$$

Where

k_e = the cost of equity. The alternative methods of calculating the cost of equity were set out with the Dividend Valuation Model.

k_d = the cost of debt. This is the after-tax interest rate paid by the company.

E = the market value of the company's equity.

D = the market value of the company's debt.

Alternatively, if the cost of equity and the cost of debt are known, the WACC may be derived directly from the company's gearing or debt/equity ratio.

Example

The cost of equity is 10% and the after-tax cost of debt is 6%. Gearing (the debt/equity ratio) is 0.5x. Calculate the WACC.

$$WACC = k_e \times \frac{E}{D+E} + k_d \times \frac{D}{D+E}$$

While we do not know the absolute market values of debt or equity, we know that the market value of debt = 0.5 × the market value of equity. Therefore, we simply set equity = 1 unit and solve for the WACC as shown below.

$$WACC = 10\% \times \frac{1}{1.5} + 6\% \times \frac{0.5}{1.5}$$

$$= 8.67\%$$

6.10 Net present value

Having identified our explicit period free cash flows and a terminal value, the net present value is simply the sum of these items discounted at the WACC.

$$\text{Net present value} = \frac{FCF_1}{1+WACC} + \frac{FCF_2}{(1+WACC)^2} \cdots \frac{FCF_n}{(1+WACC)^n} + \frac{TV_N}{(1+WACC)^n}$$

Where FCF_{1-n} = the explicit forecast free cash flows from t_1 to t_n.

TV_N = The terminal value at t_n

6.10.1 Illustration

An analyst has identified the following free cash flows for a company.

Year 1	100
Year 2	200
Year 3	250

After that steady growth of 3% is assumed in perpetuity.

The WACC is 10%.

Calculate the net present value.

Our first step is to calculate the present value of our three explicit free cash flows at the WACC.

$$\text{Present value of explicit free cash flows} = \frac{100}{1.1} + \frac{200}{(1.1)^2} + \frac{250}{(1.1)^3} = 444.$$

Next we calculate the terminal value at Year 3 based on our perpetuity with growth formula. Note that we need to use a Year 4 cash flow, which we calculate by growing the Year 3 cash flow at our steady state 3% growth rate.

$$TV_3 = \frac{250 \times (1.03)}{10\% - 3\%} = 3{,}678.57$$

Then we need to discount the terminal value at Year 3 back to t_0 again using the WACC.

$$TV_0 = \frac{3{,}678.57}{(1.1)^3} = 2{,}764$$

The net present value is therefore the sum of the present value of the explicit free cash flows and the present value of the terminal value.

Net present value = 444 + 2,764

= 3,208

6.11 Uses of cash flow based-valuations

In general, a cash flow based valuation is considered the superior valuation method as it focuses on the ultimate driver of value creation: cash.

It is of particular use when

- Assets are difficult to identify and measure and are expected to change through time. This makes an asset-based valuation inappropriate.

- The company is experiencing rapid growth. In particular, if expected growth is higher that the cost of equity the dividend valuation model cannot be applied. Where a company is experiencing rapid growth, it is appropriate to forecast cash flows separately over this high growth period, since growth in excess of the required return to investors is not sustainable indefinitely.

- There are few comparable quoted companies, accounting policies vary or the quality of earnings is suspect.

- The desired valuation is an enterprise valuation as opposed to an equity valuation.

6.12 Limitations of the cash flow-based approach

- Meaningful forecasts of cash flows are difficult to make due, for example, to lack of data or uncertainty over future trends.

- For an asset-based business such as a property or investment company.

- There are comparable quoted companies with similar capital structures, the quality and earnings are not distorted by dubious accounting policies.

- The company is experiencing steady growth, the market is fairly valued and the valuation multiple is not expected to change.

7 ILLUSTRATION

7.1 Introduction

The following illustration demonstrates the first three valuation techniques explained in this chapter, assets, dividends and P/E using an example company, Pacino Limited.

The following are financial details for Pacino Limited.

7.1.1 Profit and loss account for the year ended 31 august

	2003 £'000	2004 £'000	2005 £'000
Profit after tax	300	359	435
Dividends	(150)	(155)	(163)
Retained profit	150	204	272

7.1.2 Balance sheet as at 31 august

	2003 £'000	2004 £'000	2005 £'000
Fixed assets	750	900	1,120
Working capital	400	460	520
Loans	(100)	(106)	(114)
	1,050	1,254	1,526
Share capital	100	100	100
Reserves	950	1,154	1,426
	1,050	1,254	1,526

The required return on the company's equity is estimated to be 20%. The P/E ratio of similar listed companies is around 9x. The net dividend yield of similar listed companies is 4%. The fixed assets are shown at cost that is approximately £200,000 below market value. The loans are shown at market value.

7.1.3 Requirements

Estimate the value of Pacino Limited, using the following methods.

- Dividend valuation model (DVM).
- P/E ratio.
- Asset value.

7.1.4 Dividend valuation model

The first requirement is to estimate the anticipated growth in dividends. This could be done by extrapolating from past dividend growth.

$$150(1 + g)^2 = 163$$

$$(1 + g)^2 = \frac{163}{150}$$

$$g = 4\%$$

Alternatively, the dividend growth rate of similar quoted companies could be roughly estimated as the cost of capital less the net dividend yield, i.e. (20% − 4%) 16%.

Further investigation would be needed to establish the appropriate growth rate to use. Factors to consider include

- Whether the past growth for Pacino is likely to continue.

- Whether the higher growth rate for earnings will translate into higher dividends at some stage. Dividend cover has been improving over the three years.

- Whether the comparable quoted companies are in the same area of the sector or in higher growth areas.

Using a growth rate of 4%, the value of the company is given by

Formula to learn

$$MV = \frac{D_0(1+g)}{k_e - g}$$

$$MV = \frac{163,000 \times 1.04}{0.2 - 0.04} = \textbf{£1,060,000}$$

Note that the £163,000 is the historic dividend. Next year's prospective dividend needs to be estimated by using the expected growth in dividends of 4%.

7.1.5 Price to Earnings ratio

Formula to learn

$$\frac{P}{E} = \frac{Price}{EPS} = \frac{Equity\ value}{PAT}$$

$$\therefore Equity\ value = PAT \times \frac{P}{E}$$

$$MV = £435,000 \times 9 = £3,915,000$$

This needs to be discounted to reflect the lack of marketability of the shares, say by 30%.

$$£3,915,000 \times 70\% = \textbf{£2,740,500}$$

The P/E ratio method gives a much higher valuation than the dividend-based method. This is because Pacino Limited's earnings have been growing at a significantly higher rate than dividends, meaning that earnings are much higher than dividends. So long as the retained earnings are being reinvested wisely and will give rise to higher earnings and dividends in the future, the P/E ratio method may give a fairer valuation.

7.1.6 Assets

The book value of the assets needs to be adjusted for the market value of the fixed assets. The value of the company is given by

$$MV = 1,526,000 + 200,000 = \textbf{£1,726,000}$$

7.1.7 Summary of valuations

Basis	Equity Value
DVM	£1,060,000
P/E	£2,740,500
Assets	£1,726,000

Therefore, the value of the equity of Pacino Limited lies in the range £1,060,000 to £2,740,500.

With suitable cash flow information, this valuation range can then be cross-checked to a free cash flow valuation before arriving at a final valuation range.

8 SUMMARY OF VALUATION METHODS

Valuation Approach	Principal Uses
Asset Based Valuation	■ Asset-intensive business ■ Liquidation value ■ Security in a share value ■ Company with no profits or cash flows ■ Equity value
Dividend Valuation Model	■ Minority investors ■ Equity value ■ Good estimates of k_e and g available ■ Steady state growth
P/E Ratio (comparable companies approach)	■ Comparable quoted companies ■ High quality earnings ■ Steady state growth ■ Equity value
Discounted Cash Flow	■ Generally superior approach ■ Growth companies ■ Assets hard to measure/likely to change ■ Sufficient information to make meaningful forecasts ■ Few comparable quoted companies ■ Enterprise value

CHAPTER ROUNDUP

- The enterprise value of a company represents the total value of a company to all investors, both equity and debt.

- Equity value excludes debt, preference shares and minority interests from enterprise.

- The stock market value of a company is suitable for small stakes in listed companies.

- The transaction value of a company reflects the cost of buying the whole company in an acquisition.

- The break-up value of a company is the value from selling off its separable assets.

- The asset based method is used to assess a minimum price for a company if it were to be broken up.

- A dividend based valuation is useful for small shareholdings in unquoted companies using the dividend valuation model formula of $MV = \dfrac{D_1}{k_e - g}$

- Relative valuation measures use comparable quoted companies.

- The P/E ratio $= \dfrac{\text{Price per share}}{\text{Earnings per share}}$

- Cash based methods reduce accounting distortions and allow a company to be valued on a cash dividend basis or as a present value of future cash flows.

BPP
LEARNING MEDIA

TEST YOUR KNOWLEDGE

Check your knowledge of the chapter here, without referring back to the text.

1. What are the main components of enterprise value?

2. Which value is appropriate to use for a change in control?

3. Why is it inappropriate to use an asset based valuation method for a service company?

4. Which period's dividend is divided by the cost of equity minus growth in the dividend valuation model?

5. What is indicated by a relatively high P/E ratio of a company compared to others in that sector?

6. What does EBITDA stand for?

7. What is enterprise free cash flow?

8. What is the formula for the weighted cost of capital?

TEST YOUR KNOWLEDGE: ANSWERS

1.   Market capitalisation + Gross debt – Cash + Preference shares + Minority interest.

      (See Section 2.1)

2.   Transaction value.

      (See Section 2.2.2)

3.   They tend to have relatively few assets on their balance sheet.

      (See Section 3.4)

4.   It is the dividend at the end of Year 1 that is used.

      (See Section 4.2.4)

5.   A high P/E ratio indicates good growth prospects as investors are prepared to pay a higher multiple of the
      current earnings.

      (See Section 5.2.1)

6.   Earnings before interest payable, tax, depreciation and amortisation.

      (See Section 5.6)

7.   The cash flow generated after tax, funding purchases of fixed assets and increases in working capital.

      (See Section 6.3.1)

8. $K_e \times \dfrac{E}{E+D} + K_d \times \dfrac{D}{E+D}$

      (See Section 6.9.3)

11

Acquisitions and Disposals

Acquisitions can be made for a variety of reasons. We look in this chapter at the positive reasons and some more dubious ones.

Different structures for the acquisition involve varying degrees of participation by existing or new management. This gives rise to many different terms and expressions that you are required to be familiar with.

CHAPTER CONTENTS

CHAPTER LEARNING OBJECTIVES

Acquisitions and Disposals

- **Know** the key features of an acquisition or disposal and the reasons why they happen.

    - Listed or private.
    - Hostile or recommended.
    - Owner/manager exit.
    - Existing/continuing/new management participation.

- **Understand** how acquisitions are typically financed and by whom.
- **Understand** the basic tax considerations of acquisitions and disposals.
- **Know** the key features of and differences between a trade sale and a spin-off.

Private Equity and Debt Financed Transactions

- **Know** the key features of and differences between

    - A management buy-out (MBO).
    - A management buy-in (MBI).
    - A leveraged buy-out (LBO).
    - A leveraged buy-in (LBI).
    - A buy-in management buy-out (BIMBO).
    - An institutional buy-out (IBO).
    - A public to private (PTP).

- **Understand** the key terms and phrases typically used in private equity and debt transactions

    - Debt/equity ratio.

    - Capital structure, i.e. types of shares and their rights (e.g. dividend, liquidation preference, redemption conversion, anti-dilution, pre-emption, voting).

    - Ratchets.

    - Investment hurdles.

    - 'Drag and tag' provision.

    - Good leaver/bad leaver.

    - 'Pay to play'.

    - Bridge finance.

    - Burn rate.

    - Capitalise.

    - Carried interest.

    - Co-investment.

    - Convertible debt.

    - Down/follow-on round.

    - Founder shares.

- **Understand** the investment process and the funding components of a typical

    - Trade sale.
    - MBO/MBI.
    - PTP.

- **Understand** how to identify the principles applied in determining the levels/ratio of equity and debt that may be available in such transactions.

1 INTRODUCTION TO ACQUISITIONS AND DISPOSALS

The purpose of this chapter is to cover the key areas to consider when making an acquisition or disposal. It considers specifically the acquisition process for both private and public companies. Additional regulations relating to the takeovers of UK public limited companies are found in the chapter on the City Code.

We also consider the financing methods that can be used to acquire a new company, and in particular, the participation of the existing management in some form of a management buy-out.

2 MOTIVES FOR ACQUISITIONS

In considering whether an acquisition is appropriate or not, a company should always address the underlying rationale. The key reason given why most acquisitions fail is that they are not planned properly and insufficient thought is given to the financial benefits likely to arise from the transaction. In all cases, a bidder should be able to isolate and quantify the anticipated synergies.

2.1 Synergies

Synergies are the financial benefits arising as a result of a transaction. They can be derived from three sources.

- Cost savings.
- Revenue enhancement.
- One-off cash inflows.

2.1.1 Cost savings

Synergistic cost savings can arise in the combined operations from operational reasons, such as eliminating duplication in the merged entity, as well as improvements in the financing structure of the business.

- Examples of both types of cost savings are as follows.

- Reducing head-count in administrative functions.

- Economies of scale leading to improved production efficiencies.

- Gaining critical mass and market dominance, giving ability to set prices and negotiate bulk ordering discounts.

- Eliminating excess production capacity.

- Reducing the group's effective tax rate. This could for example result from acquiring foreign operations that are taxed at a lower rate than the UK.

- Improving free cash flow. The acquisition may have the effect of reducing business seasonality, leading to an improvement in the entity's credit rating and an overall cheaper cost of debt.

2.1.2 Revenue enhancement

The merged entity can benefit from the following.

- Cross-selling products to two separate customer bases.
- Common distribution channels.
- Common advertising, sales promotion and warehousing.

2.1.3 One-off cash Inflows

Non-recurring cash savings arise from the following.

- Disposal of surplus assets.
- One-off tax credits.
- Disposal of non-core elements of the business.

2.1.4 Quantifying synergies

Once the source of the synergies has been highlighted, it is necessary to estimate the financial effect and also the timing of the cash inflows. A discounted cash flow forecast can then be prepared which computes a present value of the synergies. The valuer should also consider the negative impact of the transaction, for example, cash outflows arising due to reorganisation and redundancies or delays in anticipated revenue streams being realised.

2.2 Motivations for making acquisitions

Possible motivations for acquisitions that could lead to the realisation of synergies, include the following.

2.2.1 Horizontal integration

Acquire a company in a similar line of business. This may give access to different geographical markets or new market segments. It could also protect market position by helping eliminate the competition.

2.2.2 Vertical integration

Acquire a supplier or customer. Such integration may enable a company to secure an important source of supply for its business. It may enable a company to obtain supplies more cheaply than its competition. Alternatively, it may enable a company to control its outlets to the final buying public, as is the case, say, with breweries and public houses.

2.2.3 Purchase an undervalued company

It may be the case that the target is currently undervalued by the market and that there is an opportunity to buy it cheaply. If the acquirer thinks that this is the case, then he should have very good justification for his view as opposed to the general view of the market.

2.2.4 Acquire to gain expertise

Acquire technical or other expertise. This could enable a company to seize market share from competitors or retain competitive edge in a sector facing rapid technological change.

2.2.5 Market penetration

Market penetration means developing new and larger markets for a company's existing products. A market penetration policy will often be used within markets that are becoming more international or globalised. Cross-border mergers and acquisitions can be a means of becoming a major player in such markets.

2.2.6 Acquire for growth

The quickest way of achieving growth is usually by acquisition. In the short term, it is probably the most expensive of all the options. It does, however, enable a company to acquire new expertise, avoid the need to build a market presence gradually and may result in synergies that give extra benefit to the company as a whole.

Acquisition also entails many risks. For example, the acquirer may pay too high a price, may buy a very poor company with hidden liabilities or may buy into an area that it does not really understand and which becomes a drain on its resources.

2.2.7 Financial rationale for acquisitions

The acquisition could be made in order to generate potential financial benefits for the purchaser, for example

- Improved earning quality (consistency of annual profits) through acquiring a more consistently or counter-seasonally profitable business.

- Greater and cheaper access to financing through acquiring a more cash generative subsidiary.

- Possible use of tax losses of the target company. However, as most tax authorities dislike acquisitions which are entered into simply in order to reduce tax, these tax losses **may not be usable post acquisition**.

- Enhanced asset backing for the bidder's shares (where the bidder has a lower ratio of net assets to share price than the target company). This would increase the assets available to secure loans, thereby probably improving the terms and amounts of any borrowing.

2.3 Some dubious motivations for acquisitions

2.3.1 Diversification

Diversification is achieved by acquiring a business that faces different risks from an entity's existing operations. Diversification may bring benefits to a group, for example by reducing the overall beta of the group and thus its equity cost of capital.

However, diversification is not, in itself, necessarily a sufficient reason for an acquisition. If investors are already fully diversified, then the acquiring company is not bringing any benefits to its shareholders by diversifying its business portfolio. The shareholders have already done this for themselves. With the globalisation of capital markets, it is increasingly easy for investors to diversify for themselves rather than relying on companies to do it for them.

In certain circumstances, diversification can actually be detrimental for a business, where the acquiring company has little or no expertise in the area into which it is diversifying. An inexperienced management may be unable to devote sufficient time or have the inside business knowledge to develop the acquired operations to their best potential.

Inclusion in a larger group that does not understand its business will merely demotivate a new subsidiary's management and probably result in higher administration and other overheads.

2.3.2 Accounting considerations

It has been possible for acquisitive conglomerates to achieve growth in earnings per share solely by acquiring new companies every year. Since accounting earnings are less important than the fundamentals of the business and its cash flows, acquisitions made on this business cannot be guaranteed to succeed in the long term.

2.3.3 To avoid takeover

The larger the company, the less likely it is to be the subject of a bid itself. However, recent experience has indicated that size is not necessarily a deterrent to a determined bidder, who may see benefits in acquiring the group and breaking it into smaller segments.

2.3.4 Empire building

Existing management may feel that the existing group is too small for their talents or the nature of the businesses is not interesting enough for them. In such a situation, rather than returning any surplus cash to shareholders by way of dividend, they may reinvest the cash in new businesses to enable them to demonstrate their management skills fully.

2.4 Why do acquisitions fail?

Success of mergers can be judged by reference to the returns generated post-acquisition versus those received by the acquirer's shareholders pre-acquisition. Mergers may not be successful for the following reasons.

2.4.1 Diversification into an area outside company expertise

The acquirer's management do not understand the business they now control and are not able to expand it in order to maximise possible returns.

2.4.2 Premium priced transaction

The acquirer overpaid for the target. Insufficient synergies are generated by the combined entity post-acquisition to justify the bid premium paid. Experience fails to deliver the financial benefits that were quantified prior to the deal completing.

2.4.3 Inappropriate financing structure

The capital structure put in place to fund the transaction is inappropriate. In particular, the combined entity post-acquisition generates insufficient cash flow to service the borrowings necessary to fund the transaction. Borrowings as a source of funding are cheaper for the company than equity. However, borrowings require a fixed cash payment relating to the interest charge for servicing the debt and a repayment of the capital amount outstanding. The greater the volatility of the underlying operational cash flows the more problematic it will be to service the debt finance. Riskier acquisitions should always be funded by a higher proportion of equity, which is a more permanent source of finance.

2.4.4 Ineffective rationalisation

Inappropriate or ineffective rationalisation of the businesses post-acquisition and inclusion in a larger group that does not understand its business will merely demotivate a new subsidiary's management. Consequently, this will probably result in higher administration and other overheads.

Empirical research indicates that the main beneficiaries of takeover activity are the offeree shareholders and that the post-acquisition returns of the offeror shareholders are negative.

3 MOTIVES FOR DISPOSAL

3.1 Introduction

Having identified the reasons why a company might be seeking acquisitions, it is also important to identify the reasons why a business is for sale. Once these are known, it will be possible to establish whether the business is actually saleable, how much it can be sold for and to whom it can be sold.

3.2 Corporate disposal of a subsidiary or division

Corporate disposals should be determined by strategic considerations. The same strategic ideas that determine whether a company should make acquisitions and in what area to expand will be relevant for disposals. The only difference is that the company should be disposing of businesses which do not fit into its strategic plans and which are non-core to the group.

3.2.1 Trade sale versus spin-off

Where a company, usually a large group, wishes to dispose of just one part of its business, this can be achieved by a trade sale or a spin-off.

In a **trade sale**, the disposal will be of the division or subsidiary **as a whole to one acquirer**. This will be of the assets and liabilities of the division as a going concern.

In a **spin-off**, the shares of the subsidiary company, currently 100% owned by the parent company in the group and therefore not publicly traded, will be **sold off to many investors** through either a public offer of securities or more likely a placing with institutional shareholders.

3.3 Personal disposal of a family business

A disposal of a business by an individual is unlikely to be motivated by strategic considerations of core businesses and growth areas. It is more likely that the entrepreneur has developed the business over a number of years and now wishes to realise his or her capital gain.

The motives of such a vendor may include the desire to

- Realise a cash sum after building up a business.
- Achieve a level of security.
- Enable his family to have a good education and good prospects.
- Let the business grow through combining with a larger concern.
- Obtain status through becoming a director of a listed company.
- Get out while the going is good, anticipating the demise of the business.

The motives of the vendor will determine what is a satisfactory form and level of consideration. A vendor who wishes to realise a cash sum and believes that the company is not going to prosper is going to want a cash deal and will possibly be prepared to sell for a smaller sum than would otherwise be the case. A vendor who believes that the company will continue to be successful, wants continued involvement in the business and wants to ensure the continued well-being of his staff, will probably only accept a higher price and may be happy to have an earn out deal and shares consideration.

4 STRUCTURING THE DEAL

4.1 Introduction

Now that we have identified the reasons and motivations behind the corporate finance transactions, we will consider the manner in which the acquisition or disposal is to take place and how it is to be financed. The finance may arise through the issue of more shares or bonds and other forms of long-term finance. The effect on the financial gearing of the acquiring company has already been considered in the Accounting Analysis chapter. In this chapter, we will consider the role of Venture Capital in the acquisition process.

4.2 What to purchase: shares or assets?

When buying a business in a private deal, it is possible to acquire either the shares of the company that is conducting the business or to buy the business and the related assets from the company. The factors to consider in deciding which route to follow include the following.

4.2.1 Share deal

- The deal will put the cash directly in the hands of the vendor, whereas selling assets would keep the cash in the company selling the assets. Taking the cash out of the company will involve additional tax charges. Receiving cash directly will only incur capital gains tax liabilities. If the consideration being paid is not cash, but shares or loan stock, then any capital gains tax liability may be deferred.

- The share deal will **preserve tax losses** in the business being sold, if applicable. Selling the business would mean that the acquirer would probably be unable to use these losses, as they can only be offset against future profits of that same subsidiary.

- Transferring shares may make it easier to keep the business of the target company intact, e.g. preserving long-term contracts with key customers.

- Transferring shares will avoid potential problems with loss and clawback of capital allowances that may occur with an asset sale.

4.2.2 Assets purchase

The acquirer can pick and choose which assets he wishes to buy.

- The business can be put into a 'clean' company. Any tax or other liabilities of the business will not have been assigned across and, hence, there is no risk of unpleasant surprises or liabilities in the future. This avoids the need for many of the detailed warranties and indemnities in the sale agreement.

- If the acquirer has previously disposed of certain business assets, such as land and buildings or plant and machinery, then it may be able to claim rollover relief when it replaces these by purchasing the assets of the target company.

- Purchase of assets will result in different capital allowances being received when compared to the purchase of shares in the company, which may be disadvantageous.

- Purchase of assets will create goodwill in the acquirer's accounts, whereas this may be avoided in the case of a shares purchase.

4.3 How to pay: shares or cash?

4.3.1 Cash bid

- The vendor's connection with the company is severed. He will, therefore, feel no concern as to whether or not the company does well in the future. Cash consideration provides the vendor with an exit route from the business and a way to realise his investment.

- The vendor will have to pay capital gains tax immediately on any gain.

- The acquirer's gearing will increase, if borrowings have been raised to finance the purchase. For a group with little debt, this may have the desirable effect of lowering the overall WACC (weighted average cost of capital) of the company. For a highly geared company, the increase in financial risk of the entity may have a negative impact on credit rating and therefore overall cost of capital. In the latter scenario, it may be appropriate to raise the cash via a rights issue, termed a 'cash underpinning'.

- The earnings of the acquiring group will be boosted by the profits of the target but reduced by the additional interest expense on increased borrowings or the lower interest income due to reduced cash balances. The net effect is likely to be an increase in earnings per share, but the quality of the earnings will have fallen as a result of the increased gearing.

- All the gains of the acquisition after allowing for the cost of the deal will go to existing shareholders of the acquirer. Their interest in the group has not been diluted through the introduction of additional shareholders.

- Instead of borrowing from outside providers of finance, the acquirer may issue loan stock to the vendor. This will enable the vendor to defer any capital gains tax liability until the loan stock is disposed of. It may also reduce the effective price of the acquisition if the coupon on the loan stock is below a market rate of interest.

4.3.2 Shares bid

- The fortunes of the vendor are tied in with the acquirer. It is, therefore, in his interests to ensure that the company does well in the future. It provides a way for the acquirer to incentivise the existing owners to maximise value in the post-acquisition period. Typically, the vendor of a private company will not be allowed to sell the shares for several years via a 'lock-in' arrangement.

- The vendor will be able to roll over any capital gains tax liability until the shares are disposed of. This will assist in tax planning.

- The gearing of the acquirer will reduce as a result of issuing shares, although this does depend on the level of gearing in the acquired company.

- The earnings of the acquirer will be boosted by the profits of the acquired company, but these will be spread over more shares, with the effect on earnings per share being uncertain. Generally, if a company acquires another company on a P/E ratio lower than its own, then the earnings per share subsequent to the acquisition should improve.

- The gains arising from the acquisition will have to be shared with the new shareholders. The interests of the existing shareholders will have been diluted by the issue of new shares to outsiders.

- The total dividend will need to be increased in order to maintain dividend per share after the acquisition.

4.4 Earn outs and deferred consideration

4.4.1 Advantages of earn outs

The **final consideration for a deal** is often paid several years after completion and is **linked to the profit** performance of the acquired company. This is termed as 'contingent' consideration or using an 'earn out'. The obvious advantage for the acquirer is that it ensures that a full price will only be paid if the acquisition is an unqualified success. It will also often mean that the vendor will stay on to manage the acquired company for several years. This will ensure continuity of management, enable a smooth transition to be made in terms of management over the period of the earn out and keep in the company an individual who may well be instrumental in the company's past success.

Deals can also be structured using deferred consideration where there is certainty at the outset as to the total consideration to be paid; however this is paid in instalments, thus helping the cash flow of the bidding company.

4.4.2 Problems of earn outs

- Calculation of profits for the purpose of working out the deferred consideration will need to be exactly defined. The temptation is for both sides to adjust the profits to suit themselves. The vendor, who is still the key director of the acquired company, may argue for reduced provisions for doubtful debtors, etc., whereas the acquirer may seek to impose excessive management charges against the company.

- The level of integration of the subsidiary with the group will need to be established. The group will want to integrate it as fully as possible in order to realise the anticipated benefits of the acquisition. However, it will need to be kept separate for the purposes of profit calculations. If central services are provided by the group, then this will reduce the costs in the subsidiary but a management charge will be made. Such charges can be difficult to negotiate and be seen as fair.

- The acquiring company's directors will seek to control the direction in which the subsidiary is heading, for the benefit of the overall group. This may conflict with the desire of the vendor to maximise profits over the period of the earn out. It will be difficult to ensure goal congruence between the vendor and the acquirer.

- The vendor will find it difficult to operate within the constraints of a large organisation and with budgets imposed from outside. His or her ability to run a successful business may have stemmed from the ability to make decisions quickly without reference to any outsiders. Furthermore, the vendor's status in the company will have changed and this may be hard for him or her to take.

- Earn outs can work against the long-term good of the business. The managers may be incentivised to focus too much on short-term profit targets and avoid making difficult decisions that have a detrimental impact on profit today but benefit the business as a whole in the long term. For example, if targets are based on a measure of free cash flow, capital expenditure could be put off until after the earn out period is completed.

4.4.3 Good leaver/ bad leaver

When a vendor is retaining some shareholding, or there is a phased buyout of their remaining shares, the sale and purchase agreement may need to address the **expected behaviour of the vendor** during and after the completion.

The price that will be paid for the vendor's remaining shares will be only be paid at market value (or a pre-determined fair value) if the leaver has 'behaved' during the handover period. A 'bad leaver' would normally be determined as someone who is in breach of their employment contract or has resigned from the company within a stated time period. A 'good leaver' is then simply someone who has not resigned or breached their contract.

4.4.4 Ratchets

The private equity firm could be prepared to offer other incentives to management to motivate them towards making the venture successful. These can take the form of a **ratchet**.

A ratchet is an arrangement whereby **managers get a larger share of the company's equity if the business performs well** and achieves certain specified targets in the business plan. The ratchet allows the exact division of the ordinary share capital between the entrepreneurs and the private equity firms to be decided after the success (or failure) of the venture is known.

Example

A company is the subject of an MBO. It is currently making annual after-tax profits of £2m, which are forecast to rise to £5m after three years. The private equity organisation financing the buyout has estimated that to achieve its target return on investment, it would have to own 40% of the company's ordinary share capital if annual profits are £5m at the end of three years. However, if annual profits are £6m, it will only need to own about 30% of the ordinary share capital to earn its target return.

Analysis

A ratchet arrangement could be agreed whereby for every £100,000 of profits over £5m per annum after three years, up to a ceiling of £6m, management should be entitled to an extra 0.5% of the equity. If profits reach £6m, management will therefore raise their stake in the ordinary share capital from 60% to 65%.

Ratchets can be both positive and negative. If profits are below a target amount, management could be required to give more of the equity to the private equity firm.

Ratchets will usually operate by means of convertible redeemable preference shares held by the private equity firm. Management's overall percentage stake in the equity could be increased, under the ratchet agreement, by the private equity firm choosing not to convert them into ordinary shares. Ratchets might also be in the form of options to buy new shares at a price below their current value. The exercise date for the options is linked to the payment of a cash bonus to management, who could then use the cash to pay for the new shares.

5 PRIVATE EQUITY AND DEBT FINANCED TRANSACTIONS

5.1 Introduction

Acquisitions can be made by directly by existing companies (public or private). In addition, many acquisitions are financed by private equity and debt funds that provide finance to other parties such as the management of a division to acquire a company. Examples of private equity acquisition funding, such as Management Buyouts, are outlined below.

Sometimes, the investment by an equity fund (often referred to as venture capital) is topped up with a further investment directly by members of that venture capital fund. This is referred to as **co-investment** and has the advantage of strengthening the investor's commitment and interest in the success of the new venture.

5.2 Acquisitions ('buyouts')

Venture capital funding can be invested to finance a change of control of the company in an acquisition or buyout situation. Two examples of acquisition funding are as follows.

- A management buyout **(MBO)** is the purchase of an existing company or a business unit by a group of its **own managers**, with the support of external investors.

- A management buy-in **(MBI)**, in contrast, is the purchase of an existing company or a business unit by an **external management** team, with financing from venture capitalists and banks. The buy-in team must have the necessary experience and/or expertise to run the business they are purchasing.

- An alternative is the buy-in management buyout **(BIMBO)**, where the **existing** management team is **supplemented with outside** expertise.

- Where there is a **significant proportion** of the finance provided by **debt finance** and a comparatively small financial stake held by the management team, this is referred to as a **Leveraged** buyout or buy-in **(LBO/LBI)**.

Sometimes, the buyout will be financed using very short-term finance known as **'bridge finance'** and subsequently replaced by longer term funding.

A key concern with start-ups will be their **cash burn rate**. This recognises that a start-up company will require significant cash upfront to pay for initial outlays to establish the business. Even when the business is up and running, there will be a delay in receiving the cash proceeds from the company's turnover. Therefore, it is important to monitor the extent to which net operating cash flows remain negative. The company must ensure that it has sufficient cash resources to cover this initial stage before net operating cash flows become positive.

If the cash burn rate is too high, the company is likely to require a further injection of capital. This is sometimes referred to as a **down round** or **follow-on round** of capital raising, as the original investors are called on to contribute a further tranche of capital into the firm, often at a lower share value than the original round.

5.3 Exit routes

Given the investor's need for a capital gain, a feasible exit route is vital from the very start. The exit is likely to be either a flotation, a trade sale to another company or a restructuring whereby the investor's shares are repurchased by the company. The most likely of these is a trade sale since many companies will not be sufficiently large to be floated or may be unsuitable for flotation for some other reason. A share repurchase scheme may not realise a realistic sum unless the company gears up to an unacceptable extent.

5.4 Investment hurdles and the principle of leverage

In order to compensate for the high-risk levels, the return on the investment will need to be substantial. The actual return required will vary from investment to investment but an internal rate of return of around 30% to 35% would not be unusual. The setting of a minimum return is known as an 'investment hurdle'. The venture capitalist will aim to maximise this return by introducing debt funding to help partly fund the purchase price. Since debt finance is repaid at par value on exit, any upside can be for the benefit of the Ordinary shareholders, namely the venture capitalist and the management. This is known as the 'Principle of Leverage' or 'financial gearing'.

Gearing (leverage) is the ratio of debt to equity in a company's finance structure. High gearing is associated with greater financial risk for two reasons.

A very high-geared company is a potential credit risk, as it might be unable to repay its debts or interest on schedule, particularly if interest rates rise.

Annual earnings (profits remaining for ordinary shareholders) are generally more volatile as gearing increases, as debt interest must be paid before profits are available to shareholders.

Additionally, a highly geared company may find its ability to raise further finance to be restricted, particularly if its existing borrowings have gearing covenants.

5.5 Public to private transactions

A public to private transaction (PTP) involves the buyout of a quoted company. The following is a list of scenarios when a public to private transaction might be appropriate.

- The company is a small cap share that has been underperforming the market as a result of general underperformance in the small cap sector.

- There is poor liquidity in the shares such that it is difficult for shareholders to realise value other than through some form of offer for the shares.

- There is at least one major shareholder who can influence the outcome of the bid.

- The proportion of shares in public hands falls such that there is not the marketability of share required in the Listing Rules.

- The institutional investors can add something to the company that it does not have in a public context as a separate entity, such as management skills or links to other companies.

5.6 Institutional buyouts (IBOs)

Here, an institution identifies a possible company, arranges the finance and then approaches a potential management team. IBOs tend to be the larger venture capital deals, with management often receiving a very small share of the overall equity.

5.7 Investor protections

In a small private company acquisition, there are specific concerns around the original owners of the business. They hold and may continue to hold significant shareholdings in the company and therefore the acquirer may require certain provisions to be inserted into the sale and purchase agreement to protect their interest.

5.7.1 Drag-along

A 'drag-along' provision will protect the acquiror in that, should a sufficient proportion of the shareholders of the company decide to dispose of their holding, they can 'drag-along' a reluctant minority. In effect, this is a **compulsory purchase agreement** when say 70% of the shareholders agree to sell, that none of the original shareholders can block.

5.7.2 Tag-along

A 'tag-along' provision states that, should an original shareholder decide post-acquisition to dispose of their shares, they must allow the acquiring investors the same proportional access to the new investor. For example, should a founding investor retain 40% of the shares in an acquisition, and then is approached later by a third party wishing to purchase half their remaining shares, the founder must ensure that the new third-party investor makes the same proportional offer to buy half of the other investors shares on the same terms.

However, there is no compulsory purchase element. If the investors are happy to retain their 60% holding, there is no obligation on them to sell. Therefore, the acquirers have just maintained a right to **participate equally in any exit route** being used by the founder.

5.7.3 Pay to play

This provision ensures that if the founder shareholders wish to **retain special entitlements** and protections, such as convertible preference shares, they **must participate pro rata in any subsequent issue** of new shares.

We might envisage a scenario where a relatively young company needs a vital injection of further equity in order to see it through a period of high cash burn. If the founder shareholders enjoy longer term equity upsides in convertible preference shares, then they have to 'pay' for the possibility of good long-term rewards by 'playing' along with the need to raise more equity finance along the way.

CHAPTER ROUNDUP

- Positive reasons for an acquisition include synergies of cost savings, reserve enhancement and one-off cash flows.

- Financial reasons include access to cheaper finance due to more cash generation or more asset backing, improved earnings quality and possible use of tax losses.

- However, acquisitions for more dubious reasons, such as to avoid being taken over or empire building may well lead to failure.

- A trade sale is the disposal of a company or division as a whole to one buyer.

- A spin-off is the sale of shares in a subsidiary to many different investors.

- If an acquirer purchases the share of a company then tax losses will be preserved. The purchase of individual assets will avoid any hidden liabilities in the company.

- An earn out clause will link the final consideration for a deal to the performance of the company post-acquisition.

- Buyouts can involve existing management (MBO), new management (MBI) or a mixture of old and new (BIMBO).

TEST YOUR KNOWLEDGE

Check your knowledge of the chapter here, without referring back to the text.

1. What are the main synergies anticipated by an acquirer?

2. What is vertical integration?

3. Name three dubious reasons for an acquisition.

4. What is the difference between a trade sale and a spin off?

5. What are the capital gains tax consequences for the vendor of a cash versus share consideration?

6. What is a good leaver/bad leaver clause?

7. What is a ratchet clause?

8. What is a PTP transaction?

TEST YOUR KNOWLEDGE: ANSWERS

1. Cost savings, revenue enhancement and one-off cash inflows.

    (See Section 2.1)

2. Acquiring a supplier or a customer.

    (See Section 2.2.2)

3. Diversification, accounting considerations, to avoid being taken over and empire building.

    (See Section 2.3)

4. A trade sale is to one buyer, whereas a spin off is to many investors.

    (See Section 3.2.1)

5. If the vendor receives cash then capital gains tax is payable immediately. If the consideration is shares in the new company then gains will be rolled over until the shares are disposed of.

    (See Section 4.3.2)

6. The final payout to the vendor is dependent of certain standards of behaviour and co-operation post– acquisition.

    (See Section 4.4.3)

7. An arrangement where managers get a larger amount if they perform well in terms of exit value achieved or speed of exit.

    (See Section 4.4.4)

8. When an acquirer buys a publicly quoted company and de-lists it.

    (See Section 5.5)

12

Corporate Finance Documentation

Throughout the acquisition it is important that appropriate documentation is maintained. To aid the understanding and memorisation of the different documents, we have divided the chapter into the four stages of initial, acquisition process, completion process and financing documentation. You need to know the purpose and scope of each document.

CHAPTER CONTENTS

CHAPTER LEARNING OBJECTIVES

General documentation in corporate finance transactions

- **Understand** the purpose and scope of an engagement letter in the context of a corporate finance transaction.

- **Understand** the meaning of representations, warranties and indemnities in the context of a corporate finance transaction.

- **Understand** the purpose, limitations and scope of representations, warranties and indemnities in the context of a corporate finance transaction.

- **Understand** the purpose of a disclosure letter in the context of a corporate finance transaction.

- **Understand** the use of vendor protection clauses in the context of a corporate finance transaction.

- **Understand** the purpose and scope of a Confidentiality letter in the context of a corporate finance transaction.

- **Understand** the purpose and scope of Shareholders agreement in the context of a corporate finance transaction.

Buying and selling documentation in corporate finance transactions

- **Understand** the purpose and key contents of an Information Memorandum.
- **Understand** the purpose of a Letter of Intent and Heads of Agreement.
- **Understand** the purpose of an Exclusivity Agreement.
- **Understand** the purpose of Comfort letters and Side letters.
- **Understand** the purpose of a Hold Harmless letters.
- **Understand** the purpose and scope of a Sale and Purchase Agreement.

Loan and security documentation in corporate finance transactions

- **Understand** the concept of taking security in the context of a corporate finance transaction.
- **Understand** the purpose and scope of a term sheet.
- **Understand** the purpose and scope of a loan agreement.
- **Understand** what guarantees and indemnities are in the context of a debt transaction.
- **Understand** the purpose, scope and limitations of loan representations and warranties.

Public company documentation in corporate finance transactions

- **Understand** the purpose and scope of subscription/placing agreements.
- **Understand** the purpose and scope of underwriting agreements.
- **Understand** the purpose of Verification notes.
- **Understand** the purpose and scope of a prospectus.
- **Understand** the purpose and scope of Longform and Shortform reports.
- **Understand** the purpose and scope of a legal due diligence report.

1 INTRODUCTION TO DOCUMENTATION

The purpose of this chapter is to cover the key documents that are required in corporate finance activities, i.e. mergers and acquisitions and financing transactions. Throughout the process, it is important that communications are clearly recorded and documented to ensure all agreements are legally valid and enforceable.

We have separated the documentation into the various stages of a typical transaction as follows.

- Initial documentation.

    - Engagement Letters with advisors.
    - Exclusivity Agreement.
    - Confidentiality Letter.
    - Hold Harmless Letter.

- Acquisition process documentation.

    - Information Memorandum.
    - Initial Letter of Intent and Heads of Agreement.
    - Representations, Warranties and Indemnities.
    - Disclosure Letter.
    - Comfort Letter and Side Letter.
    - Longform and Shortform Reports.

- Completion process documentation.

    - Sale and Purchase Agreement.
    - Shareholders Agreement.
    - Vendor Protection Clauses.
    - Verification Notes.

- Financing documentation.

    - Term sheet.
    - Loan agreement.
    - Guarantees and indemnities.
    - Loan Representations and Warranties.
    - Subscription/placing Agreements.
    - Underwriting Agreements.
    - Prospectus.

A summary table of the above is provided at the end of the chapter.

2 INITIAL DOCUMENTATION

When considering whether an acquisition is appropriate or not, a potential bidder may approach the target to request some initial information. Assuming the target does not treat it as a hostile bid, or indeed is actively seeking a disposal, they will wish to provide sufficient information to entice the bidder, without overly compromising their own commercial interests should the deal not go through. The release of this information and restrictions as to who may act on or communicate this information are set out in various initial documents.

2.1 Engagement letters

Both the bidder and the target will need to appoint specialist advisers right from the outset of the proceedings. These will not only include the corporate financiers – usually from an investment bank – to cover the financing and mechanics of the bid, but also lawyers for the legal agreements, accountants for reviewing the financials, pension actuaries to check for hidden pension liabilities, chartered surveyors to revalue properties and any other professional required for due diligence work.

2.1.1 Purpose

The purpose of the Engagement Letter is to **formally record**, in a legally binding document, **the nature of the relationship** between the professional adviser and their client. Should there be any disputes arising with the adviser during or after the corporate finance transaction, either party can sue in the courts for enforcement of the terms of the Engagement Letter.

2.1.2 Scope

The Engagement Letter will set out the nature of services to be provided by each adviser and will vary from adviser to adviser. This may be set out quite generally to allow for any circumstances arising, but at the same time it should clearly state any areas that would not be covered, for example where there is known to be another adviser appointed for that area such as a lawyer covering legal issues. There is likely to be a limitation of liability clause to accompany any restriction of scope as professional indemnity insurance costs are high and grounds for claims need to be minimised by the adviser.

The Engagement Letter will need to address the issue of fees to be paid to the adviser. It will not usually be possible to agree a fixed fee from the outset but the basis of the fees, together with their scheduling and payment terms can all be agreed upfront.

The engagement letter will then contain any other terms and conditions that are appropriate to the nature of the service each adviser is providing. There may also be certain requirements of the adviser's professional body to be included.

Finally, there will be a section which deals with any arbitration or complaints procedures that may be available, with ultimately an agreement as to which legal jurisdiction will apply in case of legal action.

An engagement letter will also be used when specialist advisers are appointed in connection with a stand alone financing transaction, e.g. IPO or rights issue.

2.2 Exclusivity agreement

2.2.1 Purpose

The Exclusivity Agreement prevents the vendor from entering into negotiations with any other potential purchasers for a limited time period. The acquirer therefore **secures sole negotiating rights** with the vendor for a period of time.

2.2.2 Scope

The Exclusivity Agreement may specify a two-stage time period (for example, exclusivity may be granted for four weeks, to be extended provided the purchaser can furnish proof of available funds at the end of the initial period), or more simply allow a single period of exclusivity. To be enforceable, the agreement must be for a fixed period and made under the official seal of the company, or consideration must pass to the vendor.

Exclusivity clauses or 'lock-out' clauses may be included in the Heads of Agreement (discussed below) or as a separate document.

2.3 Confidentiality letter

2.3.1 Purpose

If the target company board is not averse to the initial approach, then negotiations may be taken further. At this stage, it is likely that a Confidentiality Agreement (or Letter) will be signed by both parties. The objective of this is to ensure that any information released as part of the negotiations is not misused by the recipient, although other clauses may also be inserted.

The Confidentiality Letter is normally entered into prior to the release of any non-public information about the target (such as an information memorandum or management accounts), and would normally be a condition of the release of that information to the recipient. This can be included in the Heads of Agreement.

2.3.2 Scope

Typical points that would be covered in the Confidentiality Letter, also called a 'non-disclosure agreement' include the following.

- The nature of information that will be disclosed by each party.

- To whom the information will be made available in each company and who will not be permitted to see it.

- A prohibition on photocopies being made of information provided and an agreement to return all originals should negotiations fail.

- A prohibition on any information made available being used by the recipient for the benefit of their own business, unless they had already received the information from another legitimate source.

- Agreement not to disclose the existence of negotiations to other parties and stressing the secrecy of the negotiations.

- Agreement **not to poach staff** should the negotiations fail. This should prevent a potential bidder using confidential information to identify the best staff and then lure them away with better job offers.

There is no standard form; some non-disclosure agreements may be a page long, while others are 20 pages long. There is no regulatory or statutory requirement for such an agreement to be entered into, but it has become a matter of normal commercial practice. It is also possible for the agreements to be bilateral in nature – i.e. committing the vendor not to disclose information on the potential purchaser which they receive in the course of their negotiations.

The agreement is legally binding as a contract, it may however be difficult to enforce. To claim successfully in relation to a breach of confidentiality undertaking, the aggrieved party would have to prove the breach, and secondly quantify the amount of loss resulting from the breach, in order to sue for damages.

2.4 Hold harmless letter

2.4.1 Purpose

This is also referred to as an 'indemnification letter'. As the name suggests, it idemnifies (or will not hold the person receiving the letter liable) for any harm resulting from the information disclosed or actions undertaken in relation to a specified event.

2.4.2 Scope

The letter will need to specify the information or actions concerned and which parties are covered by the letter. It will state that the parties concerned will be indemnified and saved from all liabilities and actions resulting from certain specified events or actions, hence the expression 'hold harmless'.

An example of where these may be used is when there is a hesitant party in a project who is concerned about potential liabilities that may arise. By putting this indemnity agreement in place, we are able to reassure the reluctant party to engage in the project.

3 ACQUISITION PROCESS DOCUMENTATION

Once the parties to a potential deal start to get serious, more detailed investigation work and negotiations will follow. In turn, this will necessitate further and more detailed documentation.

3.1 Information memorandum

3.1.1 Purpose

The Information Memorandum will be prepared by the vendors of a company. Having established the exact structure of the company for sale and to whom it is likely to be attractive, a selling document can be prepared which is accurately targeted to the desired acquirers.

As an Information Memorandum, it will portray the business in a favourable light. However, it should be remembered that S397 of FSMA 2000 makes it a criminal offence to make a false statement dishonestly or recklessly in order to induce someone to enter into an investment agreement. It is also an offence to withhold information dishonestly for the same purpose. The document should, therefore, be prepared with due care and attention.

3.1.2 Scope

The Information Memorandum should **give a potential acquirer sufficient information to make a decision** about whether to buy the business and how much to offer, subject to an accountant's investigation. Notwithstanding this, the vendor should be careful not to reveal confidential details until they are assured as to the seriousness of the acquirer's intent.

Contents

The key contents are likely to be as follows.

- An overview/executive summary.
- Sales marketing and product information.
- Suppliers.
- Directors, senior management and employee details.

- Administration systems and related details.

- Locations of key premises.

- Existing shareholders and their percentage holdings.

- General company information, such as the registered office, company registration number, etc.

- Financial details, being recent profit and loss accounts, balance sheets and cash flow forecasts. Budgets and forecasts for coming years may also be appropriate.

- Suggestions as to how the acquirer can develop and add value to the business.

3.2 Initial letter of intent and heads of agreement

3.2.1 Purpose

If negotiations allow, **a preliminary agreement containing the terms of the acquisition** will be reached. These will be summarised in the form of heads of agreement (also referred to as a 'letter of intent'). This is not usually a binding contract but merely formulates the key terms of the agreement. It will usually be subject to the final contract being agreed after a detailed investigation of the target has been completed.

The terms are negotiated between the vendor and the purchaser with the assistance of their financial advisers and approved by the solicitors for both sides. The document forms the basis for the Sale and Purchase Agreement that will later be drafted by the legal advisers to the parties. The document is signed by the parties to the transaction, but in the UK, it is not (apart from confidentiality clauses and exclusivity agreements, etc.) legally binding.

There is no fixed format for Heads of Agreement, with some advisers preferring a concise version and others preferring a more comprehensive one. Accordingly, they can range from a two-page document, to 20 pages or more. In smaller deals, some advisers and principals in fact prefer to sidestep this stage of the process and progress straight to the Sale and Purchase Agreement.

Many others, particularly financial advisers, prefer a more detailed form of Heads of Agreement, for the elimination of doubt or disagreement later in the sale process and to assist the solicitors in producing a Sale and Purchase Agreement that accurately meets the requirements of each of the parties. Accordingly, detailed negotiations will be involved at this stage, and considerable input of advice to the principals.

3.2.2 Scope

It is especially useful to include in the Heads of Agreement some detail on the structure of the transaction. In particular, some areas that should be decided at this stage include

The names of the vendor and the acquirer and brief details of what is being sold.

- Amount, timing and basis of calculation of any deferred or contingent consideration. (Consideration means something of value given in exchange for getting something from the other party.) This can prove to be a particularly contentious area so should be addressed in detail at the Heads of Agreement stage.

- Proposals in relation to the employees and directors of the company – will there be redundancies, will the services of the existing management be required and if so, on what terms?

- Any critical warranties or conditions required by either party. Conditions and warranties are discussed below.

- Procedures for progressing the transaction. This will include the timing and scope of due diligence, the identities of the parties and their advisers, naming the lawyers responsible for preparing the initial draft of the Sale and Purchase Agreement, determining responsibility for costs in the transaction, allowances for site visits and meetings with key personnel and putting a timetable together for the completion of the deal.

3.3 Representations, warranties and indemnities

3.3.1 Purpose

The purpose of the warranties and indemnities made in the contract is to protect the acquirer. Notwithstanding the detailed investigation made by the acquirer's accountants, the vendor will often be obliged to give warranties that the company is as stated.

> A warranty is an assurance that a particular state of affairs is correct. If this is not true, the person giving the assurance or warranty is liable for compensation for any loss suffered.

For example, a warranty could be given that a particular provision made in a balance sheet is appropriate, and another that a property is owned unencumbered, i.e. without any legal charges or restrictions attached to it.

Typically, warranties will be for a period of two to three years, although tax warranties will usually be for six years.

The warranties are usually set out in schedules to the Sale and Purchase Agreement, although occasionally a separate Deed of Tax Warranty will be signed.

> **Indemnities** are given where there is likely to be a contingent or actual liability or loss that is known about before completion and where it is appropriate for the vendor to be responsible on a pound for pound basis. An indemnity would be given where a general warranty provision does not provide adequate cover for the potential loss.

The vendor then undertakes to make good the liability in a particular set of pre-determined circumstances. There is no burden of proof of financial loss by the purchaser. Indemnities are frequently sought by the purchaser for taxation matters, or where there is an actual claim outstanding against the company, e.g. a legal claim that has been served but not yet resolved.

3.3.2 Scope

A warranty is a **statement that a particular state of affairs is correct**. Typical examples of warranties are

- Completeness of liabilities in the accounts.
- Good title to assets, particularly properties.
- Tax warranties regarding the tax position of the company.

Tax warranties focus on the target company's liability to tax of any kind arising out of its activities prior to completion, where the liability may not emerge until up to six years later. Clearly the vendor will wish to limit the warranties given as far as possible, and equally the purchaser will wish to make them as all-inclusive as possible.

Indemnities provide for compensating the acquirer for any losses suffered due to specific liabilities mentioned in the Sale and Purchase Agreement. This may include, for example, certain contingent liabilities. They will probably include indemnities in respect of tax liabilities. Indemnities provide a stronger form of protection for an acquirer than warranties. A purchaser need only prove that the state of affairs envisaged by the indemnity has arisen, without the need to quantify that a loss has been suffered as a result.

Indemnities fall into two categories.

- **General** – which will cover tax, for example.
- **Specific** – which will cover matters such as specific litigation or other contingent liabilities.

Clearly, warranties and indemnities all constitute a potential liability for the vendor. This liability is limited, however, in two main ways.

- Setting *de minimis* **limits** to avoid small unnecessary claims. One example might be that no claim could be made for a loss below £1,000, or until all claims together total over £20,000.

- There may also be a **warranty cap**, so that the total warranty claim cannot exceed, for example the total consideration or some percentage thereof.

A **Disclosure Letter** will be agreed, see the next section, and insurance can be taken out against possible warranty claims. The life of the warranties will be limited as far as possible.

3.4 Disclosure letter

3.4.1 Purpose

The purchaser cannot claim under a warranty in relation to information that was known to him prior to completion. Accordingly, the vendor and purchaser will negotiate the information that is deemed to have been disclosed to him prior to completion. The negotiation of these disclosures can also be a lengthy process with the vendor seeking wide-ranging and general disclosures and the purchaser seeking to limit them to the very specific.

3.4.2 Scope

The warranties will often be made in fairly general, wide-ranging terms and therefore, the Disclosure Letter is needed to **highlight specific exceptions to the warranties**.

As mentioned above, where a warranty is found to be incorrect, the purchaser may sue the person giving the warranty. However, it is not possible for the purchaser to seek legal redress concerning items included in the Disclosure Letter.

3.5 Comfort letter (side letter)

3.5.1 Purpose

A Comfort Letter (sometimes called a Side Letter) differs from a Disclosure Letter or other similar agreement in that the Comfort Letter is not normally legally binding. It will usually be the vendor who is setting out in writing certain statements or undertakings which will give general comfort to the purchaser.

Since the comfort letter is not usually legally enforceable, this does beg the question of whether it is worth the paper it is written on? In practice, the 'comfort' comes from the fact that the provider of the letter has put down in writing their promises or intentions and therefore this provides a certain 'moral' authority to the statements made. Were there to be any breaches of the undertakings given in the comfort letter, then the provider will suffer the potential reputational risk that they have not honoured their responsibilities as set out in the Comfort Letter.

3.5.2 Scope

As the Comfort Letter is **not legally binding**, the contents may **relate to more general matters** that would not be able to documented in a normal legal agreement.

A Comfort Letter is also sometimes provided by a parent company to support the borrowings of a subsidiary. All that the parent company is effectively saying in the letter is that they are aware of their subsidiary's liabilities under the agreement and provide comfort that it is their intention to support their subsidiary in meeting its obligations.

3.6 Longform and shortform reports

3.6.1 Purpose

The acquirer's accountants, typically their auditors, will usually conduct a detailed investigation of the company to be acquired. The objective is to ensure that the company being sold is as described by the vendor. This investigation forms what is known as **'due diligence'** and the final conclusions are often prepared by the accountants in the form of a '**Longform Report**'.

Any issues identified in the report will be examined. They may lead the purchasing company to abandon the acquisition or to renegotiate the contract to reflect the new information.

A summary of the key points raised in the Longform Report is not surprisingly called a **Shortform Report**. Unlike the Longform Report which is a private document for the potential acquirer, the Shortform Report will often form the basis of any offer document or listing requirements and therefore become public.

3.6.2 Scope

The Longform Report will normally cover the following areas.

- An overview of the company, its products and the industry in which it operates.

- A detailed examination of the company's products and industry and how the market place has developed and is expected to develop in future.

- Details of competing firms.

- Details of the company's operations in general.

- An analysis of the management team, how effective they are and whether they are essential to the company's success.

- Details of other employees.

- Details of premises occupied, leases, etc.

- An historical financial summary of profit and loss accounts, balance sheets and cash flows.

- An examination of any profit or other forecasts made by the vendor, considering how reasonable they appear to be.

- Details of any legal claims outstanding against the company.

3.7 Legal Due Diligence Report

Purpose

The acquirer's lawyers will also usually conduct a detailed investigation of the company to be acquired. The objective is to ensure that there are no hidden legal difficulties within the company. This investigation is known as **'legal due diligence'**

BPP
LEARNING MEDIA

Scope

The Legal Due Diligence Report will normally cover the following areas.

- Confirmation that statutory corporate documents are in order.

- Securities agreements in place, e.g. shareholder agreements or debt covenants

- Review of pending or threatened litigation

- Review of employee contracts and benefits and any employment disputes

- Verification of freehold and leasehold properties and associated health and safety issues

- Current status of taxation returns for the company

- Adequacy of company's insurance cover

- Intellectual property rights and adequate protections eg patents and licences

4 COMPLETION PROCESS DOCUMENTATION

Once all the due diligence work and analysis has been performed, the final stages of the corporate finance transaction will consist of some final legal documents. These will largely be based on the other documentation that has already been produced, such as the Heads of Agreement, except these final documents are ultimately the ones that count. Therefore, it could still be possible for some 'deal-breaker' to enter at this stage leading to the whole acquisition being called off.

4.1 Sale and purchase agreement

4.1.1 Purpose

Once the Heads of Agreement have been agreed, the principals and their lawyers start to prepare the Sale and Purchase Agreement. This is the contract that **sets out in detail the terms of the deal**. Once the principals sign the Sale and Purchase Agreement, they have entered into a legally binding commitment to continue with the transfer of the business in exchange for consideration.

Depending on the size and complexity of the transaction, it can be anything from 50-200 pages or more. Much of the detail will be found in schedules to the agreement rather than in the body of the text.

This document is required in almost all transactions, unless there are a large number of shareholders or when the sale involves a public company, in which case an offer document will be more appropriate.

Once the Sale and Purchase Agreement has been finalised, the purchaser and vendor will either exchange contracts with completion pre-arranged for a later date (for example, contracts could be signed and exchanged once all key terms are agreed, with completion on the final day of the purchaser's or vendor's year end, or once certain conditions precedent are met) or the principals may agree to exchange and complete simultaneously.

Ideally, all approvals and consents will have been obtained prior to completion, and at completion all that remains to be done is the signing of the Sale and Purchase Agreement, share transfers or asset transfers and fund transfers. In practice, a number of details will typically emerge in the course of the completion meeting ranging from the minor to the 'deal-breaker'.

4.1.2 Scope

The first draft of the agreement is typically drafted by the purchaser's lawyers and the vendor's lawyers will comment on this first draft. The financial advisers should also review the agreement to ensure that the terms match the requirements of their clients, and that the terms agree with those set out in the Heads of Agreement.

The main contents of the Sale and Purchase Agreement are

- Jurisdiction and definitions.
- Summary of the main terms.
- Timing and effective date.
- Consideration: amount, form, timing and conditions.
- Conditions of the transaction and obligations of the parties.
- Restrictions on the vendors.
- Agreement on costs.
- Warranties.
- Indemnities.
- Procedures for claims.

The form of the Sale and Purchase Agreement will differ according to whether the deal is being structured as an asset sale or a share sale. For example, where a share sale is involved, the purchaser acquires all risks associated with the company and its history, and so they seek extensive warranties and indemnities. In an asset sale the purchaser limits his risk by acquiring only specified assets and leaving the actual and contingent liabilities of the company with the vendor. In this case fewer warranties are required.

Either way, a significant part of the negotiation will focus on the precise terms and wording of the Warranties and Indemnities.

4.2 Shareholders agreement

4.2.1 Purpose

A shareholder agreement is most usually associated with a relatively small private company with only a few major shareholders. This may be the case for a Management Buy Out (MBO) or the founders of a company working with a venture capitalist. Its purpose is to set out any agreements which the shareholders have entered into and provide protections in light of certain corporate events, e.g. any subsequent issues or shares via a rights issue or open offer.

4.2.2 Scope

The shareholder agreement will often concern any subsequent issue of shares in the company and the right or obligation for all existing shareholders to participate in such subsequent issues. Examples of these are 'drag-along' and 'tag-along' provisions which were discussed in the previous chapter.

4.3 Vendor protection clauses

4.3.1 Purpose

The purpose of these clauses in a Sale and Purchase Agreement is to **set out limits of liability of the seller** and purchaser. As part of the legal process involved in the disposal of their shareholdings, or assets of a division, the seller's solicitors will pay careful attention to this area. Not only will they be resisting giving too much away in warranties and indemnities as discussed above, but the seller's solicitor will look to further limit the potential future liabilities that may return to haunt the seller post sale.

4.3.2 Scope

The purchaser will naturally wish to resist any limitation of liability on the part of the seller, so such clauses are likely to be very restricted in scope.

4.4 Verification notes

4.4.1 Purpose

As the documents that are published as part of a public issue of securities will be widely distributed and relied upon by potential investors, it is important that due care and attention is paid as to the accuracy of the information contained in these documents. Therefore, the directors of the company issuing the prospectus or listing particulars will be required to conduct a 'verification' exercise. It is not just sufficient for the directors to state that they believe the information included in the issue documents is correct. They must maintain **detailed notes and evidence to back up all material statements**. These then will form the Verification Notes.

4.4.2 Scope

As the directors have a very wide potential liability for all information released during the corporate finance transaction, the scope of the verification exercise will extend to all the information provided by the directors.

Any statements of fact should refer to the professional adviser who has verified this information on behalf of the directors. Any statement of opinion must be considered by each director and they must be satisfied that there is a reasonable basis for that opinion. The evidence will be recorded in the Verification Notes.

5 FINANCING DOCUMENTATION

When considering how to finance the acquisition, any approach to an external financier will give rise to the need of formal legal documentation. This will range from a loan agreement with banking financiers, to public offer documents that need to comply with the EU Prospectus Directive.

5.1 Term sheet

5.1.1 Purpose

Once the terms of the financing arrangement with a lender have been agreed in principle, a Term Sheet will usually be prepared and agreed. Although the Term Sheet itself will not form a legal document, it will form the basis of subsequent loan agreements and any warranties.

5.1.2 Scope

The Term Sheet will be a summary of the **main terms of the proposed transaction**. The lender will be concerned to cover pricing, taking security and any covenants or guarantees as discussed in the next section. The borrower will also be interested in the pricing compared to the security it is promising. They will also be concerned to ensure that confidentiality letters will be in place to protect the information they are disclosing to the prospective lender.

5.2 Loan agreement and the giving of security

5.2.1 Purpose

The Loan Agreement is the document which represents the **primary contract between the lender and the borrower**, and the one which sets out all the commercial terms and administrative detail on which the lending will operate.

If there is a dispute, the courts, once they are satisfied that a contract exists, will interpret the meaning of a loan agreement strictly in accordance with what it actually says. The main challenge is to ensure that the clauses actually say what they are intended to mean, that they are not ambiguous and that their effect is broad enough to cover all perceivable eventualities.

5.2.2 Scope

About half of a typical Loan Agreement is simply administrative covering such things as

- Notice period for drawdowns (i.e. taking out a further tranche of the loan).

- When interest payments must be made.

- Where notices must be sent.

- How long to rectify defaults.

- Who is responsible for withholding tax.

The remaining half of the Loan Agreement is an extension of the lender's credit process by which the lender formalises in writing the security it will take and restrictions surrounding the loan facility. This will normally take the form of covenants as to financial performance and then positive and negative covenants regarding other activities.

Financial covenants will often revolve around the maximum level of indebtedness that a lender will incur as a proportion of its assets. For example, the lender may undertake not to borrow more than 60% of its total asset value. This could also be measured by the ability of the lender to cover interests payments from operating profits, measured by the interest cover ratio.

The borrower's financial conditions can be specified in absolute terms (amounts) or in calculated amounts (ratios). Financial covenants will clearly vary depending on the nature of the facility and creditworthiness of the borrower.

Positive covenants compel the borrower to do certain things which the lender feels will be conducive to the well being of the borrower's business and its ability to meet its obligations under the Loan Agreement. Examples would include the borrower keeping assets fully insured and providing certain financial information to the lender at set times throughout the loan period.

Negative covenants restrain the borrower from doing things which the lenders think are undesirable and may be damaging to the borrower's or to the lender's interests. For example, a negative pledge forbids the borrower from giving any security, or from giving any further security other than that already known to the lenders, or giving security without simultaneously offering the lender equal security.

Often, the negative covenants can be a long list of a range of things the borrower is not meant to do during the term of the facility without the lender's consent, such as restrictions on dividend payments; the giving of guarantees, and the disposal of assets. The general philosophy is that the lender is trying to preserve the borrower as more-or-less the same entity that it initially analysed and approved a loan to.

5.3 Guarantees and indemnities

5.3.1 Purpose

A lender might seek the additional security of knowing that a loan is not only backed by the borrower, but also by a parent, associate or other person to whom the bank can have recourse in case of default of the borrower.

Most standard form documentation of banks describes the 'Guarantor' as providing a Guarantee **and** Indemnity.

A Guarantee alone is a separate obligation to the borrower's primary obligation to repay the loan. It can only be actioned by the lendor if the borrower has failed to honour the guaranteed obligation and any security given by the borrower has been exercised. Accordingly, if the principal obligation is void, the guarantee is also void, since the guarantee will then be in respect of an unenforceable obligation.

The inclusion of an Indemnity clause, entitles the lender to enforce the Guarantee immediately upon the borrower's non-payment following demand. Since the Indemnity is an undertaking from the Indemnifier to insulate the lender from loss (rather than an undertaking to perform in those respects which the borrower has failed so to do), the Indemnity survives any defect in the underlying loan contract. An indemnity is thus more valuable to a lender.

Similarly, it may be inappropriate for the lender to fully exhaust all legal remedies against the borrower before calling upon the guarantor to perform the guarantee. In such a case the Indemnity clause can kick in even before actions against the borrower have finished.

5.3.2 Scope

It is often convenient to have the guarantor(s) be made a party to the Loan Agreement and to include the guarantee that they are to give as part of the Loan Agreement. In terms of legal effect it makes absolutely no difference whether the guarantee is incorporated in this way or whether it is constituted by a separate document.

Although the guarantor is a party to the Loan Agreement, he is only bound by those terms, conditions or clauses which specifically are stated as applying to him.

5.4 Loan representations and warranties

5.4.1 Purpose

In signing the Loan Agreement, the Board of Directors is representing and warranting that a number of things are true. For example, that the entering into of the Loan Agreement does not infringe any other agreement to which the borrower is subject. For example, the borrower may have previously promised to another lender that it would not enter into any other Loan Agreements without that lender's permission. The new lender will specifically ask the directors of the borrower to make a representation on this point, so that they know that this prior agreement is not compromised.

These issues may actually bring something to light before the execution of the documents if the borrower's officers are honest. In addition to focusing the directors' minds, lenders can visit upon the directors' personal liability if a representation or warranty is given where it can be demonstrated that the giver of the representations and warranties knew it to be false.

5.4.2 Scope

Standard Representations and Warranties made by the borrower include the following.

- Status of the party making the Warranty or Loan Representation.

- Powers and authority.

- Legal validity – agreement is binding.

- Pari passu (i.e. equal) ranking – the Borrower warrants that its obligations under the loan agreement will not be subordinated to any unsecured creditor.

- No conflict with existing agreements.

- No pending litigation or insolvency proceedings.

- No default exists.

A further clause is normally included to ensure that the borrower repeats the representations and warranties at each drawdown and on the first day of each new interest period, with reference to the facts and circumstances then existing.

5.5 Prospectus

Note that we are now considering the issue of securities as a way of raising finance rather than a lender giving security over an asset in order to support a loan.

5.5.1 Purpose

The Prospectus is the **marketing document** intended to persuade potential shareholders to buy the shares or other securities offered, such as bonds. It is prepared by the financial advisers and solicitors. An additional prospectus may be issued, known as a **Pathfinder Prospectus**, containing **outline details** of the initial public offer.

5.5.2 Scope

The Prospectus will contain a full description of the company, its plans for future operations and development, the key managers along with all the necessary information required under the EU Prospectus Directive. The financial information contained in the Shortform Report mentioned above is likely to be contained in the Prospectus. Further details as to the scope of the prospectus and the requirements of the Prospectus Directive are contained in the chapter entitled *Equity Capital Markets*.

5.6 Subscription/placing agreements

5.6.1 Purpose

The Subscription Agreement is a contract between the issuer of a security, e.g. a share or bond, and the corporate financiers who are responsible for marketing and placing the security with investors. Its purpose is to set out the terms on which the lead manager and other members of a syndicate of banks will purchase the new securities. This will normally follow on from a period of book building during which the banks will have lined up the investors who want to buy the new issue.

5.6.2 Scope

The Placing Agreement will set out the price of the issue and any fees payable or who will incur certain costs. Just as with the other major agreements surrounding the issue of new securities, the placing banks will wish to receive representation and warranties both at the outset of the agreement and at the date on which the securities are to be issued.

There may be a supplementary agreement between the lead manager and any co-managers in the syndicate to determine the allocation of securities to each syndicate member.

5.7 Underwriting agreements

5.7.1 Purpose

The Underwriting Agreement is very similar to the Subscription Agreement in that it will state the responsibility of the underwriting banks to purchase any securities which are not taken up by investors during the offer.

5.7.2 Scope

The main contents of the Underwriting Agreement are as follows.

- Conditions to be fulfilled, e.g. passing of relevant resolutions, listing of the securities.

- The obligation of the underwriter to take up the shares at the agreed price.

- Representations, warranties and undertakings made by the company, e.g. compliance with all relevant regulations, truth and fairness of the accounts.

- Circumstances in which the underwriting agreement will be terminated, e.g. force majeure (an act of God).

- Fees payable. The fees payable will be linked into the risk that the underwriter takes on in relation to the whole issue of the shares and will not just be driven by the actual number of unsold shares the underwriter is required to take on

6 SUMMARY

6.1 Introduction

As this chapter makes up around 20% of the exam, we recommend that you memorise the purpose of all these documents.

6.1.1 Initial documentation

Document	Parties	Purpose
Engagement Letter	Advisors and Clients	Set out the nature of services to be provided and responsibilities of both parties
Exclusivity Agreement	Seller (vendor) and buyer (acquirer)	Prevent other potential buyers negotiating for a set period
Confidentiality Letter	Seller and buyer	Agreement not to disclose or use information received other than for the purpose of that transaction
Hold Harmless Letter	Provider and user of information	An indemnity to the provider of information or participant in a potential transaction that they will not be liable to any legal liabilities

6.1.2 Acquisition process documentation

Document	Parties	Purpose
Information Memorandum	Seller	Provide information to potential buyers
Initial Letters of Intent and Heads of Agreement	Seller and buyer	Set out the key terms of an initial agreement to buy a company that will form the basis of further negotiations
Representations, Warranties and Indemnities	Directors of selling company	Protection for the buyer against hidden or unforeseen liabilities or impairments arising after acquisition
Disclosure Letters	Directors of selling company	Disclosure of any known important facts by the seller
Comfort Letter and Side Letter	Directors of selling company	Not legally binding but indication of goodwill on certain matters by the seller
Longform and Shortform Report	Buyer's accountant	The results of due diligence work on the potential acquisition including financial reviews
Legal Due Diligence Report	Buyer's lawyers	The results of the legal due diligence work.

6.1.3 Completion process documentation

Document	Parties	Purpose
Sale and Purchase Agreement	Buyer and seller	The definitive legal document concerning the transaction
Shareholders Agreement	Shareholders in the new entity	An agreement concerning the rights and responsibilities of the shareholders of a new company
Vendor Protection Clause	Buyer and seller	Limitation of the liability of the seller
Verification Notes	Seller in a public offer	Evidence and verification work performed for key information contained in offer documents

6.1.4 Financing documentation

Document	Parties	Purpose
Term Sheet	Borrower and lender	Initial outline of key terms of a loan
Loan Agreement	Borrower and lender	Formal legal document concerning a loan transaction
Guarantees and Indemnities	Borrower's parent or other person with the lender	A guarantee will be called to meet the legally valid loan obligations if the borrower defaults. An indemnity will be agree to meet any loss arising from a loan default even if the loan is declared invalid
Loan Representations and Warranties	Directors of borrowing company	The directors give various undertakings to give comfort to the lender
Prospectus	Issuing Company (responsibility of directors approved by sponsor)	Marketing document for new securities (shares or bonds). May initially be issued in outline form as a pathfinder prospectus.
Subscription/placing Agreements	Issuing company and lead manager	Sets out the process to be followed in placing the new securities with potential investors
Underwriting Agreements	Issuing company and underwriters	Agreement of underwriters to buy any unsold securities in an Initial Public Offer or other sale of securities

Congratulations on completing the Certificate in Corporate Finance Study Book. We recommend the following final steps to prepare for your exam.

1. Ensure you have completed the chapter-by-chapter questions in your Question Bank.

2. Attempt the Practice Exams in the Question Bank.

3. Review areas of weakness by reviewing those areas in the Study Book.

4. Contact a BPP tutor if you require further help.

5. Complete the Practice Exams a second time and check on BPP Online for any latest questions or updates.

> # GOOD LUCK IN YOUR EXAM

TEST YOUR KNOWLEDGE

Check your knowledge of the chapter here, without referring back to the text.

For each of the following purposes, identify the document that is most appropriate.

1.   Sets out the nature of a professional relationship with advisors.

2.   Prevents poaching of staff by a failed acquirer.

3.   Protects providers of information from actions.

4.   Sets out the information for potential buyers.

5.   Assures buyers that a material fact is correct.

6.   Gives the full details of financial due diligence.

7.   The definitive completion document.

8.   Set out the key factors of a potential loan.

TEST YOUR KNOWLEDGE: ANSWERS

1.   Engagement letter

      (See Section 2.1)

2.   Confidentiality letter

      (See Section 2.3)

3.   Hold harmless letter

      (See Section 2.4)

4.   Information memorandum

      (See Section 3.1)

5.   Representation or warranty

      (See Section 3.3)

6.   Longform report

      (See Section 3.6)

7.   Sale and purchase agreement

      (See Section 4.1)

8.   Term sheet

      (See Section 5.1)

INDEX

BPP
LEARNING MEDIA